THE

YEAR

GOD

DIED

THE
YEAR
GOD
DIED

JESUS AND THE ROMAN
EMPIRE IN 33 AD

JAMES LACEY

BANTAM
NEW YORK

Bantam Books
An imprint of Random House
A division of Penguin Random House LLC
1745 Broadway, New York, NY 10019
randomhousebooks.com
penguinrandomhouse.com

Originally published in hardcover in the United States by Bantam Books, an imprint of Random House, a division of Penguin Random House LLC, in 2024.

Hardback ISBN 978-0-593-35522-0
Ebook ISBN 978-0-593-35523-7

Printed in the United States of America on acid-free paper

1st Printing

First Edition

BOOK TEAM: Production editor: Ted Allen • Managing editor: Saige Francis • Production manager: Maggie Hart • Copy editor: Muriel Jorgensen • Proofreaders: Claire Maby, Kathy Jones, Amy Harned

Book design by Jo Anne Metsch

The authorized representative in the EU for product safety and compliance is Penguin Random House Ireland, Morrison Chambers, 32 Nassau Street, Dublin D02 YH68, Ireland.
https://eu-contact.penguin.ie

To the three new family additions since I started writing this book—
my grandchildren Calvin, Emma, and Elle

Contents

THE

YEAR

GOD

DIED

THE

YEAR

GOD

DIED

A Very Roman Murder

Sejanus strode triumphantly to his accustomed place in the Senate chambers. After decades of unremitting toil, his life's quest was finally in striking distance. The emperor Tiberius had sent word from the isle of Capri, where he had sought refuge from Rome's continuous clamor, that Sejanus was this day to receive tribunician powers. Sejanus, who had long wielded the power of an emperor, would, with the granting of the *Tribunicia Potestas*, officially have powers equal to those of Tiberius. Just as crucially, Tiberius was aged and increasingly infirm. No one expected him to live much longer, a couple of years at most. His remaining dynastic heirs would still be children without protectors when he died. In the tumultuous and often deadly conflicts that marked Roman politics, they could be easily pushed aside in favor of a man experienced in wielding power. With the *Tribunicia Potestas* in his hands and having carefully removed most of his serious rivals, Sejanus was perfectly positioned to make the final leap and make himself emperor of the Roman Empire.

As he took his reserved seat in the Senate chamber, Sejanus beamed. Always alert to danger from any quarter, Sejanus failed to suspect that Tiberius, the one man more experienced in the deadly arena of Roman politics than himself, had outwitted him. For Tiberius, who had only recently begun viewing his protégé as a dangerous rival to himself and his posterity, had not sent orders raising Sejanus to ultimate power. Instead, he had ordered Sejanus's removal from all offices and to be placed under arrest. Although Tiberius did not order Sejanus's execution, the old emperor certainly knew that once he had set events in motion, that was the only possible outcome.

Sejanus, dumbfounded by the rapid reversal of his fortunes, was led off to prison. Within the hour, the Senate had reconvened at the Temple of Concord, where they took measure of the people's mood and, more crucially, that of the Praetorian Guard—commanded until that morning by Sejanus. Seeing that the Guard had not stirred from its barracks, they became confident that they were fulfilling the will of the emperor. Assured that the always dangerous Roman mob gloried in Sejanus's fall and that the Praetorians' passivity had been bought, they condemned Sejanus to death.

Sejanus was dragged from his cell and brought to the Gemonian Stairs—the Stairs of Mourning—where only the most dishonorable persons were executed. After being strangled, his body was thrown down the stairs in full view of the Roman Forum. In keeping with tradition, the body was left for three days of abuse—beaten by the mob, scavenged by dogs, and pecked at by birds—before being tossed into the Tiber River.*

Not yet finished, the Senate, despite every indication that the mob's desire for blood was satiated, ordered the execution of Sejanus's children. Both children were immediately carried off to prison, unaware of their impending doom. Sejanus's daughter, not yet in her teens, was bewildered by her treatment and repeatedly asked why people were mad at her and what she had done wrong. As she was dragged along in tears, she told everyone in earshot that she was sorry and begged forgiveness for whatever she had done. Because Roman law forbade the execution of a virgin, her executioner took it upon himself to rape the child before she

---

* Dio, *The Roman History*, 58.11.5–6.

and her brother were strangled and also thrown down the Gemonian Stairs.*

This brutal act set in motion a series of events that established the context for Jesus's trial seven months later. Simply put, if Sejanus had not been executed, it is unlikely that Pontius Pilate would have ordered Jesus's crucifixion either.

* Tacitus, *The Annals*, 5.9.

PART I

THE NEW TESTAMENT AND ITS CRITICS

ONE

Did Jesus Exist?

I have authored many histories and biographies and never, until now, had to spend a single word making the case that the subjects of my books were real persons who actually existed. Historians and their audiences take it for granted that Alexander the Great and Julius Caesar were men who walked the earth. The same historical courtesy is often not given to Jesus. While most of the scholarly community concedes that Jesus was a real person who walked the earth, there is a significant segment of scholars who have cleared entire forests to supply paper to publish works denying Jesus's historical existence. As this book requires that Jesus existed as a real flesh and blood man, it is worth reviewing the evidence of his existence.

Unfortunately, one of the first things one discovers when studying the ancient world is that precious little of what the ancients wrote has made its way down through the ages. For instance, scholars possess less than a third of what Aristotle wrote. Only 35 volumes of Livy's 142-volume magisterial history of Rome survive intact, and we only have seven of the more than eighty plays written by Aeschylus. Through tantalizing fragments and mentions of earlier books in later Byzantine volumes, historians know of hundreds of major historical works written by ancient authors that are no longer available.

Over the years, I have contributed several chapters to edited volumes on Alexander the Great without anyone ever concerning themselves with Alexander's actual existence, even though every ancient reference we have to Alexander was written 250 or more years after his death.* Why? Mainly because we know that the later historians used multiple sources written by persons who are also part of the historical record and that these ancient writings, despite many contradictions among them, all confirm the central narrative of elements of Alexander's life. Moreover, these surviving narratives are buttressed by substantial archaeological evidence attesting to Alexander's existence and importance in his own time.

Still, for other events and persons in ancient history, we have far less evidence than we do for the life of Alexander. For instance, historians only have a single account, by Herodotus, to prove that the Battle of Marathon ever took place. If Herodotus's account is wrong, we must admit that we know nothing about what was arguably the most important battle of the ancient world.† Historians, however, believe Herodotus presents an accurate account of the battle. Why? There are several reasons, but the most crucial is that we know how history was related during the period. Greece did not harbor thousands of scribes patiently transcribing Herodotus's work for distribution to a mass audience. Instead, Herodotus earned his silver by reciting passages from his work to paying audiences. As his audiences demanded wonder and entertainment, Herodotus filled his works with fantastic stories about gold-mining ants in India and the rising of the phoenix in Egypt.‡ But they also paid to

---

* That Alexander did exist is attested in biographies written by such ancient historians as Diodorus Siculus, Quintus Curtius Rufus, Arrian, Plutarch, and Justin. None of these writers, however, lived while Alexander was alive. The closest, Diodorus Siculus, was born approximately 250 years after Alexander's death, and most of the others were writing one or two centuries later than that. They did, however, employ sources handed down by persons who knew Alexander, such as Callisthenes, Alexander's official historian, and Ptolemy, one of Alexander's generals. Unfortunately, only minute fragments of these earlier original works survive.

† Herodotus, *The Histories*, 6.109–115. Other ancient writers—Plutarch and Nepos—wrote about the battle, but they did so centuries later and added little to the narrative.

‡ Herodotus, *The Histories*, 3.102–105 and 2.73.1, respectively. A possible answer to the myth of the gold-mining ants was offered in *The New York Times* in 1996. The article speculated that the ants were large marmots that dug up gold as they burrowed into the ground. See Marlise Simons, "Himalayas Offer Clue to the Legend of the Gold Digging Ants," *The New York Times*, November 25, 1996.

hear their own stories' histories, paying to have them recorded by poets and historians. Fathers who fought at Marathon or in the battles of the Second Persian War—Thermopylae, Salamis, and Plataea—would bring their children to hear the stories of these battles and expect them to be truthful as well as correct in every particular. If Herodotus dared to tell a story that did not align with the known facts, there were literally thousands of eyewitnesses to the events he was narrating who would not hesitate to correct him.

Herodotus was not the only historian who earned his living in this way. In a mostly illiterate society without television, smartphones, and all the other entertainments of modern life, storytellers were always in demand. Many historians discount historical narratives rooted in a prior oral tradition, claiming they are prone to letting in changes with every retelling. In this regard, historians view oral traditions through the prism of the grade school game of telephone. In that game, one child is given a statement to be whispered in succession to all the students in the class. Inevitably, when the final student repeats the message, it has little resemblance to the original statement. But this discounts the importance that such societies placed on the oral transmission of ideas. Novice storytellers were drilled for years by master storytellers until they could recite every story entrusted to them word for word. Moreover, these stories were recited before sophisticated audiences who had heard most of them many times before and fully expected to listen to them without errors each time. These were societies that valued their traditions and were quick to spot any deviation from the accepted canon. If we extend the telephone game analogy just a bit, picture the game where everyone in the class has already heard the message and where each successive student must repeat the message aloud for all to hear. In this version of the game, the entire student body is on hand to correct anyone who deviates from the original canon immediately.

This is almost certainly how the Gospel stories were spread among the first generation of Christians. Before they were written down, these stories circulated among the small Christian community that was already intimately familiar with them. Most of them, in fact, had lived through these stories either as participants or interested onlookers. These early

Christians were not making up stories as the basis of a new theology; they were retelling their lived experiences. Moreover, as we will discuss later, this oral storytelling was written down within a generation of Jesus's death when their exactness could be verified by still-living participants in the events surrounding Jesus's life. Given how the Gospels came into existence, historians should give them a better reception as accurate historical documents than is typically the case. Likely because the Gospels are also the foundation of Christian theology, historians, instead, tend to look for any and all possible reasons to dismiss the New Testament books as historical documents. In doing so, historians employ methods that are the reverse of those they use for all other ancient texts. Typically, when historians encounter ancient works that tell two different versions of the same event, their correct and immediate impulse is to try to merge the two accounts into a seamless narrative. What they do not do is toss aside the contradictions as fabrications of the author's imagination. For instance, Polybius and Livy's accounts of the Second Punic War vary remarkably. No reputable historian ever considers throwing out those portions where the two authors disagree. Instead, they work to discover evidence to help develop reasonable explanations for the differences, hoping to synthesize narratives into a seamless tale. Where that is impossible, historians present both versions to their readers, usually along with some analysis of which version is likely more accurate based on the preponderance of all available evidence.

As we shall see, the Gospels are rarely given the same courtesy. Too often, Gospel narratives of events are considered suspect unless proven by other unrelated sources. Frequently, even this is not enough, as a rather large community of historians have declared all of the Gospels as myths written by a burgeoning Christian cult to defend its existence. Unfortunately for those holding this position, there are near-contemporary, non-Christian sources unrelated to the gospel writers who testify that Jesus did exist. Therefore, if we return to the central question of this chapter—Did Jesus exist?—we can first employ the words of the foremost historian of the early Roman Empire, Tacitus, who wrote about the great fire in Rome during Nero's reign:

Therefore, to scotch the rumor, Nero substituted as culprits, and punished with the utmost refinements of cruelty, a class of men, loathed for their vices, whom the crowd styled Christians. Christus, the founder of the name, had undergone the death penalty in the reign of Tiberius, by sentence of the procurator Pontius Pilatus and the pernicious superstition was checked for a moment, only to break out once more, not merely in Judaea, the home of the disease, but in the capital itself, where all things horrible or shameful in the world collect and find a vogue.*

Those historians claiming that Jesus is a myth employ two main arguments to discount this passage by an author considered the most careful and reliable of all the historians of ancient Rome. The first and most damning is that a Christian interpolated this passage at a later date. There are two points worthy of note here: First, those holding this position know they are making a claim that cannot be disproven through any available evidence. And second, they are, in an oft-repeated pattern, doing something they do not do with any other passage in the ancient texts: They are declaring a passage as a fantasy purely because it does not suit their preferred narrative.

Thankfully, most of us are not blinded by preconceived notions and can employ some common sense to determine whether Tacitus wrote the passage. For instance, one wonders what determined Christian zealot—picture a Dark Ages monk working alone in a dank cell—patiently copied Tacitus's manuscript and then decided that there was an excellent opportunity to mention Christ in this one spot. That done, he considered that he could stop now as his single contribution was surely enough to help propagate the faith for generations of readers to follow. He is a remarkable man indeed, who, once having inserted this single mention of his beloved Christ, resisted all temptation to do so anywhere else in the manuscript. Moreover, one wonders how he managed to capture Tacitus's exact flow and syntax without having had training as a forger. And lucky

* Tacitus, *The Annals*, 15.44.

for him, no other monk working in some other dank cell ever just copied out the original version without adding Christ to the narrative, leaving our overly zealous monk's version in perpetual dispute.

Not enough yet? Take a moment to consider the rest of the passage and note what else our supposed interpolator added or failed to edit out. Would a Christian, willing to add his own passage to Tacitus's work, also have allowed the line referring to Christians as a "class of men, loathed for their vices" to remain in the work? Similarly, our supposed Christian editor is unlikely to have inserted Christ into the work and then call his own faith a "pernicious superstition" and a "disease"—one of many infecting Rome—"where all things horrible or shameful in the world collect." Just for a moment, consider the brilliance of this solitary figure plotting how he could add Christ into Tacitus's text so that it would be believable two thousand years hence. His eureka moment came when he decided to write in the name of Christ and make its inclusion believable by using the rest of the paragraph to blaspheme his god and insult the religion he had dedicated his life to. Does that sound reasonable? This entire passage is the work of a Roman pagan who took a dim view of Christianity. It is also written proof, outside of the Gospels, that Jesus existed.

The fallback position historians take is easily dispensed with. Here, those who are intent on proving Jesus is a myth claim that Tacitus's mention of Jesus is a transcription error. This claim is based on a passage in Suetonius, which states that Claudius removed the Jews from Rome because they "constantly made disturbances at the instigation of Chrestus."* In this telling, Chrestus is a different Jew who was causing trouble during Claudius's reign, one who is never mentioned again or found in any other text. However, there is general agreement that Chrestus is a misspelling of Christus, one that frequently appears in Christian works, particularly in Greek writings—*Chrēstianos* in place of *Christianos*. Moreover, anyone claiming that Tacitus meant someone other than Jesus would have to explain how this other person—Chrestus—managed to get himself exe-

---

* Suetonius, *Claudius*, 25.4.

cuted by Pontius Pilate, as Tacitus spells out, and then started the Christian community that so bothered Nero.

The second ancient historian mentioning Jesus is Josephus, born four years after Jesus's crucifixion. He is the author of *Jewish Antiquities,* a history of the Jewish people from their earliest days to about the middle of the first century, and *The Jewish War,* which relates to the story of Jerusalem's destruction and the fall of the Masada Fortress in 73 AD. His extensive works are often used to supplement what is found in the Gospels, as he wrote extensively on many of the personalities found in the New Testament. Thus, if Jesus existed, one would expect to find him mentioned in Josephus's works, and he is. The first time in *Jewish Antiquities:*

> About this time there lived Jesus, a wise man, if indeed one ought to call him a man. For he was one who performed surprising deeds and was a teacher of such people as accept the truth gladly. He won over many Jews and many of the Greeks. He was the Messiah. And when, upon the accusation of the principal men among us, Pilate had condemned him to a cross, those who had first come to love him did not cease. He appeared to them spending a third day restored to life, for the prophets of God had foretold these things and a thousand other marvels about him. And the tribe of the Christians, so called after him, has still to this day not disappeared.*

Following the lead of Catholic priest John P. Meier, historians often remove, without justification, what they consider later Christian testimony, inserted decades or centuries after Josephus wrote his account. If these passages are removed, we get:

> About this time there lived Jesus, a wise man. For he was one who performed surprising deeds and was a teacher of such people as accepted the truth gladly. He won over many Jews and many of the Greeks. And when, upon the accusation of the principal men

* Josephus, *Jewish Antiquities,* 18.3.3.

among us, Pilate had condemned him to a cross, those who had first come to love him did not cease. And the tribe of the Christians, so called after him, has still to this day not disappeared.*

Once again, one wonders about the Christian interpolator who may have added the offending phrases but possessed sufficient restraint to limit himself to changing just this paragraph while refraining from the many other opportunities available within *Jewish Antiquities* to mention Jesus—remarkable restraint indeed. In fact, there is good reason to believe that there were no later alterations to the passage. Historian Gary J. Goldberg has pointed out that Josephus's account is so similar to the Emmaus Narrative in Luke—24:19–27—that they were likely both drawn from the same source.†

Finally, there is another mention of Jesus in Josephus that makes it clear that there had been some discussion of Jesus as Christ or the Messiah at an earlier point in the manuscript:

> Having such a character, Ananus thought that with Festus dead and Albinus still on the way, he would have the proper opportunity. Convening the judges of the Sanhedrin, he brought before them the brother of Jesus who was called the Christ, whose name was James, and certain others.‡

This passage shows no signs of later Christian interpolation. If a later Christian had entered this passage, one could assume he would have given

---

* Josephus, *Jewish Antiquities*, 18.3.3.
† See Gary J. Goldberg, "The Coincidences of the Emmaus Narrative of Luke and the Testimonium of Josephus," *The Journal for the Study of the Pseudepigrapha*, Vol. 13 (1995), pp. 59–77. This paper also discusses Agapius's "Arabic Testimonium," which likely presents a version of Josephus's work written before any Christian could possibly tamper with it. In Agapius's work, the passage reads: "At this time there was a wise man who was called Jesus. And his conduct was good and his learning outstanding. And many people from among the Jews and the other nations became his disciples. Pilate condemned him to be crucified and to die. And those who had become his disciples did not abandon their discipleship. They reported that he had appeared to them three days after the crucifixion and that he was alive; accordingly, he was perhaps the Messiah, concerning whom the prophets have recounted wonders."
‡ Josephus, *Jewish Antiquities*, 20.200.

more praise to James, who is almost always referred to in the New Testament as the "brother of the Lord" and not the brother of Jesus. Also, Josephus is clearly working from sources other than the Gospels, as succeeding passages tell the story of James's martyrdom, which is not mentioned in the New Testament.

None of the arguments relating to the possibility of later Christian interpolations of Josephus's works impact the basic question of whether Jesus ever existed. His mentions of a historical Jesus are widely accepted as part of his original work. Only Josephus's references to Jesus's divinity as the Christ or Messiah have been seriously questioned by historians.

Suppose the works of Tacitus and Josephus stood alone. In that case, they are sufficient evidence that a man named Jesus, who many of his contemporaries believed to be the Messiah or the Christ, lived in Palestine during the reign of Tiberius and was executed by order of Pontius Pilate. But these two works do not stand alone. They are joined by the Gospels, which, although meant to explain the teachings of Jesus, also provide a substantially coherent historical narrative. Thus, we must turn our attention to their reliability as historical documents. But before we do so, it is important to make a first stab at dating the various Gospels. Historians generally agree that most of the Gospels were first written within the lifetime of many of the participants. While there have been extensive debates on the dating of the Gospels, the overwhelming majority of historians believe the Gospel of Mark was written before 66 AD (before the destruction of the Temple by the Romans in 70 AD), while Matthew and Luke were written around 85–90 AD.* The Gospel of John was likely written in the 90s, but possibly as late as 110 AD. That means that Mark was written barely three decades after Jesus's death when most of the apostles were still alive (Peter was likely crucified two to four years before).

---

* Historians and New Testament scholars are in general agreement that Mark's Gospel, having been written first, was known to Matthew and Luke, and may have been used as source material. It is also certain that Luke wrote Acts. When Acts ends, the apostles Peter and Paul are still alive. As both were killed in the Neronian persecutions between 64 and 67 AD, Mark has to have been written prior to the later date. There is even a strong possibility that it was written a decade before, while Mark was traveling with the apostle Peter.

TWO

Who Wrote the Gospels?

A s in all things related to the Gospels, a substantial number of historians claim that we have no idea who the gospel authors are. We can discount almost all of these commentaries as the authors present almost no evidence contradicting the early fathers of the Church beyond asserting that the ancient sources are wrong. As I have previously pointed out, if we are going to discount all the ancient sources without any other contradictory evidence, then we must admit that we know nothing. As a general rule, one must be very reluctant to dismiss the conclusions of early Church historians—who spent considerable energy on discovering who were the true gospel authors, as well as their sources—as they provide the only evidence still extant.

For instance, one of these, Papias of Hierapolis, wrote a five-volume work, *Exposition of the Sayings of the Lord*, at the turn of the first century. This work is, unfortunately, lost to us, except in some excerpts in the works of Irenaeus of Lyons and Eusebius of Caesarea. But we need to pay attention to Papias's surviving writings because he personally knew the Apostle John and was well acquainted with the daughters of the Apostle Philip, who lived in Hierapolis, where Papias served as Bishop. He likely also knew Philip personally, as the apostle spent the last years of his life in the city and was probably martyred there in 80 AD. As Bishop, he had the opportunity to meet many of Jesus's first disciples. These were the men and women who, in their youth, would have witnessed Jesus's actions and heard his words. At worst, Papias received testimony from the first generation, who learned of Jesus's actions and teachings from those who knew him. Papias was a careful recorder of all he had learned and, in the preface of his volumes, bequeathed us his methodology:

> I shall not hesitate also to put into ordered form for you, along with the interpretations, everything I learned carefully in the past from the elders and noted down carefully, for the truth of which I vouch . . . And if by chance anyone who had been in attendance on the elders arrived, I made inquiries about the words of the elders—what Andrew or Peter had said, or Philip or Thomas or James or John or Matthew or any other of the Lord's disciples, and whatever Aristion and John the Elder, the Lord's disciples, were saying.*

A historian employing such close personal testimony to tell the story of any other figure in the ancient world would rightfully claim that, without contemporary contradictory evidence, such a source is unimpeachable. But, as the subject is Jesus, accounts such as that of Papias are often treated as mythmaking despite the absence of clashing evidence. Modern scholars should, at the least, give the voluminous evidence left by early Church historians the same weight they do other ancient sources, as it is often built upon a foundation of eyewitness testimony. Thus, my account of who wrote the Gospels will closely follow the traditional accounts, and not just because of the warning Papias placed at the end of his works, aimed at anyone who doubted his work:

> If anyone does not agree to these truths, he despises the companions of the Lord; nay more, he despises Christ Himself the Lord; yea, he despises the Father also, and stands self-condemned, resisting and opposing his own salvation.

---

* Eusebius, *Ecclesiastical History*, 3.39. Note: Aristion was the Bishop of Smyrna, who was one of the original disciples, a witness to Jesus's life, and a close companion to the Apostle Paul.

Alas, my editors would never allow me to add a similar sentiment to my own publications.

Although none of the gospel authors are named in the Gospels, there is every reason to believe that the author of Mark is John Mark, who first appears in the New Testament in Acts 12:12.* He was a close associate of both Peter and Paul and was apparently with Peter in his later years in Rome. Thus, the Gospel of Mark is the story of Christ's life and teachings as Peter related them to John Mark.† As a close associate of Paul, John Mark was almost certainly with him when he visited the leaders of the early Church in Jerusalem, giving him ample opportunity to hear the testimony of others who had personally known and walked with Jesus, including his brother, James.

The Gospel of Luke is actually written by a later disciple of Jesus. Luke, a doctor and a learned man, was a close friend of Paul's and is often mentioned in Paul's epistles. Luke is also the author of Acts and tells us that he joined Paul on his second and third missionary journeys and later went with him to Rome. At the very start of his work, Luke tells us that he is not a witness to the events detailed in his Gospel. Instead, he takes on the role of a historian from the start, stating: "Since many have undertaken to draw up an account of the things fully attested among us . . . it seemed good to me also, having meticulously traced everything again from the top, to write it down in sequence."‡ Among the early Christian

---

* Despite the Gospels not naming the authors within their text, every surviving ancient text of the Gospels, dating from the second century forward, name the same four writers in their titles, e.g., The Gospel According to Matthew or The Gospel According to Luke. Clearly, the first Christians knew who had written the four canonical Gospels.

† Papias of Hierapolis, a father of the Church who spent much of his life gathering information on the origins of the Gospels, mostly by interviewing eyewitnesses toward the end of the first century, wrote: "Mark, having become Peter's translator, wrote down accurately whatever he remembered. It was not, however, in exact order that he related the sayings or deeds of Christ. For he neither heard the Lord nor accompanied him . . . He accompanied Peter, who accommodated his instructions to the necessities of his hearers, but with no intention of giving an ordered narrative of the Lord's sayings. Wherefore Mark made no mistake in writing things as he remembered them. Of one thing he took special care, not to omit anything he had heard, and not to put anything fictitious into the statements." None of Papias's multiple volumes exist today. Most of what we know about his writing comes from excerpts used by Eusebius in his history of the early Church, written in the fourth century.

‡ Luke 1.1–4.

fathers, there was no doubt that Doctor Luke was the author of a Gospel and that he was a close associate of many of the original apostles.

Although there is a bit of room in the ancient sources to believe that the Gospel According to John was written by someone other than the Apostle John, the overwhelming amount of evidence indicates that the apostle wrote the final Gospel. This evidence includes many references to the author as the apostle Jesus loved inside the Gospel. Also, there are several instances in the Gospel of John where the author places himself in proximity to Peter, indicating that the author was part of Jesus's inner circle. To this could be added many small references to trivial details, such as the number of water jars at the wedding in Cana, that indicate the author was a firsthand witness.* Finally, the early Church father Irenaeus, who had access to Papias's volumes, claims that he was told by Polycarp (Bishop of Smyrna, and the Apostle John's close friend and disciple): "Afterwards, John, the disciple of the Lord, who also had leaned upon His breast, did himself publish a gospel during his residence at Ephesus in Asia."†

The problem that John's Gospel has always presented to historians is that it is so different from the three other Gospels—the synoptic Gospels. Once again, forests have been cleared discussing all aspects of these differences and how they impact the quest to discover the true authorship of the Gospel of John. At their core, the arguments that John was not the author are based on the presumption that the Apostle John, having lived the same experiences as the other apostles, would have written a work similar to the synoptics—Matthew, Mark, and Luke. But John, writing sometime after 80 AD, was well aware that the other three Gospels were already circulating and he likely had read them. He also could see that these earlier gospel authors were writing for particular audiences: Mark

---

* John 2:6.
† Polycarp, *Against Heresies*, 3.1. Polycarp, drawing from and supporting Papias, states the following about the authorship of the other Gospels: "Matthew also issued a written Gospel among the Hebrews in their own dialect, while Peter and Paul were preaching at Rome, and laying the foundations of the Church. After their departure, Mark, the disciple and interpreter of Peter, did also hand down to us in writing what had been preached by Peter. Luke also, the companion of Paul, recorded in a book the Gospel preached by him."

was writing for Jews and early Christians in Rome, Matthew was writing for those in Palestine, while Luke was writing for a particular person, Theophilus, with the aim of introducing Jesus's story to a Greek-speaking population.

All of these authors were writing in the generation after Jesus's death for an audience keen on hearing what Jesus had said during his lifetime. This, however, was not John's audience. He had little interest in addressing an audience spread across the breadth of the Roman Empire who were already familiar with the synoptic Gospels. John was writing at a time when the burgeoning Christian community had accepted the Gospels and was looking for someone to tell them what they meant in their present lives. As Clement of Alexandria, writing toward the end of the first century, stated: "John, last of all, seeing that the plain facts had been clearly set forth in the Gospels, and being urged by his acquaintances, composed a spiritual Gospel under the divine inspiration of the Spirit."* But even if we accept that John the Apostle wrote most of the Gospel of John, it is almost certain that he had help. There are even indications, toward the end of the Gospel, that John died before completing it, leaving it to one of his disciples to add the finishing verses and make internal edits.

Matthew is the most difficult of the Gospels to attribute to a particular person, as the internal hints in the Gospel itself are minimal, and there is no evidence otherwise available. The early Church fathers were convinced that the Apostle Matthew was the author. This includes Papias, who wrote: "Matthew put together the oracles [of the Lord] in the Hebrew language, and each one interpreted them as best he could."† As there is no existing text of the Hebrew version of Matthew's Gospel, and the earliest versions in Greek do not appear to be a translation, some have doubted Papias's statement. But it is supported by Eusebius, who, writing in the fourth century, states that one of the Church leaders at the end of the second century, Pantaenus, had acquired a Hebrew version of Matthew's Gospel in India. As Eusebius wrote: "It is reported that among

---

* Eusebius, *History of the Church*, 6.14.
† Eusebius, *Ecclesiastical History*, 3.39, is currently the main extant source for Papias's writings.

persons there who knew of Christ, he found the Gospel according to Matthew, which had anticipated his own arrival. For Bartholomew, one of the apostles had preached to them, and left with them the writing of Matthew in the Hebrew language, which they had preserved till that time."* As for the internal evidence, we have to limit ourselves to the fact that the author of Matthew presents far more information on financial matters and taxes than all of the other books of the New Testament combined, which is precisely the kind of information one might expect from a man who was a tax collector before Jesus recruited him as one of his apostles.

The most common reason scholars employ to dismiss the idea that Matthew the Apostle was the author of the Gospel bearing his name is that a large part of his work appears to be copied from the Gospel of Mark, and that a true apostle would rely on his own memories rather than copy those of another.[†] This is poor gruel for rejecting scholars such as Papias, who personally knew several of the apostles. Also, it neglects a very human tendency toward laziness. If the stories that Mark wrote are substantially true, why not use them and add one's own personal recollections to that collection, as Matthew does? For those who track such things, approximately a quarter of Matthew's Gospel is unique to that work.

---

* Eusebius, *History of the Church*, 5.10.3–4.
† This is currently the position of the United States Conference of Catholic Bishops. See https://bible.usccb.org/bible/matthew/o?bk=Matthew&ch=.

ARE THE GOSPELS RELIABLE?

In his magisterial work, *The New Oxford Annotated Bible*, Michael D. Coogan plainly lays out the current historical consensus on the Gospels:

> A historical genre does not necessarily guarantee historical accuracy or reliability, and neither the evangelists nor their first readers engaged in historical analysis. Their aim was to confirm Christian faith (Lk 1.4; Jn 20.31). Scholars generally agree that the Gospels were written forty to sixty years after the death of Jesus. They do not present eyewitness or contemporary accounts of Jesus' life and teaching.*

When I first started writing my previous book on the strategy of the Roman Empire, the consensus opinion was that the Romans were incapable of planning or executing a long-term strategy.† In fact, most historians held that the Romans were incapable of even thinking in strategic terms. No historian believes that today. When I asked one leading historian of ancient history why I was not getting any pushback on my belief that the Romans were very sophisticated strategic thinkers, he replied, "You convinced us." Similarly, I hope to convince all of you that the above statement is ahistorical nonsense and needs serious parsing.

First, no one claims that a historical genre guarantees historical accuracy, as thousands of published history books get much of their narrative wrong. Moreover, at a minimum, the synoptic Gospels were not written to confirm the Christian faith, as, during Christianity's first centuries, it was assumed that anyone reading the Gospels had already accepted the faith. If we look at the passage of Luke that Coogan mentions, it is clear that Luke is not confirming the Christian faith. Instead, Luke confirms that the recorded history of Jesus's life and teaching are true—

---

* Michael D. Coogan (ed.), *The New Oxford Annotated Bible* (Oxford University Press, 2010), p. 1,744.
† James Lacey, *Rome: Strategy of Empire* (Oxford University Press, 2022).

the exact opposite of what Coogan states.* Finally, even if the Gospels had been written to confirm the faith of believers, that would not mean that the history within them is inaccurate. In fact, the opposite is true, for if the historical portions of the Gospels were shown to be false, it would undermine the faith.

The reliability of the Gospels as contemporary accounts of Jesus's life must rely primarily upon who wrote them and what sources they employed. Coogan, in fact, tries to create doubt about the authenticity of the Gospels by declaring that they were not written by contemporary authors. How could they possibly be, as they were written "forty to sixty years" after Jesus's death? Coogan and those who accept his consensus view apparently believe that no eyewitness to Jesus's life could possibly have been alive so long after Jesus's death. Moreover, as explained a bit later, the evidence calls for a much earlier dating for Mark and Matthew's accounts than Coogan states. I mostly agree that the Gospels were written between 64 and 80 AD, with a strong possibility that Mark and Matthew were written as much as twenty years earlier. I also believe there is strong evidence that the Gospels were almost certainly written by eyewitnesses (Matthew and John) or were related by the apostles directly to the authors (Mark and Luke).†

Those who believe that the Apostles would all be dead by the time

---

* Luke 1:1–4: Now many have undertaken to compile an account of the things that have been fulfilled among us, like the accounts passed on to us by those who were eyewitnesses and servants of the word from the beginning. So it seemed good to me as well, because I have followed all things carefully from the beginning, to write an orderly account for you, most excellent Theophilus, so that you may know for certain the things you were taught.

† Many scholars state that Matthew must have been written after 70 AD, as the Parable of the Wedding (Matthew 22:7) indicates he was aware of the destruction of the Temple. But there is nothing in the text to indicate that this is the case. One has to imagine it to be true. Moreover, if Matthew was written post–70 AD, it would likely be a much different Gospel, as the audience he would have been writing for was much different than that after the Great Jewish Revolt. It should also be noted that Matthew, Mark, Luke, and John are the titles in the English versions of the Bible. But these Gospels, when written, were not called the Gospel of Matthew or the Gospel of Luke. These titles are later additions.

the Gospels were written are misinterpreting the data. Although the average life expectancy within the Roman Empire was only twenty-five, this low number is a consequence of high infant and child mortality. If you made it to adulthood, your chances of a long life hugely increased. An examination of the surviving Roman gravestones (epitaphs) in North Africa indicates that 30 percent of the Roman adult population was over age seventy, and over 4 percent made it to one hundred.* If we assume that most of the gospel writers or their informants were Jesus's age, with at least John being a decade younger (he was known as a young firebrand), there is a decent chance that most of them were still alive fifty years after Jesus's death, when they would have been in their seventies or eighties. In fact, ancient sources state that John lived past one hundred. We also know that Peter was killed during the Neronian persecutions in 64–67 AD, meaning if he was about Jesus's age, he was approximately seventy years old when he was crucified. In any event, Peter's execution took place more than thirty years after Jesus's death, leaving him plenty of time to tell his story to John Mark. We have no information that can attest to Matthew's date of death. As for Luke, it hardly matters, as he claims to have gotten his information from the witnesses to Jesus's life, and he was alive in the years when that was easily possible to accomplish.

Undoubtedly, all of the Gospels relate what was already being told as part of an oral tradition of Jesus's life and ministry. Remember, this oral history of Jesus's life was presented to audiences that had witnessed the related events. Moreover, a significant percentage of these audiences were still alive when the oral traditions were first written down. These first written Gospels were publicly recited before audiences that would be quick to spot any deviation from their lived experiences.

There would have been far fewer actual witnesses to the events of Jesus's life when Luke's Gospel began to spread. But fewer does not mean

---

* Tim G. Parkin, *Old Age in the Roman World: A Cultural and Social History* (Johns Hopkins University Press, 2003), pp. 36–37. Parkin then arbitrarily reduces this number by two-thirds based on his assumption that the Roman economy could not have supported that many old people. As I point out in my book, *Rome: Strategy of Empire*, and will discuss later in this work, the Roman economy was far richer than it is often credited by historians relying on outdated analyses. Also, in lowering this number, Parkin seems to believe that few of these aged persons were capable of work, which is unlikely to be the case.

none. Even in 80 AD, there would still have been a few—by now, esteemed Church elders—in a position to call out any errors Luke made. Moreover, the second generation of believers was the main audience for the written Gospels. These were men and women who may not have been witnesses to Jesus's life but were likely to have met the apostles and other original disciples of Jesus. This meant that they had first heard the Gospel stories from the original witnesses and would have been a difficult audience to sneak a new tradition past.

But what if all of the Gospels had been written by non-witnesses to Jesus's life, as is the case for Mark and Luke's works? Should that bother a historian? Consider that no one considers Herodotus's accounts of the Greco-Persian Wars unreliable because he collected them from living witnesses, having never witnessed the events of those wars for himself. Do we throw away Thucydides's history of the Peloponnesian War because he only witnessed a portion of it and had to rely on the accounts of others to build out a complete history? Is Polybius's history of the Second Punic War to be discarded because he was not present and had to build his narrative second- and thirdhand? Unfortunately, historians are willing, even eager, to reject Gospel sources for reasons that they would never countenance for any other ancient historical work.

By using modern historical methods, which historians employ for every other ancient source, we arrive at a default position that we will adhere to throughout this work. That is that the Gospels relate a mostly accurate historical narrative, requiring substantial contrary evidence before discarding their version of Jesus's life and times. That does not mean that every story told in the Gospels is entirely accurate. And no historian would ever make such a claim for any ancient source. There are passages in different Gospel accounts that contradict one another. But when this occurs, many historians have been much too quick to dismiss these events as fantasies or myths. But, when working with other ancient sources, historians instinctively try to reconcile them. This courtesy, however, is never extended to the Gospels. Too many historians are also quick to discount portions of one Gospel if that story is not found in any other Gospel. Here, we have another example of historians employing a methodology for the Gospels that they eschew in every other case. For instance, the four ancient accounts we have for Alexander the Great all include multiple events not found in the other accounts. Historians do not routinely dismiss these events, only attested to in a single source, as fabrications of that author. Instead, they work assiduously to blend all the ancient accounts of Alexander's life into a seamless whole, as they should. Historians accept that the histories of Thucydides and Herodotus accurately depict events, although we have no other written sources to corroborate them. But when we have "four" Gospel narratives that, at their core, tell the same story, suddenly historians believe they must start finding ways to dismiss their historical accuracy.

Even the telling of fantastic origin stories rarely causes historians to discount the remaining historical material found in such works. For instance, Plutarch relates that Alexander's mother's womb was struck by lightning on her wedding night and that her husband, Philip of Macedon, suspected a snake had impregnated her. None of this is ever used to discount the rest of Plutarch's narrative. But as the supposed virgin birth of Jesus is a matter of faith that defies science, it is often used to declare the entirety of the Gospels as myths.

Let us go back to the start of this section, where I pointed out that many ancient historians made their livings reading their histories to crowds who had personally experienced the events related in these readings. Thus, if any readers recited anything wrong, they would have been called out on the spot. We have no evidence of anyone listening to the first written versions of the Gospels calling out inaccuracies, nor are there any contemporary counter-narratives that tell a different story. On the other hand, we do have thousands of ancient texts, in whole or fragments, attesting to the factual reliability of the Gospels. Only centuries later do we begin to get apocryphal stories and Gospels. These apocryphal works were produced to satisfy the ancient Christians' insatiable appetite to know more about Jesus's life than can be found in the Gospels or the twenty-seven canonical works in the New Testament. While these stories are often interesting, their provenance is uncertain, their veracity doubtful. Thus, they should not be part of any historical work focused on Jesus and the years he was alive. However, they often offer historians insights into how Church thinking developed in its early centuries.

THREE

The Jesus Quests

Before leaving the topic of the gospel authors and their reliability, I would be remiss if I neglected what has been called "The Quest for the Historical Jesus," particularly its latest incarnation, the Jesus Seminar. The start of the First Quest's attempts to comprehend the Gospels as historical works can be dated to the Enlightenment when scholars, starting with Hermann Samuel Reimarus, went beyond textual analysis to produce biographies of Jesus. Almost all of these First Quest works aimed to prove a particular point of view—that Jesus was not divine—which led to two immediate problems: They removed portions of the Gospels that did not support that point of view, or they would add new information to fill in gaps. Both entailed the rewriting of history without any supporting evidence. This quest picked up intellectual steam in the nineteenth century, when a series of scholars published accounts of Jesus's life that removed or explained away the Gospels' miracle stories. For instance, the theologian Heinrich Eberhard Gottlob Paulus believed that many New Testament miracle stories were natural events that the apostles misunderstood.

According to Paulus, Jesus did not walk on water. Rather, he was walking along the shore in a low mist or standing in the shallows where the apostles could not tell the difference during a storm. Similarly, the miracle of feeding five thousand people with just a few loaves of bread and some fish is dismissed as a communal feast, where everyone brings their own meal. More crucially, Paulus was the first to develop the so-called swoon theory, which claims that Jesus did not die on the cross but had somehow survived the crucifixion. The first two miracles that Paulus dismisses have no impact on the story of Jesus or his central meaning for the later Christian community. If neither was included in the New Testament, it would make no difference to the narrative of Jesus's life or whether he was the promised Messiah. Still, is it plausible that men who had spent their entire lives making a living from the sea did not know where the shallows were or could be so easily fooled by a low mist? If they were that close to shore, why were the lights burning in Capernaum or Tiberias not visible? Take a moment to picture what would have happened when the mist eventually lifted or was burned off by the sun and the apostles saw that they were only a few yards from the shore. "Good one, Jesus. For a moment there, we all thought you were walking on water." After which, much hilarity ensued. With the truth revealed, they certainly would not have written it into a Gospel story.

We may never know how Jesus and his apostles fed thousands, and it is entirely possible that Jesus fed the crowd in a normal manner, possibly by having food brought from the nearby Bethsaida. But then we must deal with the fact that five thousand people were present. If they had later heard this story repeated as a miracle, they would have scoffed, at which point it would be removed from the canon. Finally, could Jesus have just passed out on the cross? We will address this question more fully later, but for it to be true, we must assume that the Roman soldiers could not tell when a man was dead. As one of their number had pushed a spear into his side, a live Jesus would still have been pumping blood through the open wound. How likely would the Romans—professional killers of long experience—or anyone else present have been to have missed this point?

Paulus lived long enough to see his ideas cast into oblivion by David Strauss, who considered all of the miracle stories myths born entirely out of the early Christian community's imagination, which needed to invent such miracles to prove Jesus was the Messiah.* This approach contrasted with the rationalism of Paulus and others who believed miracle stories were misinterpretations of natural events by those who viewed the New Testament as an accurate account of historical events. Strauss's "Third Way," which removes everything miraculous from the Jesus narrative, leaves us with an ordinary man who was executed after falling afoul of the authorities. Strauss's reduced Jesus is so unremarkable a story that one cannot explain why anyone would have written it down, never mind it having attracted four different gospel authors. Still, in his book *The Quest of the Historical Jesus*, Albert Schweitzer claimed that all academic research on Jesus's life could be divided into two periods—before David Strauss and what came after.†

Still, Schweitzer pointed out that the works of the First Quest scholars were mostly worthless, as they had removed Jesus from his Jewish context. They also failed on account of their inability to comprehend Jesus in historical terms, which he claimed was impossible "as his ultimate aims remained a mystery even to his disciples."‡ Schweitzer's critique of his predecessor's work as nothing but subjective prattle effectively brought the First Quest for the historical Jesus to an end. Schweitzer, instead, declared Jesus an eschatological prophet, heralding the imminent coming of the end of the present world and the coming Kingdom of God. Thus, in Schweitzer's view, Jesus was not himself a divine figure. After Schweitzer's work was published, there was virtually no movement in the field for five decades. Most New Testament scholars had come to believe there was nothing left to gain from historical research into Jesus's life. Despite this widespread belief, the number of works published dealing with Jesus's life refused to slow down; after all, scholars needed to publish, and there was a continuing demand for such works. Still, none of them ever passed Schweitzer's objectivity tests. This was a consequence

* David Friedrich Strauss, George Eliot (trans.), *The Life of Jesus, Critically Examined* (Swan Sonnenschein & Co., 1902).
† Albert Schweitzer, W. Montgomery (trans.), *The Quest of the Historical Jesus: A Critical Study of Its Progress from Reimarus to Wrede* (Adam and Charles Black, 1910).
‡ Ibid., p. 560.

of their fatal conceit: They ignored or constantly challenged the essential historicity of the Gospel accounts, confident that they could either improve upon them or, if the Gospels did not fit their preconceptions, they could discount them.

This quiet period was dominated by Rudolf Bultmann, who took a new route by dismissing the idea that the historical Jesus had any importance. What mattered to Bultmann was that Jesus existed, preached, and was crucified. The details of his surrounding life are, therefore, unimportant. As an exercise in reductionism, such an outlook may be unsurpassed, but it is enormously unhelpful for historians. Moreover, Bultmann argued that it was impossible to know anything about the historical Jesus based on gospel traditions—the so-called Lessing Ditch.* It was one of Bultmann's students, Ernst Käsemann, who, in 1953, ignited the "Second Quest," which aimed to establish a continuity of Jesus's preaching to what was espoused by the early Church. Without such continuity, Christians are left with a Church based upon a mythological founder.

The Second Quest, dominated mainly by German scholars, believed that although the Gospels should be examined from a mostly theological perspective, there remained enough historical information in them to tell us at least some of the facts about Jesus's life. These new analyses, however, examined the texts through a system of textual studies looking for dissimilarities between the Gospels and Jewish traditions. If a statement was not in keeping with Jewish tradition and also accepted by the early Church, then it was judged to be part of the authentic teaching of the historical Jesus. Another and clearly overlapping method of analysis employed by Second Quest scholars was the criterion of embarrassment, which held that anything in the Gospels that would embarrass the beliefs or doctrines of the early Church was unlikely to be invented. The most common example used to describe this criterion is Jesus's baptism by John the Baptist, as the Church would have been uncomfortable explain-

---

* Lessing's Ditch, named after the German Enlightenment scholar Gotthold Ephraim Lessing (1729–1781), used the picture of a ditch to describe the difference between the historical Jesus and the Jesus found in the New Testament, which, according to Lessing, was unreconcilable.

ing how the lesser John could baptize the Messiah and, thereby, remit the sins of a man supposedly unblemished by sin. The key problem with all of these analyses is that the Dead Sea Scrolls, many of them discovered just as the Second Quest was getting started, demonstrate that it is impossible to separate Jewish traditions from Hellenic traditions. The two cultures—Greek and Jewish—had been intermingling for centuries, and even the authors of the Scrolls, a separatist Jewish sect that renounced Hellenic culture, employed many Greek expressions and ideas in their works. Moreover, textual criticism, which has some utility when studying literary works, almost always falls short when applied to historical studies, as a historical instance either took place or it did not; it cannot be voided by claiming the text does not mean what it says. The Second Quest also foundered on a belief widely accepted among New Testament scholars: that the Gospels are not histories. Unfortunately, this belief in the non-historicity of the Gospels imbues most Second Quest scholars' works, who were only hoping to find a few remnants of history in what most of them considered mythological works.

In the end, the Second Quest scholars determined that all we can possibly know for sure about Jesus can be reduced to a few statements of fact, starting with Jesus having lived in Nazareth and ending with the Romans crucifying him. In between, Jesus was baptized, preached, gathered disciples, associated with persons on the margins of polite society, challenged the Jewish leadership, and was arrested. After that, the Second Quest says we can know nothing more.

If we accept the above lists of facts agreed upon by the Second Quest scholars, we must ask: Why did they discard the supporting evidence while keeping the ultimate facts?

The Third Quest, starting in the 1960s, aimed to make up for the shortcomings revealed in earlier approaches and went back to trying to comprehend Jesus within the Jewish environment in which he lived. Many of these more recent scholars have turned away from the assumptions of those who led the charge in the first two quests and are attempting to demonstrate that there is an overwhelming amount of continuity between the Jesus narrative in the Gospels and what the early Church was teaching.

This book follows the path set by Third Quest scholars but expands upon it in several significant ways. Most crucially, while this book acknowledges that Jesus operated within a Jewish environment, he was also part of a much larger Greco-Roman world. Greek culture and Roman power are too often ignored in scholarly attempts to understand the historical Jesus. But one cannot begin to grasp what occurred in Palestine two millennia ago without coming to grips with the fact that Roman and Greek influences permeated nearly every aspect of life throughout the Mediterranean. The Jews were not cut off from global trade, outside information, or imported cultural influences—nor was Jesus. As we shall see, even specific events far removed from Palestine could impact Judea and its environs.

What happened in Rome never stayed in Rome.

The Third Quest continues, but it has been joined by a new movement that is trying to return New Testament studies to the original aims of the First Quest, and separate Jesus's preaching from the requirements of the emerging Christian Church. In short, these scholars are trying to determine what Jesus actually said and what later writers invented for him. How this movement has gone off the rails is nowhere better demonstrated than in the results published by the well-publicized "Jesus Seminar."

The Jesus Seminar, founded by Robert Funk in 1985, brought together over fifty critical biblical scholars and another hundred laymen to determine what parts of the New Testament reflected the actual words of Jesus.

The Jesus Seminar, which was supposedly made up of a cross section of leading New Testament scholars, actually consists of a carefully curated group of scholars and pseudo-scholars (at least one of its members is a movie producer famous for *Basic Instinct* and *Showgirls*). They all share a common minority viewpoint on the Gospels that they want to push into mainstream thinking. The Jesus Seminar does have a few true New Testament scholars, including John Dominic Crossan and Marcus Borg, but they share the group's desire to minimize the Jesus found in the Gospels into just a few pithy quotes. In pursuit of their agenda, members started with two dangerous propositions:

1. Anything in the Gospels that showed Jesus speaking about eschatological events (the end of days and the coming of God's kingdom) was never uttered by Jesus and was placed there at a later date by the gospel authors.

2. Everything that was authentically spoken by Jesus must adhere to the criterion of dissimilarity. In other words, if what Jesus says in the Gospels is part of Jewish or Christian tradition, he did not say it. How could this be so?

Robert Funk's *The Five Gospels* lays out the Seminar's findings.* Why five Gospels? The Seminar decided they liked the gnostic Gospel of Thomas, which is not part of the Christian canon, primarily because it consists entirely of the sayings of Jesus. Thus, the Gospel of Thomas was already where the Seminar participants wanted to be. To make this added Gospel work for their purposes, the Jesus Seminar participants decided—based on zero evidence—that Thomas was written about the same time as Mark and therefore reflected what Jesus actually said. Historians, however, date Thomas to the middle of the second century—well after the four canonical Gospels started circulating and a full century after Mark was written.

To determine which passages of the Gospels were authentic, the Seminar members voted using beads. A red bead meant that a particular selection came straight out of Jesus's mouth; a pink bead meant it sounded like Jesus, but the member was not sure; a gray bead meant that a selection could be Jesus speaking, but probably not; and a black bead was used when a member believed the selection was definitely not spoken by Jesus. Each bead was assigned a number, which was added up as a weighted average, and the authenticity of each New Testament selection was determined based on the final score. It is hard to imagine a more ahistorical approach to any ancient writings.

When all was said and done, the Seminar did away with 82 percent of the passages the Gospels attribute to Jesus. For instance, the Lord's Prayer was reduced to two words. According to the Jesus Seminar, the words

* Robert W. Funk, *The Five Gospels* (Scribner Book Company, 1993).

"Our Father" were said by Jesus, and the rest of the prayer was declared rubbish and a later invention by unknown authors. Also dismissed as mythical inventions were the resurrection, the virgin birth, and every gospel miracle. According to *U.S. News & World Report*, the founder of the Seminar, Robert Funk, declared that "Jesus was the first stand-up Jewish comic . . . starting a new religion would have been the farthest thing from his mind."

The Seminar succeeded in removing Jesus from the world of a first-century Jew living in Palestine. It also did away with Jesus's apocalyptic worldview, as well as Jesus's eschatological preaching of a coming Kingdom of God. The Jesus revealed by the Seminar is nothing but a nice Jewish boy who roamed around telling people to be nice to each other. He could not possibly have said or done anything that might anger Jewish leaders and give Rome cause to crucify him. At its core, the Seminar wants everyone to believe that the gospel authors—who all lived during Jesus's lifetime and two of whom were likely part of his core group of apostles—had, within a generation of Jesus's death, decided to discard everything they had seen or heard Jesus say. They then replaced several years of Jesus's teaching with an entirely new narrative of their own design with the aim of supporting a new religion. One wonders how these four gospel authors managed to coordinate their work over several decades. Somehow, these farseeing individuals could also determine the exact passages future Christians required to support a Church doctrine constructed a century or two after the gospel authors were deceased. As improbable as that sounds, to accept the Seminar's findings, we also need to buy into the belief that everyone hearing these stories—many of whom knew or had seen Jesus—willingly accepted this wholesale revision of what they had personally witnessed. More remarkably, those Jewish leaders trying to kill the Jesus movement from its inception did not use these revisions to call out the gospel writers for perverting the truth.

In the end, the Jesus Seminar reveals itself as an ahistorical group of modern-day zealots trying to create a postmodern Jesus who never offended anyone and could not possibly offend anyone today. Given its findings, one is at a loss to explain why the Sanhedrin and the Romans took any interest in such a bland and inoffensive person. The only explanation for this conundrum is that the Jesus Seminar got everything wrong. It is unfortunate that it has received the publicity that it has over the years. But this was the intent of the Seminar's founders, who hoped to create a new Jesus more in tune with the modern era and make sure their creation was well publicized, the facts be damned.

PART II

THE ROMAN WORLD

FOUR

What Was the Roman Empire?

From its inauspicious start in the middle of the eighth century BC, on the banks of the Tiber River, Rome grew to become one of history's most powerful empires. It was certainly the longest-lasting, taking longer to decline and fall than most empires existed. In 33 AD, the Roman Empire was still at the start of its five-hundred-year run and was only on its second emperor, Tiberius. The first, Augustus, died in 14 AD and was immediately deified. One can assume that the idea that a man, upon his death, could become a god made it easier for Romans at the start of the Christian era to accept that Jesus was both a man and god. Still, one wonders how seriously the Romans, at least educated Romans, took this idea, as the emperor Vespasian satirically quipped on his deathbed, "Oh my, I think I am turning into a god."* Quite the wit from the emperor who, with his son, Titus, mercilessly crushed the Great Jewish Revolt (66–73 AD), sacked Jerusalem, and destroyed the great Jewish Temple.

Most of Rome's early history is lost in the mists of time and legend.

---

* Suetonius, *The Twelve Caesars, Vespasian*, 23.4. For another humorous view of how educated Romans viewed the deification of emperors, it is worth perusing Seneca's (attributed) *Apocolocyntosis*—The Pumpkinification of Claudius—https://www.gutenberg.org/files/10001/10001-h/10001-h.htm.

What we do know is that Rome was forced to fight for its survival from its very inception. Burnt into the historical memory of every Roman was the hostility of all of their neighbors, which Rome could only overcome by being "forced" to conquer them. Two events in this early history of the period were seared into the collective Roman consciousness.

The first was a lesson in the importance of determination when fighting a war that arose when Italy's most powerful Greek city-state, Tarantum, attacked Rome. When the leaders of Tarantum realized they had made a mistake by attacking the vicious and unforgiving Romans, they called on Pyrrhus, king of Epirus, to bring a professional Greek army to their aid. He defeated Rome in a series of battles, but at such cost that when Pyrrhus was congratulated on his victory, he replied: "If we are victorious in one more battle with the Romans, we shall be utterly ruined"—the origin of the term "Pyrrhic victory."

But Rome was also reeling, and the Senate decided to consider and vote on the peace terms offered by Pyrrhus. The senators were leaning toward accepting the offered terms when the aged and blind senator Appius Claudius Caecus rose to speak. He told the assembly that he wished he had become deaf as well as blind so he did not have to bear the shame of hearing Roman senators debate accepting terms from an enemy who still had an army in the field. After reminding his fellow senators that Rome only discussed peace after an enemy had been vanquished, he demanded the expulsion of Pyrrhus's ambassador and the immediate restarting of hostilities. With renewed purpose, Rome's battered but unbroken legions retook the field. Pyrrhus was unwilling to engage and soon departed the peninsula in hopes of easier pickings elsewhere.[*]

The second great lesson, one that dominated Roman strategic decision-making for centuries, was delivered by a force of Celtic barbarians in 390 BC. After defeating a hastily assembled Roman army at the Battle of the Allia on July 18—an accursed day on the Roman calendar—the Celts entered Rome. After the defeat, the Romans fortified themselves within the citadel on Capitoline Hill and prepared for a siege. Unfortunately, there was insufficient space on the hill for the entire pop-

---

[*] Appian, *Samnite Wars*, 10.5–6.

ulation, and priority was given to the young. The elderly were left behind, but to help reconcile them to their fate, every past Roman consul voted to join them. As the Gauls moved through the city, they saw the consuls seated around the forum in their regal gowns of office. For a long time, the Gauls were stayed from slaughter by the regal magnificence and stately manner of the consuls. Then, as Livy relates, "M. Papirius roused the passion of a Gaul, who began to stroke his beard . . . by smiting him on the head with his ivory staff. He was the first to be killed, the others were butchered in their chairs." A general massacre of the aged Romans ensued.

After withstanding a short siege on the Capitoline, the Romans agreed to pay the Gauls a thousand pounds of gold to depart.* When the Romans complained that the scales were calibrated to cheat them, the barbarian leader tossed his sword on the scale, "uttering words intolerable to the Roman ears, namely *'Vae victis,'* or 'Woe to the vanquished!'"† Before the Gauls could get away, however, they were met by another Roman army. This time, the Romans won a decisive victory and, according to Livy, the slaughter was total. When the annihilation was complete, the Roman general stated, *"Non auro, sed ferro, recuperanda est patria"*—not by gold, but by iron, is the nation to be restored.‡ Centuries later, accounts of these two events still dominated the Roman imagination and guided Rome's policies: Always negotiate from a position of strength, and Rome's salvation was always to be found in the "iron" of the legions.

The martial mindset, developed by necessity, first ensured the city's survival and was then instrumental in Rome's expansion across the Mediterranean and into the hinterlands far beyond the coast. By the time of Jesus's death, the Roman Empire was almost at its maximum size. Only Briton, gold-rich Dacia, and Mesopotamia had yet to be conquered. The latter two would be abandoned in favor of protecting the Roman core when the Empire was under military pressure all along its frontiers. But in 33 AD, what Edward Gibbon wrote about the second century was already mostly true: "The empire of Rome comprehended the fairest part

* Livy, *History of Rome*, 5.41.
† Ibid., 5.48.
‡ Plutarch, *Parallel Lives*, "Camillus," 5.29.

of the earth and the most civilized portion of mankind. The frontiers of that extensive monarchy were guarded by ancient renown and disciplined valor. The gentle but powerful influence of laws and manners had gradually cemented the union of the provinces. Their peaceful inhabitants enjoyed and abused the advantages of wealth and luxury."*

If one's goal is to spread a new religion over a large segment of the world, it would be difficult to find a better period in history to do so. Until the advent of the Roman Empire, the Mediterranean world, since the first dawning of civilization in the region, consisted of a fragmented collection of states continually warring with one another. Rome and its legions enforced unity where it had never been before—first through the iron of the legions and then through an enlightened policy of ruling with a very loose footprint. As long as there was peace and the assessed tax revenues arrived in Rome on time, the emperor, Senate, and people of Rome were content to let locals govern their own affairs. A Roman governor held sway for the big issues, but the minutiae of local governance was mainly left to the locals.

In 33 AD, the Roman Empire stretched from Spain in the east to the Syrian deserts in the west, and from north to south, it occupied all of the lands between the North Sea and the Saharan Desert. Its tentacles were already reaching deep down the Nile, and its traders were already well familiar with India and possibly beyond. When Jesus began his ministry, Rome was the most extensive unified political structure the world had ever known and would remain so until its fall in 476 AD. The Empire's population was probably pushing sixty million people, of which, according to a census in 8 BC, 4,233,000 were Roman citizens. In terms of density, there were approximately forty-one persons per square mile, which is close to half of Europe's current population density of eighty-seven persons per square mile. Compared to the next fifteen hundred years, the Roman Empire had extraordinarily high urbanization rates, with the city of Rome likely already topping four hundred thousand on its way to one million residents. No Western European city would again attain this

* Edward Gibbon, *The History of the Decline and Fall of the Roman Empire*, Vol. 1 (Strahan & Cadell, 1776), p. 1.

number until well into the nineteenth century. Over 11,500 towns have been identified outside of Rome, of which, in 33 AD, over fifty had more than ten thousand residents. A vast network of ports and eventually 250,000 miles of roads connected all of these towns and cities.

Roman power also enforced what has become known as the *Pax Romana*, which blessed the Mediterranean world with unprecedented peace and stability for at least the first two centuries of the Empire. It is difficult to overestimate the impact of such a prolonged peace in a world that had always known war. In succeeding chapters, we will discuss how the *Pax Romana* impacted the Empire's economy, including a focused look at Galilee. But for now, we can leave it with a single observation: Jesus lived during a period of peace and increasing prosperity, unlike any time in history. Such a period would not be seen again until the nineteenth century's *Pax Britannica* and then again during the still ongoing, if weakening, *Pax Americana*.

FIVE

Rome Rules the World

I t is remarkable how many works on the historical Jesus neglect the fact that he was living in a world dominated by Rome. This oversight is understandable, as in the Gospels, Rome is only directly referred to a few times, first in the birth narrative—Augustus's ordering a census of the Empire—and then again during the last week of Jesus's life, as the Roman prefect, Pontius Pilate, sends Jesus to his death. In between, Jesus interacts with only a single Roman during his entire ministry when a centurion (who may not even have been Roman) asks him for help curing a slave.* There are six other mentions of centurions in the New Testament; one is present at the crucifixion, while the others are all found in the Acts of the Apostles.†

What does this tell us about Roman rule? For one, although Rome could make its power felt at any time and anywhere within the Empire, it preferred to rule with a light hand, though its military power remained a brooding dark menace looming just over the horizon, something Rome's subjects forgot only at great peril. When the Empire's residents met a

---

* Luke 7:1–10.
† Matthew 27:54 and Mark 15:39 for the centurion at the crucifixion.

Roman outside of Italy, it was usually for two reasons. The first was trade, as Roman traders and merchants were ubiquitous throughout the Empire. The second was by coming into contact with a Roman official. In most cases this would be a centurion whose official duties brought them to the farthest reaches of the Empire, for centurions were the workhorses of the Empire's administrative apparatus.

First and foremost, a centurion was a soldier, what today might be considered a midgrade officer within a legion, combining the duties of both an officer and a sergeant. As the name implies, a centurion commanded a Roman century, which normally consisted of about eighty men (rarely a hundred). There were six centuries to a cohort, of which the first century was usually double strength, and five cohorts to a legion. Centurions were promoted by giving them control of more prestigious centuries. The centurion of the double-strength first century in each cohort was the senior century in that cohort—the *primi ordines*. He would also have a staff role as an adviser to the legion's commander. Most centurions were considered of the same rank, except the commander of the first cohort of the first century of the legion—the *primus pilus*—who would also sit on various higher-level war councils.

The centurions were only outranked by the legionary commander (the legate), the camp prefect, who was usually a former *primus pilus,* and the legion's six tribunes. At this point in the Empire, the legate was almost always drawn from the senatorial class, as were the tribunes. A tribune would likely have already served and gained military experience in an auxiliary formation before being promoted into the legions. The legate would have somewhat more military experience, but being a soldier was not his life. Both the legates and the tribunes viewed their service as required stepping stones for political advancement.

Typically, one would expect to rarely see a centurion, as they would be with their commands, and these commands were scattered along the frontiers, tasked with keeping out the barbarians and Persians. Only in Syria was there a strong enough concentration of Roman soldiers near population centers for there to be regular contact between soldiers and civilians—only necessary because the Persians (Parthians) were always a serious enough threat that the legions who would first meet them in combat required a sufficient mass to hold the line until the Empire could mobilize its tremendous and ferocious latent power.

But Rome had a problem. Its governmental structure had never gotten far beyond what it was when it was a small, rapidly expanding city-state on the banks of the Tiber. Until Diocletian's reign, which is still centuries away from our own period, Rome never created the proper administrative apparatus to run a far-flung empire. Yes, Rome had its governors, but they came with only a small staff, and they always did their best to rule through the infrastructure the Romans found in place when the legions first marched in. Moreover, even the governors and their staffs were only part-timers, as even this exalted position was considered just one more stepping stone to further advancement within Rome's political system.

As such, no governor wanted to make a mistake and limit his chances for advancement or other preferments the emperor had to give. An insecure governor, depending on the current emperor's temper and ferocity, would repeatedly seek guidance from Rome for even the most trivial items. One has only to look at the letters of Pliny the Younger, governor of Pontus/Bithynia, to the emperor, Trajan, to get a feel of just how tedious it must have been for any emperor to review the masses of such correspondence coming from all corners of the Empire. In the case of Pliny, his most famous letter was a request for Trajan to guide him on how to deal with Christians, who Pliny was encountering for the first time. Some excerpts will give us an impression of how the Romans initially felt about this new religion:

> Meanwhile, in the case of those who were denounced to me as Christians, I have observed the following procedure: I interrogated these as to whether they were Christians; those who confessed I interrogated a second and a third time, threatening them with punishment; those who persisted I ordered executed. For I had no doubt that, whatever the nature of their creed, stubbornness and inflexible obstinacy surely deserve to be punished . . .
>
> Accordingly, I judged it all the more necessary to find out what the truth was by torturing two female slaves who were called dea-

conesses. But I discovered nothing else but depraved, excessive superstition. I therefore postponed the investigation and hastened to
consult you.[*]

Trajan's response was for Pliny to avoid seeking out Christians but to
punish any who were denounced to him unless they denied their faith.
Pliny was also warned to give no credence to anonymous accusations, as
they would establish a dangerous precedent and were out of keeping with
the ethics of the time.

To somewhat make up for its administrative weakness, Rome's centurions were often pulled away from their units to handle a host of non-
military matters. That could range from delivering a crucial message
from the emperor to going off, on the emperor's order, to murder someone on the far side of the Empire. Centurions were trusted for these tasks
because they were famous for their devotion to Rome and their loyalty to
the emperor, although the centurions of the Praetorian Guard would
soon demonstrate that little faith could be placed in this latter trait. They
were also mature—over thirty years of age, literate, and determined.

Traits almost all centurions had in common were that they were hard
and determined men who could be counted upon to complete any task
or die in the attempt. In a later era, Vegetius listed the traits that made a
good centurion:

> The centurion in the infantry is chosen for his size, strength and
> dexterity in throwing his missile weapons and for his skill in the
> use of his sword and shield . . . He is to be vigilant, temperate,
> active and readier to execute the orders he receives than to talk;
> Strict in exercising and keeping up proper discipline among his
> soldiers . . . [†]

They were vicious in combat and harsh disciplinarians. To help maintain discipline, centurions were issued a cane (a vine rod) as a symbol of

[*] Pliny, *Letters*, 20.96–97. All of Pliny's letters can be found at www.attalus.org/info/pliny.html.
[†] Vegetius, *De re militari*, Book II.

their authority and a handy club to use on any soldier not meeting their standards. In a legionary mutiny covered in more detail later in this book, Tacitus tells of the fate of one overstrict centurion:

> . . . they ejected the tribunes and camp-marshal and plundered the fugitives' baggage. The centurion Lucilius also met his end [murdered]. Camp humorists had surnamed him "Fetch-Another," from his habit, as one cane broke over a private's back, of calling at the top of his voice for a second, and ultimately a third.*

In short, many hard and unpleasant jobs come up when one is running a sprawling empire, and centurions are just the kinds of men one counts on to get the hard jobs done. So, it is no wonder that centurions are the Romans we most encounter in the New Testament, as each of these encounters would certainly have been memorable.

There are several things that make Jesus meeting a centurion in Capernaum remarkable. The first is that the local Jewish leaders asked Jesus to help them, as they declared him a good man, and that he had built a synagogue for the town. Here we have evidence that Jesus's ministry and attested healing powers were becoming widely known. More crucially, there were clearly large numbers of people in the local Jewish leadership supporting Jesus's work who were on good enough terms with him to ask for a favor. Also, for a centurion to have made such an impression on the locals and to finance the construction of a synagogue indicates that he had been detached from his unit for some time.

What made Capernaum worth detaching one of Rome's precious centurions for such an extended period? Christians today visit the ruins to walk in the town that was Jesus's base for most of his ministry. Archaeologists have also discovered the synagogue Jesus often preached in, which is likely the same one built by the Roman centurion. This discovery is, of course, further proof of the historical accuracy of the Gospels, even in the smaller details. Archaeologists also believe they have found Peter the

* Tacitus, *The Annals*, 18.23.1.

Apostle's house within the town's ruins. Capernaum clearly has a deep meaning for today's Christians, but what explains Roman interest?

The explanation is simple. Capernaum was strategically important, as it sat along the main north-south road that connected Egypt with Damascus—the two most important provinces in the Eastern Empire. Moreover, the town stood on the boundary between the territories of Herod Philip and Herod Antipas, making it the nexus of any dispute between the two. Thus, almost all of the trade moving across Palestine would travel through Capernaum, where it could be easily taxed, as there were good roads over flat ground, plentiful water from the Sea of Galilee and the Jordan River, and, judging from the number of first-century mills found in the area, vast amounts of food to be had from nearby farms. Finally, a Parthian army trying to take Syria would need to use Palestine as a logistical base, which would only be possible if they controlled Capernaum.

All of this explains Rome's interest and the presence of a centurion in the town. But comments made by the centurion while he was talking to Jesus leads one to believe he was not there alone. The centurion mentions to Jesus that he was sent to Capernaum and that he has men available to fulfill his commands immediately.* Unless we assume that he could finance the building of an extravagant synagogue out of his military pay, which is unlikely, we can deduce that he had access to imperial funds. It does not take much of a logical leap to believe that Rome, or at least the governor of Syria, recognized the importance of the location and that the region could easily house and supply a contingent of troops. Whether that was the centurion's eighty-man century, or a full cohort, is impossible to determine.

The locals do not appear to be distressed at having Romans in their midst, which is a blow to the still common idea that the Galilee of Jesus's time was a hotbed of insurrectionist sentiment, a topic we will return to later in this book. The Jews of Capernaum clearly have no problem dealing with Roman officials or accepting money from them. Moreover,

* Luke 7:8.

Jesus appears very comfortable in the presence of a very dangerous Roman. As it was in Capernaum, so it was throughout the Empire. By the time Jesus began his ministry, the Empire, particularly at its core, was mainly quiet and had accepted, or at least grown accustomed to, Roman rule.

A Survey of the Roman World

During Jesus's lifetime, the legions had not yet taken Briton. Rome was aware of its presence and economic potential, as its merchants, especially traders in tin, had been busy in Briton for decades. Julius Caesar had even invaded the island in 55 BC and again in 54 BC. But he did not stay long enough for Rome to gain lasting control. Rome took almost an entire century before it became serious about taking the island again. In 43 AD, Emperor Claudius, in need of a glorious military reputation to secure his hold on power, sent four legions to subdue the island. The conquest of Briton dragged on for another forty years, until the final army of the Britons was defeated by Gnaeus Julius Agricola, Tacitus's uncle, at the Battle of Mons Graupius. Even then, the Romans never fully conquered the northern parts of the island.

Before the defeat at Mons Graupius, Rome had managed to settle much of southern Briton and secured an uneasy peace. However, Roman commercial interests soon arrived in force, bringing trouble in their wake. This was predictable, as trouble always came on the heels of Rome's merchants' first infestation of a region and as the new Roman administration began collecting taxes. But in 33 AD, the person destined to lead the revolt against Rome, Boadicea, was still a young girl, probably not yet in her teens. Later, she would marry Prasutagus, become queen of the nominally independent Iceni tribe, and raise two daughters. When her husband died, Rome annexed the Iceni territory, centered on current Norfolk, and confiscated the tribe's royal property. At the same time, Roman lenders, including the famed writer and philosopher Seneca, called in their many forced loans. Seneca had personally loaned leading Britons forty million sesterces and was ruthless in its collection with interest.* According to Tacitus, the tribal leaders were stripped of their land and wealth, while relatives of the deceased king were treated as slaves.†

Facing economic ruin, the Iceni protested. The Roman response was to have Queen Boadicea publicly flogged and her daughters raped as she impotently watched. Rome, as it was wont to do in the early decades of any new conquest, miscalculated the level of residual hatred the locals harbored against the intruders. Boadicea, who Dio claimed was "possessed of greater intelligence than often belongs to women," raised the flag of revolt, and the Britons answered.‡ Over the next few weeks, as many as eighty thousand Romans were killed. Dio gives full vent to the brutality of the Britons:

> The worst and most bestial atrocity committed by their captors was the following. They hung up naked the noblest and most distinguished women and then cut off their breasts and sewed them to their mouths, in order to make the victims appear to be eating them; afterwards they impaled the women on sharp skewers run lengthwise through the entire body. All this they did to the accompaniment of sacrifices, banquets, and wanton behavior.§

After wiping out the newly formed and barely trained IX Legion, Boadicea and her rebel army probably thought itself invincible. But on the island of Mona Anglesey, General Gaius Suetonius Paulinus, with the XIV Legion, was busily exterminating the last Druid strongholds as well as the last remaining Druids. The XIV Legion was already famous as the

---

* Dio, *The Roman Histories*, 62.2.1.
† Tacitus, *The Annals*, 14.31.
‡ Dio, *The Roman Histories*, 62.2.1.
§ Ibid., 62.7.2–3.

most effective legion in the Roman army and has been called by one recent historian "Nero's Killing Machine."* Paulinus wrecked Boadicea's massive army in a very short time, and she likely committed suicide rather than be captured by the Romans. Thereafter, Briton was rapidly integrated into the Roman Empire and was a prosperous and largely peaceful province for the next several hundred years. Interestingly, it was from Briton that Constantine, the first Christian emperor, began his march toward ultimate power.

Moving across the sea to Gaul (modern France), we find a much different picture. Eight decades before 33 AD, Julius Caesar had waged a relentless and ruthless war of subjugation in Gaul. It had taken eight years, but the slaughter and ruin were so complete that Gaul remained remarkably quiescent throughout the decades of the Roman civil war. While Rome was distracted, the Gauls worked to repair the damage left in the wake of Caesar's campaigns and return to a sense of normalcy. What they did not return to was the high levels of internecine warfare that the various Celtic tribes had waged for centuries. This was both a consequence of the Roman-enforced peace and the fact that their forces were so diminished that it would take a generation to rebuild them. But peace suited the Gauls, who were already relatively wealthy before Rome's arrival.

With its ancestral memories of Celtic invasions, Rome may have thought of the Gauls as barbarians, but by the time Jesus was born, they no longer fit the mold for how we think about barbarians. Even before Rome arrived, the countryside was rapidly urbanizing, and some of the Celts' coastal cities were as wealthy as any Greek or Roman city. Some Celtic tribes already had Republican forms of government, and most traded along extensive networks within Gaul and abroad. At the time, the Romans considered them fierce fighters because they remained aloof from Roman luxury. But this was already increasingly untrue before Caesar's invasions, and after the conquest was complete, the Gauls, at least the rich ones, found as much joy in luxury as any Roman.

---

* Stephen Dando-Collins, *Nero's Killing Machine: The True Story of Rome's Remarkable 14th Legion* (Wiley, 2004).

As Jesus was entering adulthood, problems arose in Gaul. By this time, Rome's civil wars were over, and it could pay more attention to fully integrating recently conquered provinces into the Empire. As was almost always the case, the crisis was fueled by financial matters, as Rome began increasing its demands for tribute (taxes). Rome's large tax demands for funding the campaigns of Germanicus in Germany from 14 to 16 AD (discussed elsewhere in this book) remained in place despite the fighting ending over a decade before.

Julius Sacrovir of the Aedui tribe and Julius Florus of the Treveri refused to pay and organized an army of debtors to overthrow Roman power. According to Tacitus, it was an auspicious moment to revolt, as the legions were in a rebellious mood after the death of their idolized leader, Germanicus, who many suspected was murdered. For a time, Celtic spirits ran high, and the rebels seized the city of Augustodunum (modern Autun), mobilized an army of over forty thousand, and awaited the Roman reaction. They did not have to wait long, as the legions, despite their recent troublesome attitude and possibly because of it, were spoiling for a fight. Two legions marched immediately, only slowed by the traditional burning and pillaging along the march route.

According to Tacitus, when the Romans saw the force arrayed against them, they considered it shameful for legions that had been fighting Germanic warriors to have to fight the motley Gallic army in front of them. Still, it would be a profitable slaughter, and afterward, Augustodunum would be theirs to sack. So the legionaries formed their lines and drew their swords. As for the Gauls, their leaders tried to inspire them with brave speeches. But the words fell on deaf ears, as the undrilled townspeople and farmers were no longer accustomed to war and were already edging toward panic.

The Romans surged forward and the Gauls broke. The fighting was over in minutes, although the slaughter continued for much longer. The only trouble the Romans had was encountering a mass of select warriors encased almost entirely in iron and impervious to swords and javelins. Still, the Romans did not tarry long, as they made quick work of the iron monsters. According to Tacitus, "The legionaries caught up their axes and picks and hacked at armor and flesh as if demolishing a wall: others overturned the inert masses with poles or forks, and left them lying like the dead."* Finally, Sacrovir and the other leaders retreated into a building, which the Romans set ablaze rather than assaulting it.

So ended the final revolt of the Gauls. It was over so quickly that the messengers bringing news of the victory at Autun may have arrived before Rome even knew there was a revolt. Gaul was quiet for the next two centuries, becoming as Roman as any part of Italy. Gaul would not seek to go its own way again until the middle of the Third Century Crisis. But even then, its departure resulted from needing to protect itself from Germanic raiders at a time when most of the Roman army was fighting the Persians or the Goths along the Danube.

In the years after the revolt, new towns and cities formed, major roads were constructed, masonry replaced wood, and there was a construction boon as amphitheaters, aqueducts, and baths were built throughout the province. As Gaul became rich, the tax burden seemed lighter, and the people became content. Gaul's assimilation was complete by 33 AD, and less than a decade later, the emperor Claudius made local landed aristocracy eligible to sit in the Senate and began appointing them to posts in Rome previously reserved for Romans.

To the south of Gaul lay Hispania (modern Spain), which had begun the process of Romanization much earlier than Gaul. Rome was already edging into Hispania in the late third century BC but was held at bay by the Carthaginian presence in the region. During the Second Punic War, most of eastern Hispania became a battleground. At the same time, Hannibal defeated several Roman armies in Italy but could not force Rome to surrender. Instead, unable to defeat Hannibal, the Romans sent legions under Scipio to Spain and wrested it and its silver ore bounty from Carthage. When the Punic Wars ended, Rome controlled eastern Spain and was inexorably moving inland. However, they met fierce resistance, particularly from the Lusitanians, who occupied much of what is today Portugal. The conquest was not finally completed until early in Augustus's reign and only after a decade of fighting against Celts in northern Spain.

* Tacitus, *The Annals*, 3.44–47.

Augustus, in 27 BC, created three provinces in Hispania that remained unchanged for two hundred years: Hispania Baetica, whose capital is modern Cordoba and included much of Andalusia; Lusitania, whose capital is the modern city of Mérida; and Tarraconensis, whose capital is the modern city of Tarragona. After Augustus completed the final conquest, Spain Romanized quickly, following the same pattern of economic integration we saw in Gaul: a construction boom, increased trade, an agricultural expansion, and extensive mining operations. By 33 AD, Spain was exporting large amounts of silver to Rome along with tin, gold, lead, wool, wheat, and even olive oil. It is no exaggeration to say that under the *Pax Romana*, Spain grew rich and stayed rich for a long time after the Empire's collapse. Spain, in fact, became so Romanized that it was almost an appendage of Italy and later produced three of the emperors most highly regarded by historians—Trajan, Hadrian, and Theodosius.

After crossing the Strait of Gibraltar, one enters Rome's North African provinces. Almost all of the original Roman provinces consisted of lands that previously belonged to Carthage. Rome took them at the end of the Third Punic War, and having left the city of Carthage in ruins, Utica was made the new capital. For a long time, Rome paid scant attention to its new province, which, therefore, remained pastoral and mostly poor. Agriculture in the regions was always based on small plots and herds, rarely rising much above subsistence level. Local agricultural wealth diminished further when Carthage was lost as a market for surplus food, and even further when the riches Carthage had earned through trade suddenly ended. Moreover, much of North Africa—Numidia and Mauretania—were left under the control of client kings as rewards for supporting Rome during the Punic Wars.

Of course, there were some profits to be had in North Africa; where there were profits, there were Roman traders; and where there were Roman traders, there were aggrieved local merchants. In 112 BC, an illegitimate prince, Jugurtha, led a revolt against Roman power, sacking the city of Citra and killing every Roman citizen. It took six years of bloody warfare before Gaius Marius and Lucius Cornelius Sulla finally crushed the revolt. When it was over, many of the veteran legionnaires were given land in North Africa, particularly in Numidian territory. This colonization increased the safety and stability of the region. As most of the legions left North Africa, the one remaining legion pushed out toward the edge of the Sahara and fortified the frontier and the oases along the approach routes used by raiders plaguing the province.

Interestingly, a falling-out between Marius and Sulla brought about a series of internal political fights and civil wars that collapsed the Roman Republic and established the Roman Empire. During this period, the comparative peacefulness of North Africa attracted settlers, speeding up Romanization and increasing the agricultural bounty. Both were speeded along by Julius Caesar, and even more so by Augustus, who placed approximately twenty more military colonies in the region.

By 33 AD, North Africa, not including Egypt, was well on its way to being the most prosperous region in the Empire. It produced about a million tons of grain a year, of which at least a quarter and probably as much as a half was exported. North Africa became the "granary of empire," and its grain fed Rome's burgeoning population. Josephus, writing a generation after Jesus's death, claimed that Egypt supplied Rome's grain needs for four months while North Africa did so for eight months.* As time passed, increasing amounts of Egyptian wheat were sent to Constantinople while the North African provinces filled Rome's needs. In the Empire's later years, North African grain was feeding a million Romans (the *Cura Annonae*), of which almost a quarter of a million were given free grain. Through such methods, the Roman government bought peace from the Roman mob. North Africa's importance to the Roman economy and civil stability was already apparent in Jesus's time. Even the incredibly frugal Tiberius never reduced the government's outlays for subsidized grain, saying in 22 AD that if he ended the *Cura Annonae*, it would mean the utter ruin of the state.† Civil peace bought by what Juvenal later called *panen et circenses*—bread and circuses—was, while Jesus preached, already an established fact. It was to last until the fifth century when the Vandals broke into North Africa and separated the region and its grain from the Roman Empire. Thus, the great tax

---

* Josephus, *The Jewish War*, 2.383–386.
† Tacitus, *The Annals*, 3.54.1.

spine of the Empire was broken, an insult from which Rome never recovered.

Moving east, we come to Egypt, the gem of the Empire. In 33 AD,
Egypt was by far the wealthiest province of the Roman Empire, and its
capital city, Alexandria, was, after Rome, the greatest and most prosperous city in the Empire. During Rome's great eastern expansion, Cleopatra, through her special relationship with first Julius Caesar and then
Mark Anthony, was able to keep Egypt at least nominally independent.
After the Battle of Actium and the deaths of Mark Anthony and Cleopatra, Augustus annexed Egypt to Rome.

Because of its wealth and capacity to threaten Rome by withholding
its exports of wheat, Egypt was a different kind of province. Mark Anthony, for instance, had been able to fund an army and a fleet nearly equal
to Rome's almost entirely from Egypt's resources. His defeat by Octavian
(later known as Augustus) was not preordained, and the conflict easily
could have gone the other way. All it took for any powerful Roman senator aspiring to become emperor was first to gain control of Egypt. Thus,
even as a province, Egypt remained an existential threat to Rome, or at
least the emperor. Thus, during Augustus's reign and for the next two
hundred years, a member of the senatorial class who wished to visit Egypt
had to have the expressed permission of the emperor before starting his
trip. Moreover, while a member of the senatorial class governed every
other Roman province, Egypt was always governed by someone from the
equestrian class. The belief—and it proved a correct one—was that an
equestrian, one step down on Rome's social ladder from the senatorial
class, could never muster sufficient support to make a run at ultimate
power, no matter how rich, tenacious, or brilliant he was. To further re-
inforce the emperor's writ, in what became a personal fief, three precious
legions (reduced to two by Tiberius) were maintained within the province for decades, despite minimal external threats.

Roman control of Egypt was more invasive than it was in most provinces. This reflects both the importance of Egypt to Roman fortunes and
the fact that the administrative apparatus of the Ptolemaic government
had stultified at a remarkably low level of efficiency. As was typical of
Roman provincial governments, finance, taxation, and justice were cen-

tralized and directed by the prefect and his assistants. But it was in the towns that Rome made the most far-reaching changes, primarily by importing the Greek model.

Rome appointed local administrative councils, who were responsible for running the community's internal affairs and the local agricultural area. As long as these councils handled things efficiently, which to the Romans meant ensuring the on-time payment of tax quotas, these councils were granted significant autonomy. As the rich were often able to evade taxes, the Romans forced the local elites to establish a system of "liturgies," which compelled specific individuals to pay for particular portions of the community's infrastructure, such as local roads, administrative buildings, temples, and even decorative statuary. Overseeing these local governments were *strategoi*, who led larger districts called *nomoi*. The *strategoi* were appointed by the governor and reported directly to him. Each *strategos* was assisted by a scribe responsible for the district's financial affairs. In both cases, the positions were filled by local Egyptians. As always, by allowing the *strategos* and councils to handle almost all of the provinces' local affairs, Rome was transferring the burden and expense of administration onto the local propertied classes. Such policies allowed Rome to maintain a small and unintrusive footprint. Anything larger would have sparked resentment and revolts.

Under this new administrative apparatus, Egypt's complex agricultural infrastructure attained new heights of efficiency, and the province grew rich. It helped that the Nile flood remained regular and that the Roman world was enjoying a few hundred years of what is now called the Roman Climate Optimum. Moreover, this regular bounty of grain had ready and profitable markets in the great cities of Alexandria and Rome. The rapid monetization of the economy further enriched Egypt at even the village level, which led to significant increases in internal trade, which did not peak until the end of the second century.

Socially, the Roman government maintained lists of who was Egyptian and who was of Greek descent. Since Alexander the Great's conquest of Egypt, the Greeks ruled the region. Although there had been substantial intermarriage, the Greeks mostly maintained themselves separate and apart from the general Egyptian population. As the Romans greatly respected Greek culture and were familiar with the Greeks from centuries of political and economic interactions, they preferred the Greek community in Egypt. Thus, the Greeks in Egypt paid a lower poll tax, were eligible for subsidized food distributions, and were generally at the forefront of any ruling urban aristocracy. The more numerous Egyptian population flourished under Roman rule, but nowhere near the level of the Greeks living in Egypt.

Alexandria, the Empire's Second City, prospered throughout this early period of the Empire. It had a secure food supply, was a center for industrial production, and dominated trade in the Eastern Mediterranean. It also thrived mightily as the central location for the collection of wheat destined for Rome, which was transported in a great armada of ships yearly. Also carried in these ships were many of the wares coming out of the East (mostly India) that Romans lusted for, particularly precious gems, silk, and spices, chiefly pepper, which was always in great demand. The Roman geographer Strabo mentions how much this trade grew during the years when Jesus was growing up:

> At any rate, when Gallus was prefect of Egypt, I accompanied him and ascended the Nile as far as Syene [Modern Aswan] and the frontiers of the Aksum [Ethiopia], and I learned that as many as one hundred and twenty vessels were sailing from Myos Hormos to the subcontinent, whereas formerly, under the Ptolemies, only a very few ventured to undertake the voyage and to carry on traffic in Indian merchandise.*

Pliny claims that over a hundred million sesterces' worth of gold and silver departed to India and China annually to pay for such luxuries. If that is an accurate number, that is the equivalent of what it cost to maintain the entire Roman military, legions, naval power, and auxiliary forces for an entire year. As Pliny complained, "That is what our luxuries and women cost us. For what fraction of these imports is intended for sacri-

* Strabo, *The Geography*, 2.5.12.

fices to the gods or the spirits of the dead?"* In 33 AD, when Rome was under severe financial stress (discussed later in this work), Tiberius railed against this huge export of Roman capital that returned only trinkets and spices that were consumed as soon as they arrived in Rome. This is an argument still played out in the United States, where politicians rail against China, taking all of our dollars for mere consumer items. That the trade was heavy during Jesus's lifetime is further attested to by the number of contemporary Roman coins found in India and China, which shows that Roman trade peaked with China and India in the decades following Jesus's death.†

Alexandria was also one of the Roman world's great cultural and philosophical centers. While it may have lost the support the Ptolemies lavished on Greek art and cultural events, there was a significant resurgence during the early years of the Empire. It was in Alexandria, more than any other city in the Empire, where the Latin culture of Rome merged with the Hellenistic culture of Greece. During Jesus's lifetime, Alexandria was also the home to the great Jewish scholar and philosopher Philo. Besides being an independent source for events in Judea, particularly regarding Pontius Pilate, Philo was well versed in Greek philosophical thought and brought this approach to his commentaries on the Old Testament. When Jerusalem and the Temple were destroyed during the Great Revolt (66–71 AD), Philo's work—one of the few learned documents to survive the destruction—guided the future development of the Jewish faith. Just as crucially, when Alexandria became a primary center for the development of Christian theology in the early second century, Philo's work directly influenced the interpretation the Neoplatonists applied to the Gospels. This Neoplatonist approach to gospel studies remains with us today, particularly in the Eastern Orthodox churches.

On his deathbed, surrounded by his great generals (the Diadochi), Alexander the Great was asked one question: Who should succeed him?

---

* Pliny, *Natural History*, 12.41.84.

† Alternatively, the Romans found items that the Indians wanted—glass, weapons, slaves, etc.—and shipped them east, allowing them to conserve gold and silver. This would indicate that trade did not decrease but that the terms of trade shifted. A recent discovery—the Muziris papyrus—would indicate that Roman trade was far less than Pliny states.

His supposed answer—"to the strongest"—condemned his Empire to decades of civil war.* After Alexander the Great's death, Syria became the great battlefield between two of his successors, the Seleucids and Ptolemies, until, in approximately 200 BC, Antiochus III defeated Ptolemy V Epiphanes and secured all of Syria. About a decade later, Antiochus's defeat by the Romans at Magnesia deprived him of core territories in Asia Minor and fatally weakened his hold on Syria and the rest of the Seleucid Empire. In the decades of civil and revolutionary wars that followed, the Seleucid Empire fragmented. The anarchy only ended with the arrival of Pompey and his Roman legions.

Before the great fragmentation of their empire and the arrival of Rome, the Seleucids had accomplished much. The petty kingdoms that arose around the great Phoenician trading cities of Tyre, Sidon, Byblos, and Aradus were replaced by Republics. These cities prospered as never before by taking advantage of a general peace in the northeastern Mediterranean. As their empire flourished, the Seleucids built new cities along the coast and deeper inland, which they populated with thousands of Greek and other European colonists. These new cities, including Antioch, Seleucia, Edessa, and Apamea, were rapidly integrated into an expanding Seleucid economy. So, by the time Rome arrived, the ancient cities of Palmyra and Damascus dominated an internal trading network that was growing increasingly wealthy. Damascus sat along the major north-south trade routes, while Palmyra grew fantastically rich by controlling land trade between east and west—a trunk of the Great Silk Road.

Rome, which had flirted with the idea of making the Seleucid Kingdom a client state, was, by 64 BC, in a position to do much more. After the Roman general Pompey had defeated Rome's most dangerous enemy since Hannibal, Mithridates, Rome found itself with a surfeit of military power in the eastern Mediterranean. Pompey commanded more than enough troops to dictate any terms he wished to the enfeebled Seleucids, including the dissolution of their empire and the integration of Syria as

* Diodorus Siculus, *Library*, 18.1.4.

a province of the Roman Empire. To hasten things along, Pompey ordered the execution of the Seleucid king, Antiochus XIII, and then deposed his successor, Philip II. After his almost casual destruction of the Seleucid monarchy, Pompey appointed a Roman proconsul to govern the region until the Senate formally declared it a province and sent out a governor.

By 33 AD, Syria had been a Roman province for almost a century. Because it sat on crucial trade routes and possessed several large natural ports, it was also one of Rome's wealthiest provinces. As such, it was garrisoned by three and, at times, four entire legions, along with a probably even greater number of auxiliaries. In 33 AD, Rome had not yet penetrated deep into Mesopotamia, except for some short-lived forays that had not gone well. Moreover, due to the extent of the great deserts to the east, assigning legions to guard an extended frontier was prohibitively expensive. But, as enemies could use only a few suitable avenues across the desert to attack the province, corresponding with its trading routes, it made sense to place the legions in fortifications along these routes, typically in major cities. Concentrating the legions in and near major cities helped accelerate the Romanization of at least the urban population, most of whom were already Hellenized. It also made these legions immediately available to march into Galilee and Judea at the first signs of unrest.

Outside of the cities, most of the population in 33 AD was still locked into their old traditions, speaking either Aramaic or some other Semitic dialect. It would take many more generations before Greek penetrated into the hinterlands, and Latin never did. But it is in the cities, particularly Antioch, where one can still see the ruins attesting to the might and influence of Rome. Antioch, along with Alexandria, became one of the Empire's great cities and a leading center for learning and the arts. And while the hinterlands remained wedded to agriculture, which fed the cities, the huge volumes of trade goods entering and leaving its ports truly enriched Syria and benefited the rest of the Empire. As Jerome said in the fourth century: "An innate enthusiasm for trading survives down to the present day among the Syrians, who run through the whole world in their eagerness for profit."* The Roman writer Salvianus, however, refers to Syrian traders as a worthless crowd of merchants who can be found in every corner of the earth.† Syrian traders may not have been esteemed or society's elite, but they were the crucial cog enriching the Roman Empire.‡

Moving north from Syria, we come to Asia Minor or Anatolia, which, for our reference, includes much of modern-day Turkey. Rome first entered the area during its war with the Seleucid king Antiochus III, but after winning the decisive Battle of Magnesia in 189 BC, it mostly withdrew from the region. It returned in 133 BC, when King Attalus III of Pergamon, a close ally of Rome, bequeathed his entire kingdom to Rome upon his death. His brother, Aristonicus (who ruled as Eumenes III), led a popular revolt, which Rome brutally smashed in 129 BC. Rome's sudden intrusion in the region had enormous repercussions for neighboring states such as Pontus to the north and Cappadocia to the east. For a time, both tried to live and trade peaceably with Rome until Mithridates VI became the ruler of Pontus.

Physically powerful, a brilliant strategist, and hugely ambitious, Mithridates plotted first to control the entire Black Sea and then to employ those resources to gain control of Anatolia. After gaining control of the regions making up modern-day Georgia, Crimea, and most of the Black Sea Coast, Mithridates turned his attention to Cappadocia. Rome was already allied with Cappadocia, so any attack on that state was the same as declaring war on Rome. But Rome, at that moment, was locked in a vicious Italian civil war—the Social War—and could only spare the two legions stationed in Macedonia. In 89 BC, Mithridates decisively defeated the Cappadocian army and Rome's two legions. He then swept into the Roman province of Asia, taking control of everything up to and including the Greek cities that dotted the Aegean. The following year, Mithridates organized a massacre of every Roman living within his bur-

---

* St. Jerome, *Commentary on Ezekiel*, 27.
† Salvianus, *De gubernatione Dei*, 4.14.69.
‡ For a still accurate accounting of Syrian commercial activities, see Louis C. West, "Commercial Syria Under the Roman Empire," *Transactions and Proceedings of the American Philological Association*, Vol. 55 (1924), pp. 159–189.

geoning empire. In what became known as the Asiatic Vespers, at least eighty thousand Romans perished.

Greece, including Athens, went over to Mithridates and welcomed his armies into their territory. In the east, Armenia also allied itself with the upstart, while the Mithridatic fleet besieged a Roman force in Rhodes. Unfortunately for Mithridates, the Social War was ending, leaving Rome more powerful and united than before the war. Mithridates now had Rome's complete and undivided attention, a state of affairs that had never ended well for Rome's enemies.

The resulting three wars were long and vicious, but the result was never in doubt. The increasingly professional legions eventually destroyed Mithridates's armies and subdued the entire region. In the end, Mithridates had his bodyguard kill him before he could be subjected to Rome's final wrath. Just as crucial for the political development of Rome, the legions at this time began transferring their ultimate allegiance from the city of Rome to their commanders—Marius, Sulla, Pompey, and eventually Caesar. With their loyal armies at their backs, the generals doomed the Republic to military tyranny—an Empire for the strongest was available for the taking.

In 85 BC, Rome reorganized the area into eleven assize districts, each centered on one of their already ancient cities, including: Ephesus, Pergamon, Smyrna, Miletus, and Halicarnassus, the birthplace of the father of history, Herodotus. Due to ancient antagonisms and jealousies among all of these cities, the region was always challenging to manage. By the time Augustus ruled, the area was controlled through a mostly self-governing city system that established local laws and collected its own taxes. Rome was content to let this awkward system stand as long as it got its share of the tax revenue, and no city went to war with another. As the region had a long history of being conquered, it adjusted rapidly to Roman rule. So readily did it adapt to its new status that Rome did not need to maintain any legions within its vast expanse for hundreds of years. There were, however, some auxiliary formations stationed in a few cities. Moreover, Roman armies would routinely march across Anatolia en route to Armenia or Syria during the nearly constant struggles with Persia.

In 33 AD, these Anatolian cities were prospering as never before. Like the rest of the Empire, the cities of Anatolia took advantage of the *Pax Romana* to improve their agricultural infrastructure and increase trade. In the latter, the local cities were immensely assisted by being able to trade in two seas—the Black and the Mediterranean—and by building and maintaining thousands of miles of roads linking each of the cities with each other as well as with distant hinterlands. This prosperity is still visible today in the many ruins that dot the region's landscape, which remain a testament to centuries of colossal construction efforts.

For instance, in 33 AD, the great marketplace in Ephesus had been under construction for over a decade and was still a decade away from completion. This market area was 112 meters square and was encompassed on all four sides by a two-story stoa (a covered passageway lined with columns). Inside the market, local citizens found goods from throughout the Empire, as it was connected to the city's extensive man-made harbor. Other exotic wares came along the Persian Royal Road (part of the Great Silk Road, which stretched to China). What could not be sold in the city's great market was stored in the hundreds of warehouses surrounding the port, awaiting shipment to the Western Empire. And this was just one of many building programs in a single city. What took place in Ephesus was repeated throughout Anatolia, as it joined in the greatest period of increasing general well-being until the modern era.

Due to the many Greek cities along its Aegean and Black Sea coasts and being the first region Alexander the Great stripped away from the Persian Empire, Anatolia was heavily Hellenized, with significant Persian influences as one traveled farther east. Thus, the region was a center of Greco-Roman civilization and culture, including a library in Pergamon that rivaled Alexandria's. Pergamon, a well-established center of learning, was later the birthplace of Galen, the father of medicine and personal physician to Emperor Marcus Aurelius.

Anatolia is also where the imperial cult had its first stronghold, as testified to today by the many ruins of temples dedicated to deceased Roman emperors found throughout the region. In 33 AD, temples dedicated to the divine Augustus were already well established. They would soon be followed by temples to the god Tiberius. These imperial cults helped those residing in the region integrate Roman rule with their religious beliefs, thus hastening Romanization. The belief that all-too-human Roman emperors were born again as gods was likely a crucial reason why Anatolia became a stronghold of Christianity, based, as it was, on a man rising from the dead to take his place as God. It did not hurt the cause of imperial integration that many cities vied for the honor of being declared a *neokoros* (temple warden), whereupon they could take advantage of the many privileges bestowed upon such cities by future emperors. Emperors likely maintained these privileges as a precedent they hoped would guide their successors in enriching cities where their own temples would one day be erected. In addition, many wealthy families actively pursued having one of their number made a priest in the imperial temple, seeing it as a way to gain influence and secure future prosperity.

Moving west, we come to Greece, which was officially conquered and made a province in 146 BC, when a Roman army defeated the assembled forces of the Achaean League. But Rome had been making steady encroachments into the region for decades, as it engaged Macedonia in a series of wars. The four wars with Macedonia were finally concluded when the legions smashed the Macedonian phalanxes at the Battle of Pydna in 168 BC, ending Macedonia's independence. The later Battle of Corinth gave Rome control of Greece, except for a few minor cities that were granted some autonomy and allowed to remain outside the Roman tax structure. But in 89–88 BC, taking advantage of Rome's Mithridatic distraction, Athens led a revolt against Rome. Unfortunately for Athens and those cities that supported it, Greece lay athwart the roads the legions would use on their way to Asia Minor. Lucius Cornelius Sulla, the general commanding the Roman counter-attack, not wishing to exhaust his army, took his time marching through Greece. Crushing the revolt proved to be little more than a training event for his veterans. Sulla allowed his troops to plunder liberally as a reward for their performance and personal loyalty to him. Through Sulla and his legions, Rome made an example of Greece as a warning to any other part of the Empire that might think of taking advantage of any future Roman distraction.

During the decades of the Roman Civil Wars, Greece was repeatedly turned into a battleground. At the same time, its economy was sucked dry by insatiable demands for silver, which was needed to finance a succession of brutal conflicts. Only after Augustus won at Actium was Greece reorganized into an official province of the Roman Empire, Achaea, in 27 BC. From then on, Greece took full advantage of the *Pax Romana* to recover and prosper. Rome, which always had a special relationship with Greece, took a crucial role in rebuilding many cities and repairing damaged infrastructure. Roman patrons also invested in new roads that were added to an already substantial network. Corinth prospered as the province's capital and administrative center, while Athens flourished as a hub of culture and learning. Even once mighty Sparta—now a husk of its former glory—did well, although Roman arms militarily humbled it. The Romans made Sparta a free city and allowed it to maintain many of the institutions and laws first laid down by the Spartan lawgiver, Lycurgus, nearly a millennium before. Thus, Sparta prospered as a tourist destination for affluent Romans who came to observe the quaintness of Spartan customs and life, refusing to conform to Rome's modern world.

The *Pax Romana* was the most prolonged period of peace in Greek history. As Greece was rapidly integrated into the Empire's economic networks, it became the crucial crossroads for maritime trade between the Hellenized and Greek-speaking eastern half of the Empire and Rome. Romans were, in fact, so taken with Greek history and its cultural achievements that Greek became a *lingua franca* in the eastern provinces and elite Romans throughout the Empire. Even before Greece became a province, many wealthy Romans traveled to Rhodes and Athens to complete their education. During Jesus's lifetime, Tiberius, before becoming emperor, retreated to Rhodes for many years to participate in and enjoy the many cultural and educational opportunities the island offered.

As noted, Rome's relationship with Greece differed from that of any other conquered provinces. As Horace, the greatest poet of the Augustan age, said, *Graecia capta ferum victorem cepit*—"Captive Greece captured her rude conqueror."* Throughout the Roman Empire, Romanization substantially impacted almost every facet of life, leaving only the Jews and Greece practically untouched. For the Jews, this separateness ended badly,

---

* Horace, *Epistles*, 2.1.

when Rome destroyed their temple, Jerusalem, and much of the rest of Judea during the Great Revolt (66–71 AD). But Greece was different. Although most Romans had little respect for contemporary Greeks, they deeply revered Greek civilization and were intensely imbued with its culture.* This reverence was not, however, a two-way street. In 33 AD, Greeks respected and feared Roman military power but did not believe the Romans had anything to teach them. After all, the Romans learned Greek, not the other way around. Only a few "misguided" Greeks thought it worth the time to learn Latin. Roman language was uncouth for the Greeks, and Rome's literature was just poor imitations of the Greek originals. Even the story of Rome's founding, as written by Virgil in the *Aeneid*, was, to Greek eyes, stolen from Homer.

By 33 AD, the administrative language of most of the Eastern Empire was Greek, and Latin was spoken only in a few colonies founded by Rome. Even these were soon absorbed into the surrounding Greek culture, losing their distinct Latin flavor within two generations. Only the army held out, but as early as 33 AD the eastern legions were recruiting Greek-speaking locals. Greece increasingly became the rank-and-file language, while Latin was the language of command. Everywhere in the Roman Empire, except for Greece, local elites vied with each other for Rome's recognition and the award of Roman citizenship. Roman citizenship was rarely sought in Greece and just as infrequently given, as few Greeks ever expressed a desire to be considered Roman, despite the many benefits accruing to Roman citizens. Only when Emperor Caracalla issued the *Constitutio Antoniniana*, in 212 AD, were Greeks, like all those living in the Empire, made citizens of Rome. Few wanted the supposed honor, as the benefits were, by this time, outweighed by the fact that they were now liable to several taxes from which noncitizens were previously immune.

Neither Tiberius nor any future emperor saw anything wrong with this Greek distinctiveness. They even welcomed it, creating a special department to handle all correspondence with the Greek East and ensuring

---

* A.H.M. Jones, "The Greeks Under the Roman Empire," *Dumbarton Oaks Papers*, Vol. 17 (1963), pp. 1 and 3–19.

all proclamations and other official documents were written in Latin and Greek. Moreover, every official that Rome sent east had to be proficient in Greek. Elsewhere in the Empire, the natives were forced to deal with Roman officials in Latin. But, as we said, Greece was different because the recorded deeds of its ancestors impressed the Romans.

But where it truly mattered, at least as far as Rome was concerned, Romanization did take hold. For example, the democratic nature of most city-states rapidly vanished. Rome, which had always been ruled by patrician elites who maintained an uneasy peace with the masses of poor plebeians, did not trust democratic assemblies in which every citizen had a say. Greece, they reasoned, would be much happier and more secure if the locals were ruled by their social and aristocratic betters. Of course, Rome counted on this better sort of people to put a prospering taxable economy and Rome's political interests at the top of the priority list. Rome also approved of competition between cities as a substitute for the endemic warfare of the pre-Roman era. This competition took place in the construction of massive buildings, great works of art, and athletics. In time, the cost of this competition began to damage the economy. Still, in 33 AD, it was just the kind of Keynesian lift an economy ruined by repeated wars required to grow and prosper as never before. And, like almost every region within the Roman Empire, gladiatorial combats became a theatrical sensation. Furthermore, like the Hellenized cities in the east, the Greeks were quick to see Augustus and then Tiberius as kings, and just as fast to worship them as gods. Throughout Greece, the imperial cult took hold, and it was the rare emperor, during the Principate, who did not have one or two cities with temples for his worship. Rome continued to encourage these imperial cults, as they were an effective method of building the loyalty of the locals to the imperial center. Tiberius, who was always uneasy about such honors, saw its value in enhancing Roman control and even began transplanting the imperial cult focused on Augustus into cities in the Western Empire. His successors would do the same for him.

To the north of Greece lay the Balkan provinces, which in 33 AD remained mostly unorganized. It was only during the reign of Claudius (41–54 AD) that the lands south of the Danube were organized into five provinces—Pannonia, Dalmatia, Moseai, Noricum, and Thracia— which were garrisoned by seven legions and their auxiliaries. As it was a harsh land that brought no profit and much loss, the conquest of the Balkans was undertaken as a military necessity, not in hopes of adding prospering provinces to the Empire. But the region's conquest was essential for an Empire whose basic strategy, already visible by 33 AD, was to keep Rome's enemies far from its economic core by defending the natural frontiers along the Rhine and Danube.* Moreover, the pacification of the Balkans was required to secure the land bridge to the Eastern Empire, which would facilitate the movement of armies in any direction as needed.

How important was this land bridge? At the same time the New Testament informs that Jesus was left behind in the Jerusalem Temple by his parents, Rome was mobilizing half of its total military force to crush a Balkan revolt in Pannonia (parts of modern western Hungary and western Austria). This was not done to increase trade, as long-distance land trade was never profitable unless one traded in precious items, such as silk, jewelry, spices, or slaves. The only long-distance trade that could probably come across the Danube, worth taking to the coast, were amber from the North Sea region and slaves. Some wealth was accumulated along the Adriatic and Black Sea coasts, but this was mostly generated by Hellenized cities, with a long history of trading contacts with Greece. In the interior, life was rougher, and agriculture was mostly at the subsistence level. In the decades after 33 AD, even this area prospered somewhat during the long Roman peace. But, as late as the third century, the Balkan provinces were the legions' prime recruiting grounds, as the poor land produced the most formidable and most warlike soldiers. After the third century, most of the Balkan provinces were laid bare by incessant barbarian invasions and the tramping of Roman armies during the numerous civil wars.

There is one more Roman near neighbor worthy of note—Germania beyond the Rhine. Germania, while not a Roman province, is important to our overall story primarily because of its impact on persons who be-

---

* J. J. Wilkes, "The Danubian and Balkan Provinces," in Alan K. Bowman et al. (eds.), *The Cambridge Ancient History*, Vol. 10, *The Augustan Empire 43 B.C.–A.D. 69*, 2nd ed. (Cambridge University Press, 1996), p. 585.

come crucial as we approach the year 33 AD. This full story is told in much greater detail in succeeding chapters, so there is no need to tarry long here. But, as Germania or Germany is not described later in this work, this is an appropriate place to provide a few background notes on the region.

In 9 AD, three Roman legions led by Publius Quinctilius Varus plunged deep into the German forest, set on crushing a rumored revolt before it could gain traction. As we will see, Varus was not new to crushing revolts, having crushed a previous revolt in Galilee and Judea a bit over a decade before. In the process, he destroyed the city of Sepphoris, only a few miles from Nazareth. Jesus, who would have been about two years old at the time and possibly recently returned from Egypt, would have grown up in the shadow of a destroyed Sepphoris. But in Germania, the result was radically different, as the Germans ambushed Varus's three legions—an almost irreplaceable 10 percent of Rome's total military power—and annihilated them. According to Suetonius, Augustus was so shaken that for a long time afterward, he would wander his palace shouting *Quintili Vare, legiones redde!* ("Quintilius Varus, give me back my legions!").* In the wake of what became known as the Varian Disaster, Augustus ordered a series of invasions of Germania with but one aim: to wreak vengeance. Although, once Tiberius became emperor, he quickly shut down these costly assaults into the wilds of Germania and pulled the legions back to the Rhine.

It is difficult to overstate the impact of this decision, as it ended all plans to conquer Germania at least as far as the Elbe River and possibly beyond. For the next five hundred years, Roman territory ended at the Rhine, although Roman military and economic power reached far beyond it. Echoes of Tiberius's decision to halt at the Rhine and also the Danube are still felt two millennia later, as Europe continues to cope with Latin-Teutonic and Slavic-Teutonic divides, which, in the twentieth century, were the foundational cause of two world wars.

But in 33 AD, Germania was a wild country, heavily covered with forests. Its level of development, although far higher than historians credited

---

* Suetonius, *Augustus,* 23.2.

just a couple of decades ago, was still far below that of Gaul when Rome first sent its legions north of the Alps. When the Romans occupied Gaul, they took over thousands of thriving farms, cities along the Mediterranean that were as advanced and prosperous as any in Italy, and a flourishing trading economy along the north coast that reached deep into Briton and Scandinavia. Most crucially, Gaul was governed by tribes with an organized elite who were accustomed to trading and working with one another. Little of this existed in Germania, where the soil defied deep plowing until the moldboard plow was invented in the early Middle Ages. The tribes in Germania only appeared content when they were slaughtering one another. In short, when Rome looked at Gaul, it saw a vast expanse of lands ready to be rapidly integrated into its economic structure. But when it looked at Germania, it saw lands that would not give any financial return for a century or more, and only then, after a vast expenditure of blood and treasure. Tiberius was smart enough to understand that Germany was not worth the cost, Roman pride be damned.

What we know about Germania in and around 33 AD comes to us from Tacitus's monograph, *Germania*, written in about 98 AD, and drawn from several sources, as there is no indication that Tacitus ever traveled there. According to Tacitus, the German people were fierce-looking with blue eyes, reddish hair, and large frames. He thought they were unnaturally strong and prone to proving their strength and worth through violence. But, despite their strength, they could not endure long toil or fatiguing tasks, nor could they bear thirst or heat, though they were accustomed to cold and hunger.

In battle, giving up ground was considered good tactics rather than cowardice, provided one planned to return to the attack. But, in echoes of the Spartan tradition to "come home shield in hand or carried dead upon it," throwing away one's shield was a supreme disgrace. Anyone who so dishonored himself was forever barred from attendance at sacrifices or the assembly. According to Tacitus, most such battlefield survivors ended their shame by suicide. Moreover, a tribal chief could disgrace himself if one of his followers surpassed him in courage. Similarly, his followers considered themselves humiliated if they did not equal the courage of their chief. The chiefs fought for victory; their followers fought for their chief. And to make sure they fought hard, the German tribes often brought their women and children on campaign:

> Close at hand, too, are their closest relatives, and they can hear a woman's shout or a child's cry. Here are the witnesses who are in each man's eyes most precious, here the praise he covets most. They take their wounds to mother and wife, who do not shrink from counting the wounds and demanding to look at them. They serve the combatants food and encouragement.*

Finally, when a period of peace lasted too long, many youths departed their tribe to seek out tribes that were at war, for, according to Tacitus, the Germans had no taste for peace.

As for the German economy, Tacitus tells us that the accumulation and employment of capital for lending or to finance infrastructure improvements is unknown in Germany. He blames this on ignorance of modern methods rather than any prohibition. Agricultural lands were divided by a person's rank or standing within the tribe, and although expansive tracts of cultivable ground were available, the Germans failed to prosper "because they do not work sufficiently hard." In such statements, one can clearly hear the prejudice Tacitus and other Romans had for the barbarians.

Tacitus mentions about three dozen Germanic tribes and briefly describes many of them. Crucially, in 33 AD, these tribes could only act in concert when there was a serious threat and, even then, just for a short time. The inability of the various tribes to cooperate was Rome's greatest protection from their wrath. When there were no Roman legions on the east side of the Rhine, they fell to squabbling among themselves. By rewarding friendly tribes with trade and gifts, usually of silver, while keeping them at each other's throats, Rome maintained a general peace along its frontiers for over two centuries. The Germanic tribes only became a genuine danger to Rome toward the end of the Principate, when wealthier tribes consolidated their power by absorbing the lesser tribes. These

---

* Tacitus, *Germania*, 7.0.

amalgamations—Alemanni, Franks, Burgundians—were far more powerful than any group Rome had to deal with in 33 AD, and a genuine threat to the Empire.

Thus ends our tour of the Empire and its near abroad in and about the year 33 AD. But there remains a much wider world out there. Romans knew some parts of this world existed—India and China—but in 33 AD, these lands were shrouded in mystery. Other regions of the world—North America, South America, and most of Southern Africa—were unknown to the Romans. However, they knew that a vast continent stretched below the Saharan wastes.*

* Anyone interested in more extensive and specific information on what the Romans knew about global geography during the period covered in this book is encouraged to read the works of Strabo, who died in 24 AD. For an online copy of Loeb's English translation, by H. L. Jones, see penelope.uchicago.edu/Thayer/E/Roman/Texts/Strabo/home.html.

SEVEN

The Roman World Grows Rich

As far as any resident of the Mediterranean Basin was concerned, there was one inescapable fact of life: They lived in a world dominated by Rome. For those who gave the matter any thought, there was widespread agreement that they lived within the civilized world, and all that stood beyond the Empire's frontiers were barbarians. That was literally true of the tribes beyond the Rhine and Danube frontiers, but your learned Roman would admit to knowing there were other thriving civilizations beyond Rome's Mesopotamian frontier; just beyond the Empire's eastern deserts stood the Parthian Empire. If not as powerful as the Romans, the Parthians were strong enough to repeatedly challenge Roman authority in portions of the Eastern Empire. Beyond Parthia stood the great civilizations of the Indus and China, both of whom were going through periods of inner turmoil at the start of the first century.

For the average citizen, this meant that, although they lived under what amounted to a military-based dictatorship, it was one with a remarkably light touch. Rome's touch had to be light, as virtually all of the military force the Empire possessed was, by necessity, stationed on the Empire's frontiers. Rome could do this because it had long learned that the secret to controlling many disparate populations over a vast expanse of territory was to let them govern themselves to the greatest extent possible. When Rome conquered a new territory, it ruthlessly exterminated its most potent enemies and then co-opted what remained of the local leadership. That done, Rome placed the smallest possible governing infrastructure—a governor and his staff—atop whatever local administration had been in place before Rome arrived. In many cases, large portions of the conquered state's surviving military forces were integrated into the Roman army as auxiliaries.

To the greater part of the population, this meant that unless they lived close to the frontiers or along a major military road, they could go their entire life without ever seeing a Roman soldier. Moreover, Rome left them free to honor their traditional gods and maintain their local traditions without interference. As the centuries passed, Roman culture, and later an amalgamation of Greek and Roman culture, expanded throughout the Empire, particularly in urban areas, even though much of the countryside stubbornly held to their old ways.

The influence of Rome was most felt in the marketplace. Without exception, wherever Rome's legions treaded, Roman merchants traveled in their wake. How massive this influx of Roman commercial interests was can be measured by the destruction wrought by the allies of the ruler of Pontus, Mithridates VI, in 88 BC. As discussed earlier, in the opening act of what turned out to be the hardest war Rome fought since the destruction of Carthage almost sixty years before, Mithridates convinced his local allies to murder all of the Romans in Anatolia in a single bloody day, in which eighty thousand Romans were slaughtered.

This slaughter was part of an ongoing crisis and was instigated by Pontus, a state that was previously allied to Rome but not yet conquered or integrated into the Empire. It was also the Asiatic Vespers that brought Rome to Judea, as Rome relentlessly pursued their vendetta against Mithridates over the course of three wars. It was at the end of the Third Mithridatic War that Pompey led his legions into Syria and Judea in 63 BC. Although the areas in which the dispute began were not yet part of the Roman Empire, it is clear from the slaughter of tens of thousands of merchants that the locals hugely resented Roman economic imperialism. Moreover, economic integration always caused the most trouble within the Empire's provinces, particularly during the transition period in the years immediately after they were conquered.

Roman merchants would rapidly move into new provinces to establish centers of trade, particularly in ports and other major inland commercial centers. Once there, they often replaced many established commercial interests in the province's towns and cities. By establishing a new economic hierarchy, Rome created a new urban elite loyal to Rome, and a previous local elite who were now dispossessed of much of their income and rightfully resentful. If that had been all there was to it, the integration of conquered provinces would have been relatively easy and peaceful, as disgruntled elites would have had no one to lead in revolt. But there was a further element to Rome's economic imperialism resented by everyone, including the mass of the peasantry: taxes.

It is essential to remember that during the years Jesus lived, Rome and its Empire were in the midst of a significant political and economic transition, one in which no one was certain of the ultimate outcome or its consequences. During the centuries of the Roman Republic, Rome had discovered how to make its imperial expansion and nearly continuous warfare pay for itself. As the legions advanced, they pillaged and looted with reckless abandon. And then, when the pain became too great to bear, Rome would offer peace in return for huge wealth transfers (tribute) from its defeated enemies to the coffers of the Roman treasury. Only then would the legions desist in their predations. Often, the cost was so great that Rome's victims had to pay in annual installments for decades.

But, by the time of Jesus's birth, all of this was ending. Augustus, Rome's first emperor, continued a policy of expansion. While he probably added more territory than any past Roman general, he was increasingly conquering regions of marginal economic value. Still, it took two disasters to give Augustus pause. In 6 AD, the newly acquired province of Pannonia rose in revolt. Crushing the revolt took three years and almost half of the Roman army. But Augustus had discovered how dangerous it was to conduct further operations before previously conquered provinces had been thoroughly cowed and fully integrated into the imperial system.

No sooner had the Pannonian Revolt ended than a second calamity struck: the previously discussed Varian Disaster. As a consequence, upon his death, Augustus left in his final testament a warning to be content with what had already been gained and to give up on further expansions. Unfortunately, future Roman emperors, feeling the call to enhance their reputation by acquiring military glory, would often forget Augustus's caution. Still, for the most part, the boundaries bequeathed by Augustus remained the extent of the Roman Empire for the next five centuries.* Thus, Augustus's immediate successor, Tiberius, after allowing his nephew Germanicus to conduct several punishment expeditions into Germany, called a halt to Roman expansion for the duration of his reign.

Ending the era of Roman expansion brought a sudden halt to Rome's confiscation of the vast treasuries that the states of the eastern Mediterranean had been stashing away since the death of Alexander the Great. From now on, the revenues required to maintain the Empire would have to come from within the Empire itself through taxation. As the destruction of three legions deep in the dank German forests demonstrated, the imposition of Roman taxes was a perilous time. One may ask why this was so, as new Roman taxpayers would have already been used to paying taxes to their prior rulers. But here is the rub: Those local taxes still had to be paid. For instance, Herod still needed revenues in Palestine to run his own government, build new cities and buildings, and maintain his own military forces. Rome added its tax burdens atop what was already a steep taxation load. It was no wonder that the provincials so resented Roman taxes.

But there was another reason why Rome's revenue collections were despised, and that had to deal with how they were collected. Rome, usually after the completion of a census, would determine the minimum taxes a region would have to pay. After that number was announced, private contractors called tax farmers would bid for the right to collect the taxes. These bidding wars often reached numbers far in excess of what Rome initially considered reasonable. As the winning bidder was responsible for collecting the entire amount bid, a bit of ruthlessness in the collection procedures was baked into the system—think modern

---

* The emperor Claudius would later add Britain, Trajan would temporarily add Dacia, and Trajan and Severus would, in different centuries, temporarily add Mesopotamia.

debt collectors on steroids. But it gets worse, for we have not accounted for the contractors' profits, which were earned through excess collections, as the tax farmers kept everything collected in excess of the amount bid. The more tax farmers collected, the greater their profits, and to help them earn their profits, the full power of the Roman legions supported them. If New Testament readers ever wondered why everyone hated tax collectors found within the narrative, look no further.

One wonders why every province was not in a constant state of revolt, even long after they had all become accustomed to being part of the Empire. The answer likely lies in understanding the impact of the *Pax Romana*. Rome had profited handsomely through war and conquest—truly making war pay for itself. But the long peace of the *Pax Romana* allowed the Empire and its provinces to flourish as never before. To understand why, one must comprehend just how much gold and silver was released into the economy during Rome's final century of conquest and civil wars. In relative terms, this release of stored wealth created the greatest wealth transfer in history.

Before the advent of the Roman era, rulers had a strong incentive to stockpile gold and silver for a rainy day—a euphemism for the next war. Wars were expensive, and in an age before modern ideas of debt financing were conceived, a ruler could only fight for as long as the state treasury held out. Fighting Rome forced everyone to open their treasuries. If anything was left after a state's eventual defeat, Rome took it as tribute. Rome, over decades of rapaciousness, also took most of the wealth of the defeated state's wealthiest persons, the gold and silver stored over centuries by temples and the working treasuries of cities and towns.

The trapped wealth of eons was suddenly set free. Rome, on the other hand, did not stockpile money. It rarely amounted to much when it did so and would never stay stored for long. Even a frugal emperor, such as Tiberius, only left a full treasury for his successor to immediately spend and then some. Almost as quickly as money came into Rome's coffers, it would flow out again. During the late Republic, most of this money was spent on adding new conquests or fighting civil wars. Even as the Empire settled, the army continued to demand vast expenditures. But money was also increasingly going into civil construction, allowing Augustus to boast that he found Rome "a city of bricks, but left it a city of marble."[*] Not content with beautifying Rome, Augustus also sponsored building projects across the breadth of the Empire. Such constructions were in addition to what provincial and local governments spent on their civic projects. As no local leaders had to concern themselves with defense any longer, there was no need to maintain expensive armies or to squirrel away silver or gold as a hedge against a future conflict.

The Roman Empire was experiencing something akin to what England and parts of Europe witnessed when England's Henry VIII dissolved the monasteries, thereby freeing huge amounts of capital from what has been called the dead hand of the Church. When Henry VIII seized the land and the rest of the Catholic Church's riches and put it to more productive use, he set the conditions for England's rise to great power status and supplied the capital underpinning the start of the Industrial Revolution. Similarly, the great wealth freed from state bondage by Rome may have had an even more profound impact given the enormous geographical scope of the Empire and the number of persons directly impacted.

In short, when Rome's civil wars ended, the Empire's economy was awash in cash and stayed that way for most of Jesus's life, only temporarily pausing in the great financial collapse of 33 AD, of which we will hear more later. Although no ancient economists were toting up a statistical record for historians to peruse, the Mediterranean economy was likely vibrant and growing throughout the previous decades of conflict. For, as Rome fought its civil wars, all other conflicts ended, and the frontiers were remarkably quiet. That means the only parts of the Empire impacted by war were those areas where armies actually tread and fought— a very small area indeed, given the relative size of the Empire. Moreover, until our modern era, great conflicts tended to be exceptionally good for the overall economy of the warring parties, as states flooded the economic systems with silver to pay, supply, and transport massive armies over vast distances.[†] So, while rulers and governments might bankrupt

---

[*] Suetonius, *Augustus*, 29.1.
[†] For an analysis of this phenomenon, see James Lacey (ed.), *Great Strategic Rivalries* (Cambridge University Press, 2016).

themselves paying for endless wars, the foundational economy typically prospers mightily, except those unfortunate cities, farms, and businesses that found themselves directly in the path of armies set on devastation. But, even in these cases, agriculturally based economies typically came back from devastation far faster than a modern economy.

But rebuilding after wars does not increase wealth, as this is an example of what modern economists call the broken windows fallacy. This fallacy explains why breaking every window in a country leads to increased economic activity as the windows are repaired but does not add anything to a nation's wealth. The increased economic activity expended labor and resources only to get back to where you were before the windows were broken. As those resources and labor were not available for other uses, the opportunity cost means a state will be worse off than it would have been if no windows had been broken. Similarly, repairing war damage only brings a devastated community back to something approaching prewar levels of economic activity.

Thus, where armies have destroyed vast amounts of capital—buildings, granaries, irrigation canals—rebuilding these structures does not leave a region or state better off than it was before. Rather, it just returns the region to the prewar status quo. Moreover, in an age of endemic warfare, which is certainly true of the entire Mediterranean region before the *Pax Romana,* most societies must have been wary of investing too much in expensive infrastructure that was always a target for marauders and invading armies. Such wariness would have acted as a natural brake on economic development throughout the Mediterranean.

So what did all this mean for the average person living within the Empire? First and foremost, persons and communities had an opportunity to enhance their overall wealth for the first time in eons. By removing the threat of having one's entire economic infrastructure wrecked on a regular basis, the general peace of the Empire set the conditions for a vast economic expansion throughout the Mediterranean region. For the first time since the dawn of civilization and the creation of the first city-states, one power was enforcing peace on a large portion of the known world. Thus, capital investment was no longer continually applied to repairing

the damage from repeated conflicts but was increasingly employed toward growing the economy.

Investment funds were now going toward increasing the amount of arable land under cultivation, building industry, and increasing trade. As the various subregions of the Empire became increasingly convinced that peace was going to last, the average person became ever more willing to invest in costly infrastructure that hugely enhanced the scope, efficiency, and productivity of the agricultural economy. While there were still many subsistence farmers throughout the Empire, there is increasing evidence of a fast-growing money-based market economy centered on a growing number of cities and towns. Even the poor were generally much better off than previously.

Some historians counter this notion of general prosperity by insisting that the early emperors—Augustus and Tiberius included—ruled during a period of almost unceasing conflict. In this view, the total of Augustus's reign is as bloody a period as any other in Roman history. This outlook makes much of Tacitus's statement that the *Pax Augustus* was a "peace stained in blood." But by focusing on the many battles along the frontiers of the Empire—including the Varian Disaster—these historians overlook a significant point. No matter how violent the frontiers, or how many legionnaires were still fighting to expand the edges of the Empire, the vital inner core of the Empire went untouched. This cost of the armies was surely an economic burden, but the army for two hundred years barely grew as the economy grew steadily wealthier. Thus, the load, relative to the economy, was continually shrinking. As the army assured the *Pax Romana* and kept the barbarians from the Empire's inner core, historians should stop thinking of it as a cost center. Instead, they must recognize the army as the vital element that assured the Empire's vitality and growing prosperity.

EIGHT

What Romans Believed

Everyone believed what Pliny the Elder believed, and his influence spanned well into the next millennium. No monastery library in the Middle Ages was complete unless it held a copy of his book *Natural History*. By the start of the Renaissance, hundreds of versions were scattered about revitalized European centers of learning. Pliny, for over a thousand years, was the final arbiter of what was held to be true and false in people's understanding of the world around them. Pliny read extensively to gather the vast amount of information in his *Natural History*, and much of his work is copied from Aristotle, Theophrastus, and many others. In fact, Book One of his thirty-seven-volume *Natural History* lists the names of his sources and many of their key works, most of them lost to us. Thus, until the modern era, Pliny was believed to have captured much of the knowledge and wisdom of the ancients, and his work made a handy substitute for all that was lost. For over a millennium, learned persons throughout Europe were surrounded by the ruins of ancient Greece and Rome, continually reminding them that there were once civilizations far beyond their own in capacity and knowledge. Only during the later era of the Enlightenment would learned individuals start to question this ancient wisdom. Even so, there was much actual knowledge in Pliny, along with the many fantastical stories and superstitions. We can, therefore, use Pliny's writings as a proxy for what the ancient world in 33 AD generally believed to be true.

Pliny, or Gaius Plinius Secundus, was born around 24 AD, so he was a contemporary of Jesus for at least a decade. He was spectacularly rich, a good friend of the emperor Vespasian, and served, as almost all members of the equestrian class did, as a junior military commander. There is no evidence he ever married, and his famous son, Pliny the Younger, a Roman governor during the reign of Trajan, was adopted. During his stints as a military officer, a lawyer in Rome, and governing four different provinces, Pliny produced several great works in his life, including a twenty-volume history of Rome's German Wars that is now wholly lost to us and is the only work referenced by Tacitus in which he discusses events in Germany. He died in 79 AD, while taking a boat across the Bay of Naples in a futile attempt to rescue friends and family members caught in the eruption of Vesuvius.

Pliny's *Natural History* was likely finished just before his death and was dedicated to Vespasian's successor, his son Titus. Pliny aimed to cover every field of human knowledge as thoroughly as his sources allowed. As such, many have considered it the first encyclopedia. There was, in fact, nothing similar and of comparable scope until the mid-1700s, when Denis Diderot published his twenty-eight-volume Encyclopedia.* He claimed to be the first Roman to undertake such a work, encompassing all of the then-known fields of science. His work was popular in antiquity and was among the first books ever printed in 1470. We will limit ourselves to those aspects of his work that demonstrate the gulf in beliefs between our own time and that of 33 AD in the hope that this will allow us to better understand the peoples of the Roman Empire in Jesus's time.

Before examining Pliny the Elder's beliefs, an interesting diversion into his work habits as outlined by his son, when he was explaining how his father was able to finish such a stupendous amount of work in such a

---

* One can also credit Isidore of Seville (the last great scholar of the ancient world) with a valiant effort in this direction in his twenty-volume *Etymologiae* (*Origines*), published between 600 and 625 AD.

relatively short time, is instructive. His methods are not as important to us as what this description tells about the lifestyles of the rich in the Roman Empire, for it was only people who could enjoy such a lifestyle who could undertake this type of work. One can easily imagine the wealthy Tacitus employing much the same methods.

Does it surprise you that a busy man found time to finish so many volumes, many of which deal with such minute details? . . . Long before dawn; in winter he would commence . . . He could sleep at call, and it would come upon him and leave him in the middle of his work. Before daybreak he would go to [the emperor] Vespasian—for he too was a night-worker—and then set about his official duties. On his return home he would again give to study any time that he had free. Often in summer after taking a meal, which with him, as in the old days, was always a simple and light one, he would lie in the sun if he had any time to spare, and a book would be read aloud, from which he would take notes and extracts. For he never read without taking extracts, and used to say that there never was a book so bad that it was not good in some passage or another. After his sun bath he usually bathed in cold water, then he took a snack and a brief nap, and subsequently, as though another day had begun, he would study till dinner-time. After dinner a book would be read aloud, and he would take notes in a cursory way . . .

When he was in the country the only time snatched from his work was when he took his bath, and when I say bath I refer to the actual bathing, for while he was being scraped with the strigil or rubbed down, he used to listen to a reader or dictate. When he was travelling he cut himself aloof from every other thought and gave himself up to study alone. At his side he kept a shorthand writer with a book and tablets, who wore mittens on his hands in winter, so that not even the sharpness of the weather should rob him of a moment, and for the same reason, when in Rome, he used to be carried in a litter. I remember that once he rebuked me for walking, saying, "If you were a student, you could not waste your hours like that," for he considered that all time was wasted which was not devoted to study.*

Before returning to Pliny the Elder's works, it is worth one more glimpse into the lives of Rome's ultrarich told in another Pliny the Younger description of the daily routine of one of his close friends. This is the life Pliny claims he wants to live, as soon as he can put aside his official duties, one a world apart from that of the average Roman.

In the morning he keeps his couch; at the second hour he calls for his shoes and walks three miles, exercising mind as well as body. If he has friends with him the time is passed in conversation on the noblest of themes, otherwise a book is read aloud, and sometimes this is done even when his friends are present, but never in such a way as to bore them. Then he sits down, and there is more reading aloud or more talk for preference; afterwards he enters his carriage, taking with him either his wife, who is a model lady, or one of his friends, a distinction I recently enjoyed. How delightful, how charming that privacy is! What glimpses of old times one gets! What noble deeds and noble men he tells you of! What lessons you drink in! Yet at the same time it is his custom so to blend his learning with modesty that he never seems to be playing the schoolmaster. After riding seven miles he walks another mile, then he again resumes his seat or betakes himself to his room and his pen. For he composes, both in Latin and Greek, the most scholarly lyrics . . . he is told that the bathing hour has come—which is the ninth hour in winter and the eighth in summer—he takes a walk naked in the sun, if there is no wind. Then he plays at ball for a long spell, throwing himself heartily into the game, for it is by means of this kind of active exercise that he battles with old age. After his bath he lies down and waits a little while before taking food, listening in the meantime to the reading of some light and pleasant book. All this time his friends are at perfect liberty

* Pliny, *Letters*, 3.5.

to imitate his example or do anything else they prefer. Then dinner is served, the table being as bright as it is modest, and the silver plain and old-fashioned; he also has some Corinthian vases in use, for which he has a taste though not a mania. The dinner is often relieved by actors of comedy, so that the pleasures of the table may have a seasoning of letters. Even in the summer the meal lasts well into the night, but no one finds it long, for it is kept up with such good humor and charm.*

For those who have ever wondered why the barbarians were constantly assaulting the Roman frontiers, Pliny partially explains the massive Celtic invasions of Italy that took place well before his birth. In his telling, a Celt named Helico, residing in Italy as an artisan, eventually returned to his own people, taking samples of dried figs, grapes, olive oil, and wine with him. The barbarians were so taken with these products that they were determined to have them and the lands that produced such wonders for themselves. Hence, the barbarian hordes swarmed across the Alps—Pliny's "almost insurmountable bulwark"—to ravage Italy. The barbarians' lust for delicacies, not to mention gold and silver, was only quenched when the legions counter-attacked and annihilated the invaders. Still, by Pliny's time, the Romans were already well along in building massive and horrifically expensive defenses stretching along the entire twenty-five-hundred miles of the frontiers. Historians today hotly debate the purpose of these extensive fortified lines. But if one reflects on Pliny, the answer is simple: Historically, walls were built to protect the nice things on one side of the wall from those on the other side who want to take or destroy them. Only the advent of Communism saw walls routinely constructed to keep people in instead of keeping them out.

Pliny's belief in magic and superstition, shared by every other person then alive, helped shape, mostly for worse, the pursuit of scientific and medical knowledge for over a millennium. For instance, among the pseudoscientific methods he wrote about was the doctrine of signatures, based on the belief that the physical appearance of a plant or herb provided

* Pliny, *Letters*, 3.2.

insights into its medicinal properties. This doctrine held that plants or herbs that resembled certain parts of the body were believed to have healing properties for those same parts. For example, the yellow color of the dandelion was thought to be a sign that it could help with liver problems since the liver produces bile, which has a yellowish color. Similarly, the shape of the lungwort plant was thought to resemble the human lung, and thus it was believed to have properties that could treat respiratory illnesses. Not all magic, however, is good. As Pliny points out, the entire world should feel a debt to Rome for outlawing and doing its best to exterminate the Druids and their practices. He credits Rome with ending their evil rites, such as killing men and eating the flesh as an act of devotion.

Pliny also pushes some fantastical ideas from earlier works such as Herodotus, like the belief that beyond the Scythian tribes, whom he believes are mostly cannibals, were peoples who waged continual wars over local gold and silver mines. In these wars they employ griffins, a wild beast with wings that digs gold out of mines, which the creatures guard. Other beliefs he collects from sources that are no longer available. For example, Pliny states that in the Himalayas, there are forest dwellers, with their feet turned back behind their legs, who run with extraordinary speed and wander far and wide with the wild animals. But as these people cannot breathe in any other climate, hunters have never been able to present them to kings for examination.*

There are also tribes in distant lands whose spit cures snakebites and others whose smell puts deadly snakes to sleep. This latter tribe was also able to test the fidelity of their wives by exposing newborn children to deadly snakebites, as the snakes sought out persons with adulterous blood in them. Just a ten-day journey beyond the Dnieper, a vast and mysterious land to the Romans, were wild men who drank human blood out of victims' skulls and used the scalps as napkins hung around their necks. And another tribe, or maybe the same one, ate only once every two days. Echoing Aristotle, Pliny believed in a tribe called the Adrogyni, who can perform the function of either sex alternately, and he be-

---

* Pliny, *Historia naturalis*, 7.2.

lieved that their left breast is that of a man and their right breast that of
a woman.

Closer to home are those in Illyria, directly across the Adriatic from
Italy, who can bewitch with a glance and kill those they stare at for a
longer time. Their "evil eye" is most felt by adults; many of them have
two pupils in each eye. Another lost tribe, the Pharmaces, have sweat
glands that produce a liquid that relieves the diseases of anybody touched
by it. If the Pharmaces could not be found, one could always help cure
one's ills by finding a person with particular parts of their bodies that one
could touch to cure specific ailments. For instance, by touching the great
toe of the right foot of King Pyrrhus, one would be cured of any inflam-
mation of the spleen. When the king died and was cremated, Pliny reports that his toe would not burn and was stored in a chest in a nearby
temple.

Other marvels abound. In India, for instance, most men are over seven
feet six inches high, never spit, do not suffer from headaches, toothache,
or eye pain, and very rarely have pain in any other part of the body. There
are also men who spend the entire day staring at the sun, standing on
only one leg, others with feet turned backward and eight toes on each
foot, while there are also mountain tribes with men with dogs' heads who
talk by barking.

In Pliny's writings, we also discover a battle between an elephant and
a dragon, whose blood, once combined, created cinnabar, the source of a
scarlet pigment. Mice are also found to have their uses, such as rubbing
their feces on your head to restore hair. And if you want sparkling white
teeth to go with a new head of hair, there was nothing better than brush-
ing them with crushed and powdered mummies. But if you were searching for a cure for epilepsy, nothing worked as well as the blood of dead
gladiators. However, many Roman physicians believed it was better to eat
the livers of fallen gladiators. If you need something a bit easier to get
than the blood of dead gladiators, there was always cabbage, which cured
headaches, vision impairments, and most digestive issues, while its ap-
plication to skin healed wounds and cured open sores.

Pliny also recorded a number of other medical beliefs, most of which
still flourished many centuries later. On conception and birth, Pliny tells

us that women become faint when the embryo begins to grow hair. Additionally, at the full moon, mothers eating food that is too salty bear children lacking nails, while those who sneeze following copulation will ensure there is no pregnancy. If you want the child to grow up to be a great and victorious general, then the mother's death in childbirth is considered a good omen.

But if one wants to understand the worldview of those living within the Roman Empire, it is essential to realize that Pliny's writings were widely accepted as undoubted truths among even the most learned men. Still, Roman medicine, in general, often reached a level of sophistication not seen again until the modern era. Augustus himself formed the first professional medical corps to support the legions. This medical corps attracted many already practicing Greek physicians, lured by the promise of high pay, tax exemptions, and a retirement payout. These physicians undertook complicated surgeries, pioneered the hemostatic tourniquet, and knew how to suture hemorrhaging arteries. They also, without any knowledge of germs, enforced strict sanitation policies on all army encampments. Did it work? Well, despite almost continual frontier conflicts, the average legionnaire had a life expectancy five years greater than the average Roman citizen. That says something.

PART III

TIBERIUS AND HIS DISCONTENTS

NINE

Tiberius and the New Roman Empire

Tiberius, the man who ruled the Roman Empire for most of Jesus's life, was born in 42 BC into the Claudian family, one of the most celebrated families in Rome's powerful senatorial class. Tiberius's mother, Livia Drusilla, was the daughter of Claudius Pulcher, who opposed the rise of Octavian and Anthony's Second Triumvirate—in the wake of Julius Caesar's murder. He went so far as to take up arms and join the cause of Brutus and Cassius in the Roman East. Soon after these two Republicans were defeated at the Battle of Philippi, he committed suicide. But by that time, his daughter was married to Tiberius Claudius Nero, the father of the future emperor, Tiberius.

Tiberius's father was well respected for his bravery by Julius Caesar and joined his cause in the civil war against Pompey. He later turned against Caesar, and after Philippi he moved into Mark Anthony's camp. He was forced to flee Italy in the wake of Octavian's ferocious counterattack against Anthony's Italian supporters, who were led by Anthony's wife Fulvia and his brother, Lucius Antonius. With a pregnant wife, Livia, at his side, he joined Anthony's forces, spending the next several years trying to destabilize Octavian's hold on Italy. When Octavian and Anthony agreed to the Pact of Misenum in 39 BC, Tiberius Nero, along with many Roman aristocrats tired of ceaseless conflicts, took the opportunity to return to Italy.

Tiberius Nero's life then made an unexpected and astounding turn. Octavian took a romantic interest in his wife, Livia. Although Livia was considered by most a rare beauty, highly intelligent, and quick-witted, her true appeal may have been her Claudian lineage, which Octavian could use to enhance his lesser family background. Whatever the reason behind Octavian's sudden desire, he moved quickly to divorce his current wife, Scribonia, a legal task that was completed the same day she bore him his first child and only daughter, Julia. Octavian then ordered or otherwise cajoled Tiberius Nero to divorce Livia, despite her being several months pregnant. It was accepted at the time, and still is by most historians, that Augustus was the father of the unborn child, another son named Drusus. Adding insult to injury, Octavian ordered Tiberius Nero to escort his ex-wife to the temple and then give her away at her wedding as if he were her father. It appears that despite Tiberius Nero being pardoned for initially being on the wrong side of the civil war, Augustus was a long way from forgiving him. Livia's sons would now grow up as stepsons of Octavian, who would soon change his name to Augustus as he ascended to the position of sole ruler of the Roman Empire. Tiberius Nero died only a few years later, and his son, Tiberius, who was only nine years old, gave the eulogy.

Tiberius grew up with a ringside seat as the last embers of the Roman Republic were extinguished, as the forces of Anthony and Cleopatra were defeated at the Battle of Actium, and the initially fragile Augustan Principate established itself. From the start, Augustus made sure that Tiberius was at the center of his most crucial political maneuverings, starting with being allowed to ride one of the horses pulling the Augustus chariot during a post-Actium triumph. For much of the next five decades, Tiberius would be an on-hand witness and absorb lessons on the accumulation and wielding of power from the ancient world's greatest practitioner of such arts, his stepfather Augustus. At the same time, Tiberius's proximity to Augustus allowed much of the emperor's *auctoritas* (accumulated prestige and power) to be transferred to him.

As such, Tiberius could not help but be caught up in Augustus's lengthy and ill-starred attempts to find a successor and build a dynasty around his family. At first, Augustus centered his search around his family: the *Julii*. That focus appeared to leave Tiberius and his brother, Drusus, as both legally came from the Claudio branch of the family, with little hope of ever ascending to the rank of emperor. But Augustus always considered them important bulwarks to whomever reached the top. Still, Augustus placed his first hopes of finding a worthy successor in his nephew, Marcus Marcellus, and tried to strengthen the link to him personally by having him marry his daughter, the fourteen-year-old Julia, in 25 BC. Marcellus, however, died three years later, forcing Augustus to look farther afield. Marcellus's death was likely good for the Empire, as his rapid rise had alienated Marcus Agrippa, Augustus's closest friend and confidant. Agrippa, a brilliant battlefield commander, was, more than any other man, responsible for the military victories that catapulted Augustus to supreme power. His alienation did not bode well for the future stability of the Empire. But, with Marcellus dead, Augustus was free to make amends and bring Agrippa closer to the center of imperial power. Julia, playing the role of pawn in Augustus's dynastic maneuvering, was married once again, this time to Agrippa.

Augustus had good reasons to bring Agrippa back into the fold, as he was the one man who could be counted on to keep Rome quiet when Augustus needed to be elsewhere in the Empire. Still, what mattered most was that Agrippa was also the only one who could rally the legions to his side and contest Augustus's hold on power if there was a falling-out. One of Augustus's close advisers warned the emperor: "You have made him so great that he must either become your son-in-law or be slain."[*] To even more firmly lock Agrippa to his own dynastic ends, Augustus arranged for the marriage of his adopted son, Tiberius, to Agrippa's daughter, Vipsania Agrippina. Unusually for an arranged marriage, particularly in Roman society, where affection was often frowned upon, Tiberius and Vipsania fell in love with each other, and the relationship was likely the most fulfilling of Tiberius's life.

Although Augustus had clearly placed Agrippa in a position to suc-

* Dio Cassius, *The Histories*, 54.6.5.

ceed him, that was not what the future emperor was looking forward to. Rather, he was looking to the children of Agrippa and Julia, as his direct-line grandchildren, to succeed to the throne. The marriage did, in fact, prove fruitful enough, providing three boys and two girls, apparently enough to secure Augustus's dynasty. To ensure that they were properly prepared to meet future expectations, Augustus adopted the two eldest boys, Gaius Julius Caesar and Lucius Julius Caesar, and took personal responsibility for their education.

While Augustus waited for his newly adopted sons to grow up, an already adult Tiberius was put to good use. He was a prime mover in diplomatic negotiations in which the Parthians were convinced to return the legionary standards that Crassus had lost on the battlefield of Car-rhae (53 BC). Upon their return, the Augustan propaganda machine went into overdrive. A triumph was celebrated and a triumphal arch constructed. The diplomatic coup was treated as a decisive military victory. So, without risking a costly war, Tiberius erased the shame of Crassus's defeat and hugely increased Augustan prestige. The deal with Parthia also secured Rome's political control over Armenia, which would prove a constant source of trouble between the two great powers of the ancient world. But for now, Parthia did not have the wherewithal to challenge Rome in the east, and the region would stay quiet for two generations.

Tiberius had avoided war in the east only to find himself embroiled in a dozen years of brutal conflicts along Rome's northern frontiers. During those years, until 7 BC, he would make his mark on a series of battlefields along and beyond the Empire's northern frontier. There is no need to detail his exploits in this work except to note that, by all accounts, he was an excellent strategist and battlefield commander. He was well-liked by his men and respected by his subordinate commanders. Tiberius, however, had no liking for the political and dynastic squabbles that were the constant backdrop to his life in Rome and would try to escape them whenever possible. Far from Rome, fighting to protect and expand the Empire, Tiberius earned respect and proved his worth as a thoughtful and efficient battlefield commander who took great pride in his achievements. However, he was also prone to make enemies when he judged a man as lacking in the virtues he held dear. This included the powerful governor of Gaul, Marcus Lollius, who Tiberius replaced in 16 BC, after he was defeated in battle by several barbarian tribes. Lollius was never again trusted with a military command, but he remained friendly with Augustus, who appointed him to tutor his grandson, Gaius Caesar, a constant thorn in Tiberius's side.

Agrippa's death in 12 BC not only knocked out a key prop of the Augustan regime, it also deprived his sons, Gaius and Lucius, of the strong fatherly guidance they would require as they came of age within the world's most brutal and unforgiving political environment. But there was a more immediate problem: Agrippa's sons were children. If something happened to Augustus while Agrippa lived, he would have taken control of Rome and ensured his sons followed him. But with Agrippa gone, Augustus's dynastic plans were in peril. For, if he passed from the scene now, Gaius and Lucius would be stripped of a powerful protector and crushed in the political scrum certain to follow Augustus's death.

To shore up his exposed vulnerability, Augustus turned to Tiberius and demanded that he marry Julia, Agrippa's wife and Augustus's daughter. To clear the path, Tiberius was ordered to divorce Vipsania, with whom he was still very much in love, and who had recently borne him a son, Drusus (the same name as Tiberius's brother). By dint of his marriage to Julia, Tiberius became the legal guardian of Agrippa's sons. All of this was personally loathsome to Tiberius, as his new wife had attempted to seduce him while she was married to Agrippa, and he did not believe she would long remain loyal to him. Moreover, he detested the idea that he would soon return from the battlefields to take his place in Rome's political arena. Upon his return to Rome, Suetonius records that Tiberius once spied Vipsania out walking in the markets and followed her with "such an intent and tearful gaze" that Augustus took steps to ensure he never saw her again.*

Tiberius's marriage to Julia appears to have gone well at first but soon turned cold. There, one child died in infancy at Aquileia, and soon afterward, Tiberius and Julia were living apart, at which point Julia infamously became known for entertaining a succession of lovers. For anyone else in

---

* Suetonius, *Tiberius*, 7.3.

Rome, such behavior would have been a death sentence, but as the only child of Augustus, Julia was immune from punishment for a time. Tiberius suffered further tribulations when word came that his brother, Drusus, had fallen from a horse while returning from campaigning in Germany, and his injuries had festered. Tiberius rushed north to his brother's aid but arrived just in time to be on hand for his death. He had his brother's body returned to Rome, walking before the procession for the entire trip.

Augustus continued to pour honors upon Tiberius, along with enhancing his power within the Empire. In 7 BC, Tiberius was awarded his second consulship and presented with tribunician powers, effectively placing him on par with Agrippa and marking him as Augustus's favored successor. However, Augustus refused to promote him to the rank of Caesar or announce his preferment to the Senate. Still, Tiberius was Rome's second most powerful man and Augustus's likely successor until Gaius and Lucius came of age.

But, in 6 BC, at the height of his power, Tiberius retired to the island of Rhodes, taking with him only a few close friends and his astrologer, Thrasyllus. The reasons given were many, including that his relationships with his two stepsons had collapsed due to their licentious behavior and failure to live up to Tiberius's strict moral code. Even Augustus was put off by their arrogance and insolence.* In an attempt to show his displeasure at his grandsons' behavior, Augustus denied them tribunician powers while awarding them to Tiberius. In doing so, he offended his grandsons and made them envious and distrustful of Tiberius, who was now the only person between them and ultimate power. If Tiberius became emperor, there was nothing stopping him from putting aside Gaius and Lucius in favor of his own son, Drusus, succeeding him. At the same time, Augustus angered Tiberius by ordering him east to settle problems in Armenia. From Tiberius's point of view, removing him from Rome made the award of tribunician powers a sham. Such powers were valuable in Rome but unnecessary in the east, where all knew that Tiberius spoke for Caesar.

---

* Dio Cassius, *The Histories*, 55.9.

But such fears worked both ways. If Augustus lived until the youths were adults, they would jump past Tiberius in the succession order, putting them in a position to punish Tiberius, possibly with his life. Moreover, in the intervening years, there would be no lack of opportunities for both youths to inflict an unending series of troubles upon Tiberius. Others claimed he wanted to escape the humiliation of his wife's numerous infidelities, which he could not publicly expose, as it would embarrass Augustus. Both reasons were likely contributors to his decision to depart Rome. Still, we must give credence to the explanation he offered, "that he was weary of office and needed a rest."*

Rome was shocked, as was Augustus, who complained on the Senate floor that he was being abandoned and betrayed. But no amount of pleading from either Augustus or Tiberius's mother made an impression on him. When they went further and took more strenuous measures to detain him, Tiberius began a hunger strike. Finally, after four days, a still angry Augustus relented, and Tiberius departed for Rhodes.

Soon after his stepson's departure, Augustus turned what may only have been a rest period into permanent exile. Taking their cue from the angry emperor, everyone in Rome who mattered turned on Tiberius and publicly voiced their contempt. Marcus Lollius, the man Tiberius dismissed as governor of Gaul, went so far as to try to win further favor with the emperor by offering to go to Rhodes and return with Tiberius's head. Why did Augustus allow this disrespect to fester? After all, Tiberius was still a member of the imperial family, and it was not a great leap for such contempt to jump to others, even to the point of placing Augustus's position in peril.

The most likely answer is that Augustus still feared Tiberius's sway with the legions. Having commanded in almost every theater, Tiberius was the only man in the Empire who could contest Augustus's control of the army. Moreover, every proconsul and legate Rome sent to serve in eastern provinces considered it prudent to stop in Rhodes and pay their respects. For the most part, Tiberius shunned such visits, as the last thing he needed was to give Augustus the impression that he was attempting to

* Suetonius, *Tiberius,* 10.2.

build a power base in the east similar to that of Mark Anthony. Clearly, Augustus and Tiberius were playing a dangerous game—one that would last years. Surprisingly, Augustus did not immediately strip Tiberius of his tribunician powers, although Tiberius refrained almost entirely from using them. The one time he is recorded to have done so is when, during a philosophical debate, someone taking a position opposed to that of Tiberius became insolent. We have no idea what the scholar supposedly said, but Tiberius was furious enough to order his immediate arrest. The story calls to mind an incident when Hadrian was emperor. A certain Favorinus, who was reproached by his friends for having given in to Hadrian's arguments over a minor philosophical issue, replied: "You are urging a wrong course, my friends, when you do not suffer me to regard as the most learned of men the one who has thirty legions."*

In 5 BC, Augustus made Gaius and Lucius members of the equestrian order, one step below the senatorial class, and designated Gaius as consul five years before he was of age. He did the same for Lucius in 2 BC, leaving no doubt that Gaius was Augustus's appointed successor, with Lucius as emperor-in-waiting in the event that some calamity befell his older brother. It was also in 2 BC that Augustus turned on Julia for her immoral conduct. Tiberius was informed in a letter from Augustus that his marriage to Julia had ended and that she was being banished to the island of Pandateria. Tiberius, clearly comprehending that a significant tie bonding him to Augustus was being cut, sent repeated missives defending a wife he despised. Augustus ignored all of his pleas, leaving Tiberius more exposed to the ill will of others than ever. For now, his safety relied on his mother's continuing influence with her husband, Augustus.

Soon after Julia's disgrace, Tiberius's tribunician powers expired, leaving him with no more official power than any other Roman citizen. Fearing that his life was in danger, Tiberius wrote to Augustus and pleaded to be allowed to return to Rome. Although Livia strongly pushed her husband to allow the exile to return, Augustus refused. He did, however, make Tiberius one of his legates in the east. This act returned to Ti-

* *Historia Augusta*, 2.16.13.

berius a substantial amount of civil power in the region and gave him some protection against his enemies.

In 1 AD, Gaius was given command of the legions of the Danube during a time when barbarian activity was at a low ebb. Dio snidely remarks that Augustus placed him there so that he could learn "in quiet and safety, while the dangerous undertakings were regularly assigned to others."* But, in the east, trouble was brewing in Armenia, and Parthia appeared ready to pick a new fight. Despite his youth and inexperience, Gaius was told to head to Syria and take command of the eastern provinces.

* Dio, *The Roman History*, 55.17.

Sejanus Comes Onstage

While en route to Syria, Gaius paused at the island of Samos. While he was there, Tiberius decided it was good politics to travel to Samos and pay his respects. From the moment Tiberius arrived, Gaius and his entourage treated him abysmally. Because of his inexperience, Augustus had surrounded Gaius with advisers, one of whom was Marcus Lollius, Gaius's guardian for the trip, who still hated Tiberius for relieving him of his post in Gaul years before. Throughout the voyage, Lollius entertained Gaius with a continuous barrage of slanders aimed at Tiberius. Gaius, believing Tiberius was a spent political force, refused to countenance Lollius's suggestion that Tiberius be murdered. Still, he did nothing to restrain his followers from displaying their disdain for the man. It was a long way to fall for Tiberius, who only a few years previous had been Rome's greatest general.

But there was one man in Gaius's party who must not have gone along with the crowd: Sejanus. It would not have taken much for Sejanus to have made a favorable and lasting impression on the future emperor, as all he had to do to set himself apart from the flatterers surrounding Gaius was to treat Tiberius with even a modicum of the respect that was due to a man of his rank and position. When Tiberius returned to power, he would not forget Sejanus, one of the few Roman aristocrats still close to the inner circle of power who did not turn on him. His politeness paid off, as by the time of his death Sejanus was, next to the emperor, the most powerful man in the Roman Empire.

Yet, who was this man whom Tiberius came to trust above all others? Sejanus was born in Vulsinii, in Etruria. Tacitus tells us that he had a strong physique, designed for hard work and toil. Along with an enterprising spirit, he possessed a talent for slander and a unique capacity to intertwine a haughty arrogance for those of lower stature with a sickening sycophancy for those more connected or powerful than himself. While always portraying a personal reserve in his dealing with the powerful, Sejanus nonetheless lusted for supreme power.* Sejanus maneuvered to be trusted to accompany Gaius on this eastern mission, his first recorded step toward the ultimate power he lusted after.

Sejanus's role during this mission is not mentioned in any surviving ancient texts, but we can make several speculative but reasonable surmises based on Sejanus's continued rapid rise once he returned to Rome. We know that Gaius had a guard with him, and it is almost inconceivable that this guard was not drawn from the Praetorians. As Sejanus's father commanded the Praetorians, one can safely bet that Sejanus was part of this guard and likely its commander in the rank of tribune. As such, he would have been in close proximity to Gaius during every waking moment. During his travels, Gaius involved himself in the succession battles going on in Judea in the wake of King Herod's death. Gaius took part in at least one and likely two conferences on the matter and probably had a decisive say in the outcome, as it would be a brave man indeed who disregarded the views of the man all considered the next emperor. It is almost inconceivable that he attended a meeting with a people the Romans considered troublesome without the leader of his Praetorian Guard, Sejanus, at his side. It may have been Sejanus's first taste of the ugliness that dominated court politics in Judea in the final years of Herod's death until Rome decided it was easier to just take the region over as a Roman province. It was also likely that it was during these meetings that Sejanus developed his renowned dislike of the Jews. At some point during Gaius's grand

* Tacitus, *The Annals*, 4.1.

tour of the Eastern Empire, at least one legion engaged in combat operations in Arabia against rebel raiders. This was probably Sejanus's first taste of combat, and he apparently acquitted himself well enough in either planning or actual combat to later be trusted with crucial missions on the frontiers, as well as to command the entire Praetorian Guard. The only evidence remaining that attests to Sejanus's military abilities at this time is a tantalizing fragment from Dio. In it, the historian claims that a strong rebel force marched out of Egypt to confront Gaius while he was in Arabia: "[They] did not yield until a tribune from the Praetorian Guard was sent against them."* No name was mentioned, but Sejanus was likely the only Praetorian tribune with Gaius. He was clearly already a man to watch, and his ambition was being recognized in Rome. In Roman politics, personal ambition was not a bad thing to have people notice about your character.

* Dio, *The Roman History*, 55–10a.

ELEVEN

Succession, Chaos Returns

As Gaius's mission was winding down, Augustus's succession chessboard was again thrown into disarray. While Gaius was settling the Empire's problems in the east, Augustus sent Lucius to complete his military training in Spain. Before he arrived, the youth fell ill in Gaul and died. This was a blow for Augustus but did not change his plans, as Gaius had always been his chosen successor.

Soon thereafter, another major obstacle to Tiberius's future rise was removed from the board. At some point during the extended negotiations with the Parthians, Phraates took a strong dislike to Lollius and informed Gaius that his guardian had been taking bribes from local communities and otherwise acting in his own interest at the expense of Rome. Gaius, who had already begun quarreling with Lollius, seized the chance to rid himself of his watchdog. Gaius denounced Lollius to the emperor and ordered him out of the Roman camp. Lollius's body was found a few days later, and it was assumed that he had taken poison to avoid further punishment. This was good news not only for Tiberius; it also helped Sejanus, who moved up in the ranks of those close to Gaius and, by extension, Augustus.

Tiberius seized the moment. He and his mother, Livia, had never ceased petitioning Augustus to allow Tiberius's return to Rome. But Augustus would not consider taking any such action unless Gaius approved. That was an obvious impossibility as long as Lollius had Gaius's ear. However, when Lollius fell from grace, an opening presented itself. In 2 AD, Gaius reversed himself and consented for Tiberius to come home, but with the humbling condition that he refrain from public life. Upon returning to Rome, Tiberius took part in the coming-of-age ceremonies for his son, Drusus, before retiring to a section of Rome far from the Forum, the center of Rome's political life—but the fates were not done with Tiberius yet. Before returning to Rome Gaius, in 2 AD, took part in some minor military operations in Armenia, where he was wounded by an arrow. His health never recovered and he died early in 4 AD.

Augustus's succession plans were irredeemably shattered. There was no longer a direct bloodline that could carry on the Julian dynasty. All that was left to him was Germanicus, the son of Tiberius's brother, Drusus. He was about nineteen at the time, but Augustus considered him too young and inexperienced to rule, particularly considering that Germanicus's presence was immediately required on the Rhine frontier, where war had already erupted. Germanicus was married to Agrippina, the daughter of Agrippa and the now disgraced Julia. As such, any male offspring would be a direct blood descendant of Augustus, allowing for the reestablishment of the Julian dynasty, after a brief Claudian interlude while Germanicus ruled. Augustus's problem was that if he died in the next few years, the inexperienced Germanicus would be run over and destroyed in the deadly political scrum to succeed him. Only one possible solution presented itself: Augustus would adopt Tiberius, making him his chosen successor. In return, Tiberius would adopt his nephew, Germanicus, and designate him as his successor.

Tiberius's return to political eminence was a remarkable turnaround. His usefulness to Augustus would once again be proven on the battlefield. Over the next couple of years, Tiberius campaigned in Germany, expanding the Empire to the banks of the Elbe. By the end of 5 AD, only the barbarian Kingdom of Maroboduus, centered on Bohemia, remained outside of Rome's domains. The imperial dream of adding Germania to the Empire was, however, put on hold in 6 AD, when the province of Pannonia rebelled. As Pannonia sat on Italy's northern border, the revolt panicked Rome, as no legions resided within Italy. To manage the crisis, legions were gathered from across the Empire and rushed to the war zone, and Tiberius, still Rome's most successful living general, was sent to lead them. Commanding nearly half of Rome's total legions, Tiberius spent the next three years campaigning in Pannonia against stubborn resistance. The victory was finally gained when Tiberius turned to a scorched-earth policy, aiming to starve the Pannonians. By the end of the year, all but the most dedicated rebels made peace with Rome, and the overwhelming power of the legions rapidly overran the remainder.

Tiberius had little time to enjoy his greatest military success, as only five days after the victory in Pannonia was announced in Rome came word of a new disaster. The new Roman commander in Germany, Quinctilius Varus, was fresh from the east, where a few years earlier his Syrian legions had likely marched past Nazareth—and a youthful Jesus—on their way to Jerusalem to crush a Jewish revolt. This time, however, he led three of Rome's precious legions into an ambush and massacre. Tiberius canceled the triumph, planned to celebrate his Pannonian victory, and rushed north to restore order and seal the frontier along the Rhine. For the next three years, he campaigned across the Rhine. There were no more brilliant marches across Germany to the Elbe. Instead, comprehending that Rome could not afford any major losses, Tiberius moved cautiously. Employing what had worked in Pannonia, the restored Rhine legions were employed in laying waste to large swathes of Germany, both as punishment and to ensure that the tribes lacked the resources to continue fighting. Germanicus joined him in the 11 AD campaign, but, while he was present, the troops rarely ventured far from the Rhine. In the following year, Tiberius returned to Rome, leaving Germanicus in charge of the armies.

In 13 AD, Tiberius was elevated to the same level of power and honors that Agrippa had enjoyed. Augustus had a law passed giving Tiberius the imperium, making him coequal to Augustus throughout the Empire. This came with an extension of Tiberius's tribunician powers and honoring his son, Drusus, a consul for the first time. From the moment Tiberius reentered public life, he rapidly promoted his supporters to positions of power and influence and removed those whose allegiance was suspect. One benefit of having fallen from Augustus's favor for so long is that Tiberius knew exactly who his true friends were, as well as those who turned against him when he was down. Such networks and alliances were crucial to anyone who wanted to reign supreme in Rome. How well Tiberius did in reconstructing his power base would soon be tested.

TWELVE

The Death of Augustus

In 14 AD, Tiberius felt secure enough in power to depart for Illyricum (Pannonia) to undertake the reorganization and rehabilitation of the regions he had ravaged during the Great Revolt. He had no sooner arrived than word came from Livia that Augustus was ill and unlikely to recover. Tiberius rushed back to Italy, and likely arrived in the city of Nola just before Augustus died. At the time and later, there was considerable speculation that Augustus had died earlier, but Livia kept it a secret until her son arrived. The first order of business was the elimination of any possible rivals for the throne, of which there was only one: Agrippa Postumus. Postumus was the third son of Agrippa and Livia, after Gaius and Lucius. Physically powerful, brutish, and stupid, no one, least of all Augustus, ever considered him fit to rule. Augustus became so disgusted with his behavior that he banished him to the island of Planasia (Pianosa), where he was kept under armed guard.

Augustus was now dead, and Postumus was suddenly a dangerous loose end. He may have been unfit to rule, but he could be used as a rallying point for ambitious men seeking to dispute Tiberius's right to rule. The problem was quickly and efficiently handled by sending a trusted centurion to execute Postumus. Ever since, there has been an unending debate about who ordered the execution, as each of the ancient sources

appears to have its own candidate—Augustus, Tiberius, or Livia. Arguably, the preponderance of the evidence indicates that Augustus was the
culprit. As an adopted son of Augustus, Postumus could make a claim to
his share of the inheritance. In the final modification of his will, Augustus had named only two beneficiaries—Tiberius and Livia. He clearly did
not envision Postumus's long-term survival.

There was one other dangerous loose end: Augustus's daughter and
Tiberius's estranged wife, Julia. As Augustus's daughter, she was also vul-
nerable to being used as a focal point of any anti-Tiberius resistance.
Thus, Tiberius extended her banishment, increased her guard, and deprived her of the monies Augustus had allocated for her maintenance. By
the end of the year, Julia was dead, and there is good reason to believe she
was starved to death by Tiberius's order.

Tiberius wasted no time taking control of the levers of power. He
demanded and received oaths of loyalty from the two serving consuls and
took charge of the Praetorian Guard—the only organized military force
in Rome or, for that matter, all of Italy. Most crucially, he wrote to each
of the provincial armies, telling them of Augustus's death and informing
them that he was now the Empire's ruler. The legions, who deeply respected the man who won battles and preserved their lives from needless
loss, accepted the change without a murmur. With the legions at his
back, there was no longer any doubt that Tiberius would succeed Augustus at the pinnacle of power. Still, as Augustus was Rome's first emperor,
there was, as of yet, no tradition of succession. What was clear to every
Roman was that Augustus could declare a successor, but he could not
bestow upon him his personal *auctoritas*. To ensure his long-term rule,
Tiberius needed to establish his own *auctoritas* and make sure it was recognized by all, particularly by Rome's fractious senators. To do so, Tiberius had to overcome the fact that he was only the new *Princeps* because
Augustus, after a series of unfortunate deaths, had no other choice but to
appoint him as his successor. And even then, many believed that Augustus would still have made a different choice if he had not been influenced
by the unceasing manipulations of his wife, Livia. All of this made it
crucial, at least in Tiberius's mind, that he become emperor through the
Senate's unreserved acclamation.

When the time came for the Senate to acclaim him as emperor, Tiberius made a hash of it by publicly claiming his reluctance to rule while simultaneously extending his control of the levers of power. He wanted the Senate to override his objections and proclaim him emperor as the only man in Rome who could hold the body politic together. The confused senators had no idea what they were supposed to do, and several made statements asking Tiberius to be more forthcoming in voicing his desires. One senator went so far as to shout, "Let him take it or leave it."* Such comments angered Tiberius, who could not fathom why the senators could not divine his intentions and act accordingly. In the end, Tiberius was proclaimed emperor, even as he complained about the burdensome slavery the Senate had forced upon him. But he did so in such a way as to give the Senate hope that he would one day resign his position in favor of the far more popular Germanicus; some dared hope that he would proclaim a return to the Republic.

What was certain was that Tiberius had needlessly soured relations with the Senate right from the start of his reign. They never recovered.

---

* Suetonius, *Lives of the Twelve Caesars: Tiberius,* 24.1.

PART IV

HEROD AND THE BIRTH OF JESUS

THIRTEEN

Prelude to Herod

Since the death of Alexander the Great, Palestine, including Judea, had been ruled by his Successors, who had claimed Persia (including Syria and Palestine) in the wake of the breakup of Alexander's empire.* In 198 BC, one branch of the Successors—the Seleucids—conquered Palestine in a war against another branch—the Ptolemies. But only a generation later, in 167 BC, Mattathias, founder of the Hasmonean dynasty, and his five sons took advantage of the Seleucids' distraction elsewhere to lead a revolt against the Seleucid Empire. As a result, Judea gained substantial autonomy, although it remained a Seleucid province. Strife erupted again when a new Seleucid ruler, Antiochus VII, started bringing the Empire's lost and nearly-lost provinces back under central control. In 134 BC, he besieged Jerusalem, bringing the current Hasmonean ruler and high priest, John Hyrcanus, to heel. Antiochus was only convinced to lift the siege and leave John in power after being paid a three-thousand-talent bribe. John raided the Temple treasury to raise these funds, making him terribly unpopular with the rest of the Jewish leadership. When Antiochus VII was killed fighting the Parthians in

---

* The other portions of the Empire were each ruled by one of Alexander's top generals. Ptolemy ruled Egypt, Antigonus took over Asia Minor (Anatolia), Cassander took Macedonia and Greece, while Seleucus took Persia, which included Syria and Palestine.

129 BC, the Seleucid Empire began to rapidly disintegrate as various members of the royal family contended for power.

John Hyrcanus took advantage of the renewed turmoil to make a total break, freeing Judea of Seleucid control, and from 122 to 63 BC, Judea was, for the first time in centuries, an independent state. Then, starting in approximately 110 BC, John thought himself strong enough to launch a series of wars of conquest. He first ravaged and then occupied Samaria and Transjordan. In the process, he destroyed the Samaritan temple on Mount Gerizim. Thus, he hugely improved his relations with Jerusalem's Jewish leadership, who detested the existence of another Jewish temple outside their city. Before his death, John had turned his armies south to conquer Idumea, which did not contain a Jewish population. To remedy this, John instituted a policy of forced conversions of non-Jews in conquered areas, which Idumaea was forced to endure before being integrated into the emerging Hasmonean Jewish state. According to Josephus:

> Hyrcanus . . . after subduing all the Idumeans, permitted them to remain in their country as long as they had themselves circumcised and were willing to observe the laws of the Jews. And so, out of attachment to the land of their fathers, they submitted to circumcision and to make their manner of life conform in all other respects to that of the Jews. And from that time onward they have continued to be Jews.*

They may have continued to be Jews, but the Jews in Judea considered them second-class citizens and possibly not even true Jews. This disdain for the Idumeans was at the core of many of the problems Herod (who was Idumean) would encounter with the Jewish leadership in Jerusalem, and probably a key reason why he decided to live most of the year in his newly constructed city of Caesarea.

When John died in 104 BC, his oldest son, Aristobulus I, took power, arresting his three brothers and his mother, whom he allowed to starve to death in prison. He was the first of the Hasmonean rulers to take the title

*Josephus, *Jewish Antiquities*, 13.257.58.

of king and thereby publicly assert Judea's independence. Before dying of a painful illness in 103 BC, Aristobulus conquered Galilee, which was quickly integrated into the burgeoning Jewish state as it was already Jewish. Upon his death, his wife, Salome, released his brothers from prison, and the oldest, Alexander Jannaeus, took over the kingship while marrying the widowed Salome. During his rule, he added Iturea (east of Galilee) to the Jewish state, but he also got in the middle of an Egyptian civil war, which almost cost him his kingdom, and left most of Galilee ravaged. In his later years, Alexander's continual and costly campaigns led to civil war and the loss of Transjordan after a disastrous defeat in a war with the Nabateans to the east.

Upon his death, his wife, Salome, ruled as regent for her son Hyrcanus II, who held the office of High Priest. During her rule, 76–67 BC, the wars stopped, but the political turmoil within Judea never ended. Salome was forced to walk a tightrope between the two major religious groups, the Pharisees and the Sadducees, who, during this period, also acted as political parties. When the Pharisees demanded that her husband, Alexander Jannaeus, choose between being king and high priest, he turned on them. Throughout much of his reign, the Pharisees were persecuted and the Sadducees were favored. But Salome's brother, Simon ben Shetach, was a leading Pharisee, so the political tide reversed once she came to power. Upon her death, her oldest son, Hyrcanus II, sought Pharisee support, while her younger son, Aristobulus, sought Sadducee support. The result was civil war, eventually leading to Aristobulus becoming king, but with his brother retaining all his dignities as high priest. The peace did not last long, and with the help of a Nabatean army, Hyrcanus placed Jerusalem under siege. The war finally ended when both brothers petitioned Rome for help, assuming they could control the fox once they had invited it into the henhouse. In 63 BC, Rome's legions, commanded by Pompey the Great, marched into Jerusalem. Pompey did indeed end the civil war, as well as the independence of the Jewish state.

FOURTEEN

Herod in Power

erod was born in 72 BC in Idumea. He was the second son of
Antipater, whose ancestors had converted to Judaism, and Cy-
pros, a Jewish Nabatean princess from Petra (in modern Jordan). During the civil wars between Aristobulus and Hyrcanus II,
Antipater hooked his star onto Hyrcanus, considering him the easier of
the two brothers to manipulate and control. During the Roman Wars,
initially between Caesar and Pompey, Caesar favored Aristobulus and
took him to Rome while leaving Hyrcanus in Jerusalem as a high priest
but without political power. But Pompey's supporters in Rome, believing
Caesar was about to give both priestly and political power to Aristobulus,
poisoned the Jewish leader, leaving only Hyrcanus at the top of the Hasmonean leadership.

Later in the civil war, Caesar was besieged in Alexandria and found
himself in a potentially fatal position. Despite Caesar having previously
supported Aristobulus, Antipater (Herod's father) convinced Hyrcanus
to lead his army into Egypt to help rescue Caesar. Once Caesar was triumphant, he repaid Hyrcanus by putting aside the claims of Aristobulus's son, Antigonus the Hasmonean, and restored Hyrcanus as ethnarch
(a ruler of a region but not quite a king), while Antipater was made
epitropos (regent). Antipater oversaw Roman interests in his new position,

and as Rome was interested in everything, Antipater became the true power in Palestine. For Caesar, Antipater solved many problems; the foremost among them was that Antipater was a converted Jew, making him at least partially acceptable to most Jews. He was also an Idumean, which meant he could keep that troublesome region calm. At the same time, although he was now a mere figurehead, the fiction that Hyrcanus ruled kept Judea from becoming restive. Moreover, through his wife's relations, Antipater could keep the peace with Nabataea. Finally, Antipater was a superb administrator, capable of providing Rome with the one thing it prized above all else: regular tax revenues. Because Antipater kept the peace and secured the Roman tax base, Rome permitted him a great deal of autonomy, including being granted permission to rebuild Jerusalem's walls, previously destroyed by Pompey. To further secure his political position, Antipater appointed his son, Phasael, governor of Jerusalem while making Herod governor of Galilee, where he earned a name for himself routing bandits.

When Julius Caesar was killed, his assassins fled east to raise an army for the next round of the civil war that was clearly on the horizon. Their enemies would be Caesar's leading generals: Mark Anthony, and a rising Gaius Octavius (Octavian, later named Augustus), whom Caesar had adopted in his last will. Cassius, one of the senators who led the plot to kill Caesar, demanded in 44 BC that Judea pay seven hundred talents into his war treasury, which was only raised with some difficulty. But, even as a dangerous Roman civil war brewed in the background, local politics had not come to an end. And soon after the seven hundred talents had been turned over, a long-standing political rival managed to poison Antipater.

Without the support of his father, one might have expected to find Herod's position in Galilee threatened. But Herod had been busy during his early years as governor, starting with a brutal suppression of anti-Roman elements (often called bandits) scattered throughout the region and faithfully securing Rome's tax revenues. Rome always valued, as a friend, anyone who delivered the required tax assessment on time and without trouble. But Herod also had strong enemies. Because of his brutality, Herod made enemies within the Sanhedrin, the ruling council in Jerusalem. Still, with Rome having his back, he could ignore even such potentially powerful enemies. But to be sure, Herod made himself a close friend and ally of the Roman governor in Syria, Sextus Caesar, who could bring several legions to Herod's aid whenever called upon. More crucially, Herod demonstrated that he could adapt quickly to Roman politics' ever-changing and dangerous currents. When Cassius was defeated, Herod swiftly switched his allegiance to Mark Anthony, who would soon be sharing the Empire with Octavian (Augustus), with Mark Anthony controlling the eastern portions of the Empire. Josephus said Herod had purchased Mark Anthony's support, as he was easily "corrupted by money."* Corruption might be too strong a word, as civil wars are expensive, and Anthony's coffers were likely empty. He was also facing a Parthian invasion of Syria, which would surely cost vast sums. Much of his required funding would come from Cleopatra's seemingly inexhaustible Egyptian treasury, but Herod was well placed to supply his immediate needs.

Antigonus the Hasmonean had not yet left the political scene, and he too understood how to use cash as an enticement to gain support. So, after promising the Parthians one thousand talents and five hundred slave women, they sent a small force to help him conquer Jerusalem. Once inside the city, he seized his uncle Hyrcanus, who was still the high priest and figurehead ruler, and had his ears cut off. Such a maiming disqualified Hyrcanus from ever again being high priest. Herod's brother, Phasael, was also captured, but he killed himself by bashing his head against a stone before Antigonus could have him hideously executed. Herod, however, fled to Rome, where, on the recommendation of Mark Anthony, the Senate declared him King of the Jews.

Returning to Palestine with a largely mercenary army, Herod overran much of Galilee and Judea but could not take the refortified Jerusalem. Only after Mark Anthony had decisively defeated the Parthian armies in Syria was he able to turn his full attention to Judea. Mark Anthony sent two legions—probably *VI Ferrata* and *III Gallica*—to help Herod. With these two legions, Herod captured both Jerusalem and Antigonus, who

* Josephus, *Jewish Antiquities*, 14.13.2.

was immediately packed off to Mark Anthony for execution. After three years of fighting, Herod was now king of all of Palestine. Still, his position was weak, as a large part of the kingdom still supported the surviving Hasmoneans. Even those who detested the Hasmoneans resented that the Romans had made an Idumean, who other Jews considered impure, the king of all Jews.

To strengthen his power base, Herod married a Hasmonean princess, Mariamme, who was the granddaughter of Hyrcanus II. He and Mariamme had two sons who lived to adulthood, Alexander and Aristobulus. His marriage and his two half-Hasmonean sons helped Herod's position, but it was not enough to squelch all opposition, not even from among his new Hasmonean family. Mariamme's mother, Alexandra, befriended Cleopatra, who was now married to Mark Anthony. She asked the Egyptian queen to help make Aristobulus III high priest, and Cleopatra duly took the request to Mark Anthony. Anthony wavered, which gave Herod the time he needed to act. Herod knew he was facing a double threat. The first was that Aristobulus's elevation to high priest would allow the Hasmoneans to rebuild their power base within Judea. But just as dangerous to his long-term prospects, Herod comprehended Cleopatra's ultimate aim. If Aristiobulus III became high priest because of her support, she could use him to cleave off large portions of Herod's kingdom before absorbing them into her Egyptian dominions. When Cleopatra recommended that Alexandra bring the young Aristobulus to Egypt to meet with Anthony, the threat to Herod became real and possibly mortal.

Fearing that a face-to-face meeting might sway Anthony to support Aristobulus's appointment, Herod had the great Hasmonean hope assassinated in 35 BC. That ended the immediate threats to his rule, but a far greater one was looming. Mark Anthony and Octavian had concluded that the Roman Empire was too small for both of them. War was on the horizon, and Herod had to pick a side. The only sensible decision he could make was to put his full support behind Anthony, as he was the Roman ruler with multiple legions sitting on the frontiers of Herod's kingdom. With Cleopatra's full support, Anthony could occupy Judea and depose him long before any help from Octavian could arrive. When war broke out, it was a short one. Anthony and Cleopatra's fleet was decisively defeated at the Battle of Actium in 31 BC, and most of their legions immediately switched their allegiance to Octavian. After the defeat, Anthony escaped back to Egypt, but his cause was lost, and he was a doomed man. Herod had backed the wrong man with both money and soldiers.

Many in Judea probably assumed that Herod's fate was sealed and it would not be a happy ending, as victorious Romans were rarely kind to those who actively opposed them. But Herod had one chance, and he took it. Rather than go down with Anthony, he switched sides and left for Rhodes to meet with Octavian. To demonstrate his submission, he did not wear his crown, and to further show his worth, Herod brought bags of gold and silver. No Roman of Herod's acquaintance had ever failed to appreciate hard currency, particularly in the midst of war. Herod then put on the performance of his life. He could not deny his alliance with Anthony, so he made it the center of his proposal to Octavian. Herod pointed out all the ways he had served his former patron and how loyal he was to Anthony and Rome throughout his rule of Judea. And now that Octavian ruled Rome, which Herod said was always his ultimate master, he promised to transfer all that loyalty to Octavian.

Although he left no statue of himself or a head on a coin, as either would have violated Jewish law, Josephus leaves us a description of sorts:

> Now Herod had a body suited to his soul, and was ever a most excellent hunter, where he generally had good success, by the means of his great skill in riding horses; for in one day he caught forty wild beasts . . . He was also such a warrior as could not be withstood: many men, therefore, there are who have stood amazed at his readiness in his exercises, when they saw him throw the javelin directly forward, and shoot the arrow upon the mark. And then, besides these performances of his depending on his own strength of mind and body, fortune was also very favorable to him.[*]

---

[*] Josephus, *The Wars of the Jews*, 21.13.

Herod's presence and sheer audacity must have impressed Octavian. More crucially, Octavian was a very pragmatic man, and Herod could still be useful to him. As Anthony escaped to Egypt, Octavian was forced to rapidly follow to arrive in Egypt before Anthony could rally new forces to his cause. Such a march required Octavian's legions to march through Palestine, which would be in turmoil if Herod was removed from power. Herod had proven himself a firm and able administrator, quite capable of supplying the two things Octavian most needed: supplies as his armies marched through Herod's territory and continuing payments of silver and gold. Thus, Herod was left in power, where he soon proved his worth. Herod provided troops and funds for the remainder of Octavian's military campaign. In addition, during the campaign, Herod personally escorted Octavian through Syria and then did the same upon the Roman's return march, throwing several lavish banquets along the way. Octavian was so impressed that he not only retained Herod as King of Judea, he also returned several regions Cleopatra had managed to steal away from him, with Mark Anthony's approval. Octavian also placed under Herod's control regions that had not even been part of the Kingdom of Israel before it was diminished by Pompey's edicts in 63 BC.

Herod now possessed total power in Palestine, and, as he had the full support of Octavian, who was now sole ruler of the Roman Empire, no one could contest his hold on the kingdom. By all appearances, Herod ruled well, although he constantly had to walk a tightrope between appeasing his Jewish subjects, who despised him, and pleasing Rome.

In dealing with a hostile population, Herod relied on an extensive network of secret police, building fortresses within his kingdom and on the frontiers, and maintaining a highly trained mercenary force in Jerusalem. This force was made up almost entirely of Gentiles, and what few Jews were permitted into its ranks came from Herod's Idumean homeland or Babylonia. Nearly all of Herod's administrators were also Gentiles, who could not build an independent power base of their own in a Jewish-dominated society and therefore owed their positions and any chance of advancement entirely to Herod. Only in the priesthood did Herod retain Jews in a position of power, as he had no other choice. But he reserved the right to choose the high priest and did it from a family not traditionally associated with the role. Finally, Herod did much to destroy the power of the Sanhedrin, consisting of the population's elites, which only regained its influence after Herod's death, when Rome had taken direct rule of Judea.

As the historian Martin Goodman points out, Herod also took steps to woo his Jewish subjects. Although he was always attracted to Hellenistic culture, he never flaunted this attraction. Whenever Herod was in Jerusalem or any other major Jewish city, he did his best to abide by Mosaic Law.* Moreover, in an act meant to demonstrate his piety and pride in his Jewish heritage, he spent lavishly on projects to beautify Jerusalem and rebuild its temple. He also aggressively pushed forward the lie that he was actually a descendant of a line of Babylonian Jews. In addition, he often put forth in his propaganda that he was the protector of all Jews, wherever within the Empire they resided. Clearly, Herod was torn between two worlds: He was and wanted to be thought of as a Jew, but he also longed to be a Roman, sprinkled with a Greek cultural veneer. He was obliged to respect Jewish traditions but was always attracted to the idea of breaking free of the encumbrances of the Mosaic Law and diving into the pleasures, culture, and elegance of the Hellenistic world that surrounded him. He also hungered for power and glory, but his ambitions were constantly circumscribed by the overweening power of Rome, which held his ultimate fate in its capricious hands.

Despite being despised as an Idumean by most of the Jewish population in Judea and Galilee, Herod faced no serious threats to his power until the end of his long reign. These new, burgeoning threats came from within his family, which had always been his most pressing political concern. Soon after he was confirmed in power by Augustus, he began to suspect that his wife, Mariamme, likely bearing a grudge over the murders of her father and brother, was plotting rebellion and was guilty of serial infidelity. It is uncertain which act incensed Herod more, but in 29 BC, he had her tried and executed. Soon after that, her mother, Alexandra, summoning the last remnant of Hasmonean power, launched an-

---

* Martin Goodman, "Judea," in Alan Bowman et al. (eds.), *The Cambridge Ancient History,* Vol. X, *The Augustan Empire, 43 B.C–A.D. 69,* 2nd ed. (Cambridge University Press, 1996), pp. 737–781.

other revolt. In typical style, Herod rushed to crush the uprising with overwhelming military force. Alexandra did not survive.

Herod bought himself over a decade of domestic peace through sheer ruthlessness, but tensions were never far from the surface. He was able to abate them somewhat by sending his two sons from his marriage to Mariamme, Aristobulus and Alexander, to be educated in Rome in 24 or 23 BC. When they returned in 16 BC, Herod made it clear that he had chosen them to succeed him, setting off another round of family intrigue. The rise of the half-Hasmonean sons of Mariamme would have established a new Hasmonean dynasty that would present an existential threat to the Idumean royals. Soon, Herod's sister, Salome, and his brother, Pheroras, persuaded Herod to prefer his oldest son, Antipater, by his first wife, the Idumean Doris. In 13 BC, Antipater was sent to Rome so he could start making the connections essential to his appointment and later survival as king. Before he left, Antipater worked assiduously to further poison his father against Mariamme's offspring, causing Herod to accuse them of sedition in front of Augustus. They were guilty of the charge but still found innocent, which left them free to continue plotting against their father. Herod had them tried a second time before a Roman court in 7 BC. This time, they were declared guilty and executed. Antipater, who was senior to Herod's four remaining sons, was now the clear favorite for the throne.

By 5 BC, Antipater's power was almost equal to Herod's, and he was formally declared the king's successor. But then, Herod fell ill. Although we do not have enough information to diagnose what ailed him, Josephus gives us a horrific description of Herod's illness, one that is not for the squeamish:

> His entrails were also ex-ulcerated, and the chief violence of his pain lay on his colon; an aqueous and transparent liquor also had settled itself about his feet, and a like matter afflicted him at the bottom of his belly. Nay, further, his privy-member was putrefied, and produced worms; and when he sat upright, he had a difficulty of breathing, which was very loathsome, on account of the stench of his breath, and the quickness of its returns; he had also convul-

sions in all parts of his body, which increased his strength to an insufferable degree.*

As Herod's suffering increased, he gave full vent to his paranoia. Herod was acutely aware throughout his reign that his subjects held him in disdain. His suspicions that they welcomed his passing were confirmed when a rumor of his death caused a riot in Jerusalem, where a group of young men had torn down a golden eagle he had erected over the Temple. The rioters saw the eagle as an insult to Jewish law forbidding the reproduction of any living thing, while Herod viewed it as an offering to God. Herod's military force captured forty of the young rioters. They also arrested two renowned experts in the law: Judas, son of Sepphoraeus, and Matthias, son of Margalus, who had encouraged the rioters to attack the graven image. In a fierce passion, Herod ordered Judas and Matthias to burn alive and the rest tortured.

As Herod comprehended that his death would be a cause for rejoicing for most Jews, he ordered all of the principal men of the kingdom brought to Jerusalem and confined to the hippodrome. Upon word of his death, they were all to be slaughtered, so, according to Josephus, Israel would lament his passing, if not for him, then for the many notables who perished on his order. Upon his death, Herod's sister, Salome, rescinded the order and sent the confined men home. Only after forestalling the heinous act did Salome publicly announce Herod's death.

As Herod's death approached, his son, Antipater, already the chosen heir, apparently could not wait until his father naturally expired. But whatever plot he had concocted was betrayed to Herod, who now charged his third son with treason in a Roman court. Antipater was found guilty, but because of his rank and the possible involvement of a member of Augustus's wife's staff, the emperor was asked to declare his sentence. In the meantime, another son, Herod Antipas, was named Herod's successor. Herod was days from death when word came that Augustus had left Antipater's

---

* Josephus, *Jewish Antiquities*, 17.6.5.

punishment up to Herod. If Herod planned to take Augustus's strong hint to offer his son mercy, Antipater's actions tossed this slim chance for his survival away. Herod became incensed upon being informed that Antipater had attempted to bribe his guards to release him. Rising up on one elbow from his deathbed, he ordered Antipater's immediate execution just five days before his own death. In his few remaining days, Herod again revised his will. This time, Herod Antipas was removed from the line of succession in favor of his older brother, Archelaus. Instead, Herod Antipas was made tetrarch of Galilee and Peraea, while a half brother, Philip, was made tetrarch of several regions to the northeast—Gaulanitis, Trachonitis, Batanaea, and Panias.

FIFTEEN

Birth of Jesus

When not busy wiping out his family, Herod spent much of his long reign on a series of massive building projects, including a new port city he named after the emperor, Caesarea Maritima, which became the administrative center of his kingdom and later the center of Roman administration until the Great Revolt of 66 AD. But, by far, his most ambitious building project was the tremendous expansion of the Temple Mount, which became one of the largest engineering projects in the entire Empire during the first century. Such a project would have drawn every skilled worker within the kingdom. Hence, we may be able to employ this uncontested piece of history to reexamine the story of Jesus's birth in a way that has been overlooked before. To do that, we must look closely at Joseph, the husband of Jesus's mother, Mary. We know very little about Joseph, but there is no dispute that he was a skilled craftsman and "possibly" a carpenter. From that knowledge, can we extrapolate more about the man and his family?

The problems with discovering the historical truth about Jesus come right at the beginning, as the only evidence we have for the story of Jesus's birth are the Gospels of Matthew and Luke. These two books, unfortunately, tell differing versions, which many claim are ahistorical. Whether Jesus was born of a virgin mother is a matter of faith and far beyond the capability of historical analyses to offer any judgment. But we can, hopefully, decide on where he was born and when. Both Luke and Matthew tell us that Jesus was born in Bethlehem. Matthew does not, however, tell us how this came to be. Luke, on the other hand, gives a detailed background story as to why Joseph and Mary were in Bethlehem:

> And it came about in those days, that a decree went out from Caesar Augustus, that all the inhabited earth should be registered. This was the first registration that took place while Quirinius was governor of Syria. And all were making their way to be registered, each to his own town. Thus Joseph also went up, from the town of Nazareth in Galilee, to Judea, to the town of David, which is called Bethlehem, because he was from the house and line of David to be registered along with Mary.[*]

For historians, the problems with this narrative pile up quickly. We shall take each of them in their order in the narrative to determine if Luke is giving us a true history of events.

First, there is no historical record of Augustus issuing any such decree in the year Jesus was most likely born: 6 BC. Moreover, the Census of Quirinius did not take place until 6 AD, when Jesus would have been about twelve years old.[†] Since Emil Schürer published his supposed masterpiece on Jewish history in the time of Christ, the historical consensus has been that Luke, trusting inaccurate sources, made a historical error.[‡] Let us first assume that he did make an error. What does that change? The place of Jesus's birth remains Bethlehem, which is the key fact of the passage. Mentioning Quirinius's census is only meant to establish the dating of the event. Misdating the event has almost no impact on the narrative of Jesus's life. Rather, historians have used the possible mis-

---

[*] Luke 2:1–7.
[†] Josephus, *Jewish Antiquities*, 18.1.1 and 17.13.2–5.
[‡] Emil Schürer, John Macpherson (trans.), *A History of the Jewish People in the Time of Jesus Christ* (T. & T. Clark, 1891).

dating as further evidence that the New Testament narratives cannot be trusted or employed as historical sources.

But there are good reasons to believe that Luke did not make an error. Crucially, Luke certainly knew when the Quirinius Census in the historical record took place. In Acts, which Luke also authored, he wrote, "After him *Judas the Galilean rose up in the days of the census* and drew away some of the people after him."* Judas's revolt was in 6 AD and was sparked by Quirinius's census. As Luke was aware of all of this, he is unlikely to have made such a major error in his birth narrative. So, what could have happened here?

The first point that must be made is that Luke refers to this census as a "first" enrollment, distinctly separating it from the 6 AD census that he refers to in Acts. This earlier census was then something separate apart from the 6 AD event. So, the question now changes to: Could a census have taken place in or close to the year 6 BC? Here, we must turn to one of the more astounding testaments any ancient ruler left to us— Augustus's *Res Gestae.* Before his death, Augustus made a testament to record all of his achievements, having them displayed on bronze tablets in front of his mausoleum. Unfortunately, these bronze tablets are lost to history, but a nearly complete translation and fragments of others have been discovered in other parts of the Empire. Augustus recorded: "A second time, in the consulship of Gaius Censorinus and Gaius Asinius, [8 BC] I again performed the lustrum [census] alone, with the consular imperium. In this lustrum, 4,233,000 Roman citizens were entered on the census roll."† In the *Res Gestae,* Augustus was boasting as a Roman to other Romans, and in this case, he was particularly proud of the number of Roman citizens within the Empire. But the primary goal of a census is to record the amount of wealth and its location for tax purposes. Augustus would certainly have been as interested in the taxable wealth of the larger Empire as he was in that of Italy and Rome. Hence, it is likely that he also extended his Roman census to the larger Empire or at least substantial portions of it. Remember that a considerable number of Roman citizens

* Luke 2:1–6.
† *Res Gestae*, 8. Online: https://www.livius.org/sources/content/augustus-res-gestae/.

in 8 BC resided outside of Rome and Italy, and Augustus would want them counted. That we have no record of the order tells us nothing. We have no record of most of Augustus's orders. If not for his leaving behind the *Res Gestae*, we would not even have a historical record of the 8 BC census in Rome either. As it is, we have only one reference, apart from Luke's Acts, mentioning the 6 AD Census of Quirinius: Josephus. If we assume Augustus ordered a large Empire-wide count, we must account for the time lag involved. Getting the order out to the provinces and establishing the necessary infrastructure to collect the census data would take substantial time. This time lag would easily explain why the census in Palestine could not have gotten underway until 6 BC or thereabouts.

Some have claimed that Herod ran a quasi-independent kingdom and did not have to follow Roman dictates on when to conduct a census. Two things are wrong with this idea. The first is that Herod was slavishly attuned to Augustus's desires. In fact, his kingship, and probably his life, rested upon his ability to please Augustus. Thus, if Augustus ordered an Empire-wide census, then Herod was very likely to follow his lead. Also, it is absurd to think that Rome could not order a census in Herod's territory or oversee one that Herod had ordered. Rome had one great interest from the provinces and semiautonomous kingdoms it allowed to exist: the collection of tax and tribute revenues due to Rome. Rome may not have collected a tax for domains such as Herod's, but a large and regular tribute was certainly demanded. How much tribute Rome could require could only be determined after a census. To think that Rome would take a local ruler's word as to the taxable wealth of his kingdom is absurd. Rome cared about taxes and tributes above all other concerns, so they would undoubtedly have kept tabs on Herod's accounting processes and results. Moreover, besides collecting taxes to pay the Roman tribute, Herod also demanded revenues to support his requirements, as maintaining his own military forces and supporting a massive building program were expensive. Thus, conducting his own periodic census was in his best interest. If this census could be done in such a way as to conform with orders from Rome, so much the better.

Here it is essential to comprehend what a premodern census was. Although counting the local population, usually just males, was crucial, particularly if a state maintained a poll tax, the tabulation of property and wealth was more important. The most complete premodern census still existing was that ordered by William the Conqueror after his conquest of England in the eleventh century—the famous Doomsday (Domesday) Book. The 1085 survey of England and Wales aimed to record every piece of property and who owned it, the land's resources (agricultural and minerals), manpower, and livestock. Such knowledge established the foundation upon which the premodern state, or for that matter a modern state, was run. No ruler could run a state without having such information at his immediate disposal and regularly updated.

History thus clearly points us in a direction that makes an Augustan-ordered or -inspired census in 6 BC not only possible but probable. But what of Luke's mention of a specific census at a time when Quirinius had the power to order its conduct? To answer that, we must know where Quirinius was in 6 BC, and it just so happens that we do. Quirinius's chronology is not well established beyond the facts that he was proconsul of Crete and Cyrenaica in 15 BC, was appointed a consul of Rome in 12 BC, and was the governor of Syria from 6 to 12 AD. We also know that after his consulship, Augustus sent him east as governor of Galatia, where he fought a long war against the Homonadensians. Based on a stone inscription found in Tivoli, which states that he was "twice legate [governor] of Syria," some have tried to build a case that Quirinius was made governor of Syria twice. Unfortunately, only a fragment of the inscription was found, and it makes no mention of who "he" is. Historians have been quick to dismiss the idea that Quirinius was legate in both 6 BC and again in 6 AD, as we know for certain that Publius Quinctilius Varus was governor in 6 BC.* But they may have been too hasty in their judgment, for Quirinius did not have to be governor to have authority over Syria and Judea.

Quirinius was one of Rome's most powerful and respected senators. Augustus had so much faith in him that he appointed him as a tutor and

---

* We do not know who succeeded Varus, as there is a gap in the record from 4 BC to 1 AD. For those who believe that Jesus was born during this period, then there is an opening in which Quirinius could have been governor before a second appointment in 6 AD.

adviser to his grandson, Gaius Caesar, who was then being groomed to become the next emperor. Thus, after he finished his consulship—next to the emperor, the most important job in Rome—Quirinius was sent to Galatia to solve a specific and severe problem. The Homonadensians were a powerful mountain tribe that sat astride the main communications route between Rome's eastern provinces and the rest of the Empire. But Galatia had no assigned legions, and Quirinius did not bring any with him. The closest legions were the three maintained in nearby Syria, but for Quirinius to command them, Augustus would have had to give him proconsul power, meaning Quirinius could rule over a greatly extended region as if he were still a consul. In other words, although there was a Roman governor in Syria, he would have to take his orders from Quirinius, who spoke with the power of Augustus behind him. Without such authority, no governor would have turned over his military forces, meaning Quirinius could not possibly have waged the war for which he was awarded triumphal honors at its conclusion.

Now, let's take this one step further. When Quirinius arrived in the Eastern Empire, he would have had no idea what resources were available to prosecute a war certain to last years. He knew he had three legions at his disposal in Syria, and possibly others from along the Danube frontier or Egypt if required. But what local funding was available? Were there troops in the region to fill auxiliary roles, and how much excess agricultural produce was within easy reach to support the war effort? All of this was crucial information that would only be at his disposal if there was good census data on hand. Any previous census in the region would already be at least a decade old and of little value in assessing what was immediately available. Quirinius would need updated information if he were going to wage a major war. Thus, there is an excellent historical case, one easily made, to believe Quirinius was perfectly placed and possessed the authority to order a local census. Having just come from Rome, where Augustus had recently ordered just such a census, it is a small step to envision Quirinius sending out an order to enforce Augustus's edict, what Luke called the "first registration"—the second being the census Quirinius ordered in 6 AD.

Moreover, even if Augustus did not order an Empire-wide census, it would not have impacted what Quirinius was required to do if he was planning a major war. When a choice is available, one goes to war with as much knowledge, planning, and preparation as possible. Regardless of what Augustus ordered or did not order, Quirinius needed information only a census could provide. He would have been an incompetent fool, which he was not, to forgo demands for updated census information. Also, organizing a war requires a large concentration of resources, and Antioch was the only city in the region capable of supporting such a mobilization. As Luke wrote his Gospel in Antioch, he may have had memories of the powerful proconsul who commanded armies there during his childhood. If not, everyone who raised him would have had memories of what may have been the most significant event of their lives. Thus, any census Quirinius ordered was within the living memory of the gospel writer, his family, and his close associates.

So, where are we? In short, we have a strong case for Luke's commentary having considerably more accuracy than historians typically credit. Even if not proven, we can no longer discard Luke's commentary, as the preponderance of the evidence demonstrates the possibility of a census in or about the year 6 BC. Keep in mind that it is the preponderance of the evidence historians use to ascertain what goes in the history books.

But what of Mary and Joseph traveling from Nazareth to Bethlehem for the census? Historians' basic argument here is that this event likely did not happen and was only placed in the narrative to account for Old Testament prophecies predicting that the Messiah would be born in Bethlehem. Some of the arguments against this are trivial. For instance, many historians claim that if Jesus had been born in Bethlehem, his contemporaries would have called him Jesus of Bethlehem, not Jesus of Nazareth. This is an absurd stance, as people are most often known for the location in which they were raised and entered adulthood rather than where they were born. Where Jesus was born was an incidental fact; what he was called was based on where he was raised, and that was Nazareth.

Other arguments against the reliability of Matthew and Luke, who both state Jesus was born in Bethlehem, are more substantive. We have hopefully made mincemeat of one of the most often presented as if there was no census in 6 BC, then there was no reason for Joseph and Mary to travel to Bethlehem. But as we read above, there is every reason to believe there was a census, and that Joseph and Mary would have been counted in it. More accurately, their wealth would have been accounted for. The next strongest argument calls into question Luke's statement that "all were making their way to be registered, each to his own town."* Historians claim that it makes no sense for Rome or anyone else to demand everyone return to their hometown for the census. The very idea of such a mass movement was impractical, as it would put a considerable percentage of the Empire's population on the road at the same time, taking them away from productive activities for an extended period. But, in a time when likely 99 percent of the population was born, lived, and died all within a few square miles, one can question how many people would have to travel any great distance to register for the census.

Moreover, an Egyptian papyrus from 104 AD seems to support the idea that the Romans did order persons to return to their homes during a census:

> The house-to-house census having started, it is essential that all persons who for any reason whatsoever are absent from their nomes [regional divisions of ancient Egypt] be summoned to return to their own hearths, in order that they may perform the customary business of registration and apply themselves to the cultivation which concerns them.†

This is probably not as strong a piece of evidence as the supporters of the historicity of Luke's narrative would like, as it tells people to return to their own homes and not their ancestral homes—a huge difference. Others have pointed out that Joseph was living in Galilee at the time and would have no need to register for a census in Judea. I would contest this point. If the above analysis of Quirinius and his capacity to order a census is correct, then all of the Eastern Empire would have fallen under Quirinius's direction, meaning all of Palestine would have undergone a census. Be-

* Luke 2:3.
† Edict of Vibius Maximus, Select Papyri, 2.220. This fragment is available online in its entirety: https://www.attalus.org/docs/select2/p220.html.

sides, Galilee was still part of Herod's kingdom; it would make little sense for him to conduct a census in one province and neglect the one beside it.

But there is probably a much easier solution to this problem if we apply a bit more commonsense extrapolation. To do this, we must take several separate facts and integrate them in a way that makes sense. First, if not for Jesus being born toward the end of his reign, Herod would likely be best remembered for his massive building programs. In the two decades before Jesus's birth, Herod's most extensive engineering effort was centered on the tremendous expansion of the Jerusalem Temple, taking place only a few miles from Bethlehem.

We do not know much about Joseph, but the fact that he was a carpenter is fairly certain. Or is it? The Greek word used in the New Testament to describe Joseph is *tektōn*. This word has several translations, including craftsman, woodworker, artisan, planner, and, most often, builder. When *tektōn* is used to describe a planner, we should focus on the modern incarnation of the word *tektōn*—architect, literally "chief builder." It was not until the King James version of the New Testament was released in 1611 that the word *tektōn* became synonymous with a carpenter, mainly because wood was the building material most used in seventeenth-century England. But in the entire New Testament, Jesus only mentions wood once, which makes sense as wood was and remains a rare commodity in Israel.* However, a building material Jesus repeatedly mentions in the New Testament is stone, which makes sense, as there is one thing Israel has in abundance: stones.

> "I tell you," he replied, "if they keep quiet, the stones will cry out." (Luke 19:40)
> ". . . like a wise man who built his house on the rock." (Matthew 7:24)
> "And I tell you that you are Peter, and on this rock, I will build my church . . ." (Matthew 16:18)
> "The stone the builders rejected has become the cornerstone." (Mark 12:10)

---

*Matthew 7:3.

If the King James Bible had been written by persons living in or who were more familiar with Palestine, they would have made Joseph a stone mason. But, I would argue that a better translation is "builder," familiar with all elements of the building trade—or its modern equivalent, "general contractor."[*]

We also know that Joseph was from the House of David. Historians have made much of the probable inaccuracies in the genealogies supplied by Luke and Matthew that aimed to demonstrate this lineage. How accurate or flawed they are will remain an open debate, but several points must be made. First, the birth records of the period were available to the gospel writers in the Temple, which was not destroyed until 70 AD, and if there was one lineage that would have been meticulously tracked, it is the House of David. Even more crucial than disputing records lost to history is that no contemporary—even Jesus's enemies—contested his lineage then or later. This is important for historians because it indicates that Joseph was of a bit higher social stratum than most of the local population.

Whether being of a higher social stratum meant Joseph was wealthier than most is beyond our ability to determine. But we should ask if a simple carpenter living in Nazareth could make a living based on the carpentry requirements of those living in Nazareth. The houses were mud and stone, requiring little to no woodwork. After each of them had a table and a few chairs designed to last decades, there would have been no further need for a carpenter. What is more certain is that a small town like Nazareth could not support a carpentry business consisting of Joseph, Jesus, and his brothers, James, Joseph, Judas, and Simon.[†] But Joseph, according to Luke, had sufficient funds to travel to Jerusalem with

[*] For a readable discussion of this debate, see Jordan K. Mason, "My Boss Is a Jewish Construction Worker," *Christianity Today*, Vol. 65, no. 9 (December 2021). For a more academic discussion, see Ken M. Campbell, "What Was Jesus' Occupation?" *Journal of the Evangelical Theological Society*, Vol. 48, no. 3 (September 2005): 512. For various usages of the term in other ancient Greek works, see Henry George Liddell et al., *A Greek–English Lexicon* (Clarendon Press, 1996), 1769.
[†] Mark 6:3.

his family for the Passover festival every year. The expense of this annual trip is not trivial. Just the lodging required to attend a multiday festival would have been expensive and probably beyond the reach of a simple local carpenter.* Moreover, it is clear from the knowledge Jesus and his brothers (at least James) displayed throughout their lives—they were able to debate the most learned Pharisees and Sadducees on better-than-even terms—that Joseph was able to afford to get them all first-class educations. However, we can admit they were likely educated to take over a large and thriving business and not to become rabbis. The only reason we have to believe Jesus grew up in poverty is that when the infant Jesus was first presented at the Temple, Joseph's offering was either two doves or two pigeons, supposedly the offering expected of the poor.† This is a thin reed on which to build a case for Joseph's supposed poverty, as it reflects a single moment in time. Moreover, the offering is only from Mary and does not reflect what Joseph may have offered independently of his wife.

Given all of the above, it may be best to think of Joseph as a successful general contractor (master builder) who traveled where the work was. And for two decades, the greatest demand for builders was in and around Jerusalem, as the construction of Herod's Temple would likely have required the services of every professional builder in the kingdom.‡ Also, because of the crowded conditions within Jerusalem, most of the material used in the Temple's construction would be concentrated in small towns outside the city's gates. Bethlehem, which is still a center for stone quarrying today, would have been one of these towns, as it sits along the main route to the sea as well as ancient caravan routes. It is in towns like Bethlehem where much of the shaping and cutting of stones and imported wood timbers would have been done before the finished products were transported to the final construction site.§ As such, Bethlehem is almost

* Luke 2:41.
† Luke 2:24. See Leviticus 12:8: "But if she cannot afford a lamb, she is to bring two doves or two young pigeons . . ."
‡ While the major work on the Temple was finished in under three years, work on associated building lasted for decades.
§ The recent discovery of a large stone quarry near the Temple Mount site does nothing to negate the fact that much of the preliminary construction work, including the quarrying and shaping of stones, was done outside of the city.

perfectly situated as a base for construction activities and is only a cart ride for any *tektōn* delivering material to Jerusalem. That Jesus had close friends—Mary, Martha, and Lazarus—who lived fewer than two miles from Bethlehem, in nearby Bethany, is further evidence that Jesus's family lived in the area for a prolonged period. Otherwise, when and where these persons became close friends is inexplicable.

So, when the census was announced, why was Joseph in Nazareth? After the Temple was completed, Herod's major construction projects centered on building a series of fortresses, one of which was in Sepphoris, only a few miles from Nazareth. Once again, Joseph was going where the work was. Interestingly, a first-century stone quarry has only recently been discovered outside Nazareth, along the road to nearby Cana, where the New Testament has Jesus perform his first public miracle at a local wedding. Once again, Joseph appears to have selected a home where he has the best access to construction materials and a good road directly to the nearby construction site in Sepphoris. Joseph's profession and business interest also explain why he returned to Nazareth after spending several years away after Jesus was born. For, in 4 BC, Sepphoris, in an event we will discuss later in this work, was the origin point of a revolt against Rome. In a typical Roman reaction, the legions destroyed the city. Herod Antipas, who ruled Galilee after Herod's death, ordered the city rebuilt and turned into the "Pearl of Galilee." Thus, the rebuilding of Sepphoris would have provided Joseph and his sons enriching contract work lasting decades.

The above reconstruction explains most of Luke's narrative. Joseph was living in Nazareth, likely as a new resident, at the time of the census. He was likely there to establish his business where he could best support construction work on a major fortress in nearby Sepphoris. Before this, he had spent much of his adult life in Bethlehem, where he, in all probability, maintained a flourishing business, as despite Temple construction having ended, large building projects remained ongoing throughout the city. With this in mind, it is a safe assumption that most of Joseph's wealth—possibly the ownership of a local quarry—was still in Bethlehem. One must note that Rome's one abiding interest in conducting a census was to determine where the taxable wealth of a region was and who owned it. As the bulk of Joseph's wealth, when Jesus was born, was still in Bethlehem, it was firmly in his interest to ensure he was present and that it was assessed correctly. Indeed, some locals would undoubtedly be happy to see Joseph ruined by an overassessment, which would have bankrupted him and made his property easy pickings.

There remains a final series of interrelated major elements of Jesus's birth narrative that must be addressed: the visit of the Magi, and the ensuing flight to Egypt. These two events are only recorded by Matthew, who was not as careful a historian as Luke. Modern historians have declared these events part of a later tradition that never actually happened. There is no way to confirm Matthew's account in the final analysis, nor can it be disproven. But this work is not trying to do either. Instead, we are examining history to determine if such an event would have been possible, as my contention is that too many historians have been quick to dismiss the New Testament as a work of history without exploring the range of possibilities.

Could the Magi have followed a star to find Jesus? Over the years, scholars have examined many possible events that could explain a star moving across the sky and then becoming stationary over Bethlehem. Chinese records show that a major new light source was spotted in the night sky—probably a supernova—in 5 BC. This supernova occurred very close to the date this work presents for the birth of Jesus, but it missed by a year. Further, a supernova would appear stationary in relation to other stars, so it can also be dismissed from consideration because it was not moving across the sky. Another candidate offered is the conjunction of Venus and Jupiter in 2 BC. This event, however, would have lasted only a short time. More crucially, it occurred two years after Herod's death, so it too must be dismissed.

Simo Parpola makes an excellent case for a conjunction of Jupiter and Saturn in 7 BC as being rare enough—every eight hundred years—to be considered by the Babylonians as a highly exceptional event.* According to Parpola:

---

* Simo Parpola, "The Magi and the Star," *Bible Review*, Vol. 17, no. 6 (December 2001). This article can be found online: https://library.biblicalarchaeology.org/article/the -magi-and-the-star/. For further support see Michael Molnar, *The Star of Bethlehem* (Rut-

For the ancient Babylonian magi, however, the conjunction was not only important astronomically, but astrologically and politically . . . The conjunction of the planets in Pisces accordingly portended two things: the end of the old world order and the birth of a new savior king chosen by God.

While this event took place in 7 BC, the final conjunction was late in the year (December 1). If we account for the time it would have taken to organize an expedition, and the additional two months of travel, we get well into 6 BC. So, there is a recorded celestial event that could easily have sent the Magi heading toward Herod's kingdom that almost precisely fits with the timing of historical accounts of Jesus's birth. Once in Judea, it would have been natural for the Magi to inquire about the possible location of a newly born future king at the royal court. Once they knew that such a king was prophesied to be born in Bethlehem, they headed to that town and then returned home without telling Herod what they had found, as they had promised to do.

At some point, Herod gave up on waiting for the Magi to return to Jerusalem. But from the dates the Magi told him they had witnessed the astronomical event that set them on their journey, he calculated that the child they were looking for was under two years of age. Therefore, he ordered all infants under two years old in and around Bethlehem killed. Historians have dismissed this event, arguing that Josephus would have included it in one of his two detailed histories of the period if it had taken place. But that is an argument from silence, which is rarely a good idea when studying ancient history, as so much has been lost to us. Worse, it is looking for Josephus to record an event he was unlikely to have been aware of. Here, historians have been helped by the popular opinion that believes that many hundreds or thousands of innocents were slain. Surely, an event of such magnitude would have left some trace in the historical record outside of Matthew's Gospel. For instance, in a later Byzantine liturgy, the number of infants killed is set at 14,000. A later Syrian tradi-

---

gers University Press, 1999). This idea was put forward by Johannes Kepler, the man who first promulgated the laws of planetary motion.

tion placed the number at over 60,000, while a medieval work claims 144,000 were killed.* But are any of these sensational numbers accurate? Given the estimated population of Bethlehem and the surrounding area, the number of children under age two was likely under a dozen and possibly not even half that. Moreover, if we discount divine intervention, as historians must, Joseph was warned about the impending executions in time to make good his and his family's escape. Assuming others were similarly warned, Herod's assassins may not have found anyone to kill. Compared to the great events that Josephus was recording, the murder of a half dozen or fewer children would have been a relatively trivial affair, unlikely to have attracted his attention.

But the killing of infants is an incredibly heinous act. As such, is it credible to believe that Herod sent out his soldiers with orders to kill infants? He was undeniably ruthless, but would this be a step too far? For that answer, we have to take a step back to review some of Herod's recorded actions in the later part of his reign. As we do so, it is worth noting that there is an ancient tradition, recorded in the Talmud, that Jesus, through his father's side and possibly also through Mary's lineage, was "close to the Kingdom," which referenced the Hasmonean Kingdom.† If Herod had even a suspicion that someone met the conditions for the birth of the prophesied messiah and also had a relationship to the Hasmoneans, he surely would have reacted violently. This possible Hasmonean relationship would also explain why Herod Antipas handled Jesus with kid gloves, compared to his treatment of John the Baptist after Jesus began preaching throughout Galilee. We cannot today determine if Jesus had a Hasmonean connection. Still, the fact that it is recorded in the Talmud tells us that at least a portion of the contemporary Jewish community believed he had such a connection. If such a connection existed, it would be further evidence that Joseph was wealthier and better connected than is customarily assumed.

But back to Herod. When we left the Judean ruler, he had already

---

* Frederick George Holweck, "Holy Innocents," in Charles Herbermann (ed.), *Catholic Encyclopedia*, Vol. 7 (Robert Appleton Company, 1910).
† Talmud, Sanhedrin 43a. This can be read online at: https://www.sefaria.org/Sanhedrin.43a.25?lang=bi.

killed his Hasmonean brother-in-law, Aristobulus, to secure his throne in 35 BC. In his continual purge of the Hasmoneans, he also ordered his mother-in-law, Alexandra, executed in 29 BC, followed by his wife, Mariamme, in 28 BC. In 7 BC, a year before Jesus's birth, an increasingly paranoid Herod ordered his two Hasmonean sons by Mariamme, Alexander and Aristobulus, strangled. That same year, he had three hundred of his senior military officers executed, along with hundreds of Pharisees. The latter were killed because they predicted that Pheroras, Herod's brother and tetrarch of Perea, and his wife would take his throne from him and that their children would rule for generations afterward. Then, only five days before his death, Herod had his heir, Antipater, executed, leading Augustus to quip, "It's better to be Herod's pig than his son."* Finally, as his son was being executed, Herod's soldiers were watching over most of the Jewish leadership, who were locked inside a stadium in Jericho, awaiting execution upon Herod's death. Clearly, Herod would not shy away from killing infants if he believed doing so would do away with a potential threat to his rule. Unfortunately, few rulers in history have ever shied away from infanticide if the alternative was losing power.

The final item in the birth narrative is the escape to Egypt. Unfortunately, this is another item where the historical record fails us, as this event cannot be proven one way or another. I will, therefore, leave it with a few quick comments. If Herod threatened Jesus's life, then a retreat to Egypt made sense. There was a large Jewish community there, travel by sea or along the well-established coast road was easy, and, if we accept any part of the above analysis dealing with Joseph's life and status, he could easily afford the trip. Moreover, if we suppose the Talmud is correct, and Jesus was somehow intertwined or related to the Hasmoneans, Joseph's decision to not return to Bethlehem in favor of going straight to Nazareth makes sense, as Judea's new ruler, Herod's son Archelaus, was as anti-Hasmonean as his father, despite having two wives of Hasmonean royal lineage. Galilee, now under the control of one of Herod's other sons, Herod Antipas, who had no demonstrated Hasmonean antipathy,

* Macrobius, *Saturnalia*, Book II. Found here: https://www.loebclassics.com/view/macrobius-saturnalia/2011/pb_LCL510.349.xml?readMode=recto#:~:text=11.,(dicta%2056%20Malc.).

was a much safer location. Besides, that was where the work was, as nearby Sepphoris was in ruins and needed to be rebuilt.

This work has expended a considerable amount of time on Jesus's infancy narrative, and will do the same when we come to the last week of Jesus's life. There is a good reason for this. As we noted earlier, only two portions of the Gospels lend themselves to historical analysis—the infancy narrative and the passion week. There is little in the New Testament between these two events for historians to debate, as the remainder of the narrative follows Jesus on his travels around Palestine. One either accepts them as a true narrative of events or not. There is no historical record to prove or disprove. Historians are thus left to contest the birth and passion narrative. If these events can be shown to be historically accurate or even possible, it lends credence to the remainder of the New Testament. If, however, the Gospel narratives dealing with Jesus's birth, infancy, and death can be disproven, then doubt is cast on the entire New Testament.

Some may claim that my reconstruction of events is built on speculation. I would, however, argue that all of the above reconstruction rests upon reasonable assumptions based on the wider context of what we know about the period. Moreover, these are the same extrapolations ancient historians routinely make when examining other historical narratives. They do so because so much of ancient history has been lost to us that historians are forced to expend considerable energy filling in the blanks. What I have done above, far from being outside the bounds of modern scholarship, is consistently in the mainstream. For too long, historians have looked for ways to discount New Testament narratives rather than giving them a fair examination using the same methods they employ in every other historical appreciation of the ancient world. Readers are free to discount my extrapolations, but in doing so, they should try to replace them with something equally plausible.

PART V

THE GALILEE JESUS KNEW

SIXTEEN

Judea and Galilee Under Herod's Rule

Upon his ascent to power, Herod took over all of the existing Hasmonean fortresses and installed officers loyal to himself. He never had to worry about the loyalty of the average soldier, who followed whoever paid him. To these fortresses, Herod added nearly invincible fortresses at Herodium and Masada, as well as several smaller ones, all crucial to maintaining his power as the head of what was, in truth, a military dictatorship. Masada remains known for holding out against an overwhelming Roman force in 72–73 BC, at the end of the Great Revolt. The last defenders famously committed suicide rather than being slain or captured by the Romans. Today, Masada is remembered as a heroic last stand and is one of the cornerstones of modern Israel's national identity. At the time, however, it was a Roman message to the rest of the Empire: If you revolt, Rome will use whatever force is required for as long as necessary to ensure that everyone involved is slaughtered. It was a powerful message.

Interestingly, this powerful Herodian fortress is about the same distance from Bethlehem as Jerusalem. Thus, Joseph could just as efficiently have been working on this fortress in the years before Jesus's birth as doing work in Jerusalem. In the role of a builder or general contractor, he could also have been managing work in both locations, hence the benefits

of living in Bethlehem, as it was almost equidistant from both work locations. By working on this fortress, Joseph would also have gained the
specialized knowledge required to solicit contracts for rebuilding the
Sepphoris fortifications near Nazareth. Joseph working on Masada is, of
course, all speculation. But it is reasonable speculation and also tantalizing.

Herod had left the high priesthood in place, but it was much reduced
in power from the days of the Hasmoneans, who had made the office of
High Priest a hereditary right. Herod, who was always paranoid and insecure, with good reasons for both, made the priesthood a tool to help
control the population. First, he reduced the priests' powers, making it
much harder for the Temple authorities to become a separate core of
political influence within the realm or a focal point for revolt. He then
ended the hereditary nature of the high priest position by bringing in
new leadership from Babylon and Egypt, all men completely indebted to
Herod for their positions.

Although Herod rebuilt the Great Temple, this was done as much to
add glory and luster to his reign as to demonstrate his support of Judaism and its ethos. While Herod had to at least give lip service to Jewish
rites and beliefs lest he risk a general revolt, he did much else to show
where his heart indeed lay. In addition to the Temple, he also built the
great Antonia Fortress directly beside the holiest place in Judaism. This
fortress overlooked and dominated the Temple. It was not lost on anyone
that it was strongly garrisoned with troops loyal only to Herod until the
Romans took it over as the core of their power in middle Palestine.

Significantly, Herod's building projects were always styled in the
Roman-Hellenistic tradition, demonstrating where his heart lay. In Jerusalem, he built a theater, a large amphitheater, and a hippodrome, showing a clear preference for Roman culture and entertainment over Jewish
traditions. He also implemented a number of laws that were directly
contrary to Jewish law and tradition, and when these led to agitation and
conspiracies to overthrow his rule, he became increasingly repressive. In
his summary judgment of his behavior, Josephus recorded: "Despairing
of the traditional customs, [Herod] corrupted the ancient way of life."[*]

---

[*] Josephus, *Jewish Antiquities*, 15.267.

Beyond Herod, his family, his generals, and the Temple priests, what did the rest of the power structure in Palestine look like? Anyone with even a casual acquaintance with the New Testament or the history of first-century Palestine could not help but have come across the names of four groups: the Pharisees, the Sadducees, the Essenes, and the Zealots, all of whom had a role to play within Herod's kingdom. We will examine each in turn.

Unfortunately, just about everything we know about these groups, except for the Essenes and their societal roles, comes from a single source: Josephus, who calls them the philosophical sects.* Why is this unfortunate? Because Josephus himself was a Pharisee and noticeably preferred their arguments and way of life when he compared them to the other sects. At the very least, the Pharisees come off much better than in the New Testament, where they are often portrayed as hypocrites and enemies of Jesus.† It is also crucial to note that these groups made up a minuscule, although at times influential, percentage of the total Jewish population in Palestine.

According to Josephus, the Pharisees lived meanly, despising delicacies, while also living a life based on reason. They apparently got their start during the Maccabean era as a group dedicated to the laws of Moses and the Old Testament. As such, they are best thought of as a reaction to the growing intrusion of Hellenism into the ancient culture and religion of the Jews. During the Maccabean primacy, the Pharisees were esteemed for their exact explanations and adherence to the Mosaic Laws. They also believed in the immortality of the soul, and an afterlife where, at the end of times, the souls of the good went to heaven, while those of evil men were eternally damned. When the Romans marched into Palestine, the

---

* Most of what follows dealing with the first three of these groups—Pharisees, Sadducees, and Essenes—is drawn from Josephus's works, Book Eight of *The Jewish War* and Book 18 of *Antiquities of the Jews*.

† A good argument can be made that this reflects our modern reading of Jesus's interactions with the Pharisees. Jesus apparently enjoyed debating philosophy and the finer points of Jewish law, while the Pharisees absolutely lived for such debates. What we view as heated arguments, they may have seen as just good sport. It is certain that Jesus had supporters and friends among the Pharisees, so we may have to think hard about how they have been maligned through the centuries.

Pharisees transplanted their disdain for the increasingly Hellenistic Hasmoneans to the Greco-Roman laws and culture of the invading Romans. Josephus tells us that six thousand Pharisees refused to swear oaths to Herod or Caesar, and this is likely the total number of the Pharisee population.* Although they appear to have been accorded a measure of respect by the Jewish community, the Pharisees possessed very little institutional power during Jesus's lifetime. They are probably best viewed as somewhat of a separatist movement within the wider Jewish community, one focused on the strict observance of the Mosaic Law and against the intrusion of Greco-Roman culture and values. Jesus never condemned the Pharisees for their beliefs. Instead, he took aim at the hypocrisy of the Pharisee elites, who often failed to stay within their own strictures.† On the other hand, Jesus had Pharisee followers, most famously Nicodemus.

Outside of Herod, the real power in Palestine belonged to the Sadducees, who composed Josephus's second order. They did not believe in fate or the immortality of the soul. According to Josephus, many of their religious beliefs were contrary to the Mosaic Laws as espoused by the Pharisees. Still, they were forced to pretend otherwise, or the people would despise them and likely overthrow their hold on power. We know little else about their beliefs, as they left us no extant writings, and what little comes from other sources is prejudiced against them. As a Pharisee himself, Josephus, our main source, had nothing good to say about them.

> . . . while the Sadducees are able to persuade none but the rich, and have not the populace obsequious to them, but the Pharisees have the multitude on their side.‡

Our other source, the Apostle Paul, had also been a Pharisee before converting to Christianity and maintained a lifelong contempt for the Sadducees. Still, the Sadducees appear to have included most of the Jewish elite, aristocrats, and priesthood. Moreover, it is believed that the Sadducees dominated the Sanhedrin, the ruling and judicial body of the

* Josephus, *Jewish Antiquities*, 17.42.
† Mark 23:1–12.
‡ Josephus, *Antiquities*, 13.298.

Jewish state, which we will learn much more about later in this work. As the Sadducees were the richest and most powerful members of Jewish society, the Romans allowed them to wield significant power until the Great Revolt in 66 AD. Thus, during the years Jesus was alive, the Romans could always count on the Sadducees to do their bidding. But as they were primarily centered in Judea and Jerusalem, Jesus would have had almost no contact with them until the final days of his ministry. In his only recorded interaction with them, likely just before his trial, Jesus reveals that he believed the entire basis of Sadducee beliefs was "in error."*

The Pharisees and Sadducees most differed on the role of the Temple. Both believed or pretended to believe in the Mosaic Law, although with a crucial difference as to the central role of the Temple in Jerusalem. Both also recognized the sanctity of the Temple and its right of place among other places of worship, but the Pharisees gave much more respect to the widespread network of synagogues spread across Israel. In terms of the law, the Sadducees believed it could only be based upon the first five books of the Old Testament—the Torah, reinforced by the dictates of the Temple authorities, which were themselves. On the other hand, the Pharisees believed that there was a strong oral tradition, mostly espoused by themselves, that interpreted the law and sat alongside the law of Moses with just as much authority. For instance, Mosaic Law might say that one must not go on a long journey on the Sabbath, but the oral tradition decided how far one could go before he was considered to be on a "long" journey. In the end, the Pharisees triumphed, as the Sadducees, with their close connection to the Temple, were likely slaughtered in its defense during the Great Revolt. If any did survive, they never again appear in any works of the era. On the other hand, the Pharisees did not have as close an association with the Temple and were not primarily centered on Jerusalem. Thus, many of them survived the Great Revolt. With the Temple destroyed and the Sadducees annihilated, the Pharisees took the lead in transitioning the Jewish religion from a Temple cult to one based on a local rabbinic tradition and congregations meeting in synagogues. They

---

* Mark 12:18–24. Jesus was probably condemning the Sadducees when he mentioned priests and Levites in the story of the Parable of the Good Samaritan (Luke 10:25–37).

also continued to espouse the "oral law," which was eventually written down at the end of the second century by Judah ha-Nasi. This work is called the Mishnah and is the basis of the Talmud.

In addition to the Pharisees and Sadducees, Josephus tells us of a third group, the Essenes, who are Jews by birth but were a much closer-knit group than the other sects he discusses. According to Josephus, their total number was four thousand, and they could be found throughout Judea, living in small, self-contained groups. Their way of living resembles the modern idea of a commune, as individual Essenes possessed no money or any other belongings, as the group members commonly owned and shared everything. Like the Pharisees, the Essenes believed in the soul's immortality, which would be returned to them after death. Josephus also tells us they did not marry but that they did not absolutely deny the fitness of marriage as a means to continue mankind. One, therefore, suspects that their most pious members remained celibate and did not marry. But those who did marry were warned to be constantly on guard "against the lascivious behavior of women" and that no woman could preserve her "fidelity to one man."*

Although this group is not mentioned in the New Testament, we know more about them than other groups because of the Dead Sea Scrolls found at Qumran. As Pliny, in his book *Natural History*, mentions a community of Essenes in this area, it is reasonably certain that the Dead Sea Scrolls were the group's library, likely secreted away in a cave near the Dead Sea, east of Jerusalem, during the Great Revolt. By reconstructing their beliefs from the Scrolls, it is clear that they believed that they were living close to the end of times, and the final apocalypse would soon befall them. This belief likely explains their disdain for marriage and sex, as there was little reason to propagate if the end was near. When the end did come, the Essenes looked forward to a final climactic battle between the children of light and those of darkness and that the former would prevail. This probably explains why there is no trace of the group after the Great Revolt. If you believe your group is the elite of the true believers and God's chosen people, then it did not take much to view those subjugating

---

* Josephus, *The Jewish War*, 2.8.2.

you—the Romans—as the children of darkness. Thus, after hiding their library, the almost entirely male population of the Essenes likely marched off to war. It was a war that, without divine interference, could have but one outcome: the obliteration of the Essene movement by Rome's legions.

Josephus presents one more group, which he calls the Fourth Philosophy or sect, but then gives us virtually no information about them:

> These men agree in all other things with the Pharisaic notions; but they have an inviolable attachment to liberty; and say that God is to be their only ruler and lord. They also do not value dying any kinds of death; nor indeed do they heed the deaths of their relations and friends: nor can any such fear make them call any man lord. And since this immovable resolution of theirs is well known to a great many, *I shall speak no further about that matter.**

Josephus here references the Zealots, who took a leading and catastrophic role in the Great Revolt. But as a political movement, this Fourth Sect came later in Israel's history and did not exist in 33 AD. This leads us to a crucial question: Why do many today believe Jesus was a Zealot?

* Joseph, *Antiquities*, 18.1.6.

SEVENTEEN

Was Jesus a Zealot?

W e must spend a bit of time on the Zealots because one of the most popular recent books attempting to describe Jesus through a historical lens is Reza Aslan's *Zealot*, which declares that Jesus was nothing more than a common revolutionary set on the overthrow of Roman power.[*]

Notably, there is little of substance in Aslan's work that cannot be found in S.G.F. Brandon's *Jesus and the Zealots*, published almost forty years before Aslan's book.[†] Historians demolished Brandon's thesis long ago, so one wonders why Aslan resurrected it.[‡]

Early in his work, Aslan admits that Jesus is not part of the Zealot movement that undertook the Great Revolt against Rome in 66 AD, as there was no such political movement during Jesus's lifetime. Aslan then expends tens of thousands of words building a case that Jesus was part of a movement that he admits did not exist. In the process, he makes a hash of the period's history.

---

[*] Reza Aslan, *Zealot: The Life and Times of Jesus of Nazareth* (Random House, 2013).

[†] S.G.F. Brandon, *Jesus and the Zealots: A Study of the Political Factor in Primitive Christianity* (Manchester University Press, 1967). Aslan does mention Brandon once in a note (p. 237) dealing with Jesus's attack on the Temple.

[‡] For the seminal work on this academic destruction, see E. Bammel and C.F.D. Moule (eds.), *Jesus and the Politics of His Day* (Cambridge University Press, 1984).

The Zealot sect that Josephus refers to likely did not exist until the eve of the Great Revolt, when Jesus had already been dead for thirty years. When Jesus was alive, the term "Zealot" referred to someone zealous in their adherence to the faith, as presented in both the Mosaic Laws and the oral laws espoused by the Pharisees. By this definition, all Pharisees, Sadducees, and Essenes were Zealots. Moreover, when the New Testament mentions Jesus's apostle, Simon the Zealot, they do not call attention to any revolutionary or political affiliation of the apostle. Instead, the Gospels are calling attention to his faithfulness to Mosaic Law. Although Aslan does make a single mention of Jesus not being part of the Zealot political movement, which did not yet exist, he spends so much time discussing this later movement, its relation to the Great Revolt, and Jesus being a revolutionary character, that most readers could be forgiven for conflating the two and seeing Jesus as part of a Zealot political movement, despite it not having started until well after his death.

Since Aslan's understanding of Jesus's life and times is now accepted by so many, we require a statement of his main thesis, which is heavily indebted to the works of John Dominic Crossan, of Jesus Seminar fame, who also portrays Jesus as a peasant revolutionary. Aslan contends that Jesus was just one of many messianic pretenders of his day calling for a violent insurrection against Rome. According to Aslan, Jesus believed that his zealous religious beliefs assured him of God's support in his quest to become the king of Israel after he had overturned the current political and social order that Rome enforced. In this telling, Jesus believes that God would be so pleased with the zealous religious beliefs of his followers that he would empower them to defeat Rome's legions. As a consequence of this stance, Rome crucified Jesus as a revolutionary.

As this version of events is directly contrary to what we find in the New Testament, Aslan insists that the Christian movement made the current version up. To explain why, Aslan places the Zealot movement and the destruction of the Jewish Temple at the core of his revisionist version of Jesus's life. According to Aslan, after the Romans destroyed Jerusalem and the Temple in 70 AD, Jesus's "real" teachings were too dangerous for the burgeoning Christian community to espouse publicly. Aslan contends that the ultimate failure of the Zealot movement, in which Jesus was supposedly one of the progenitors, forced the early Christian community to find a new message that would not bring the full force of Roman might upon them. To accomplish this, Aslan declares, with no supporting evidence, that the gospel writers and Paul fabricated a story of Jesus as a peaceful preacher showing the way to God in the current world and the afterlife. Thus, Aslan would have us believe that the gospel authors removed almost everything in their works that demonstrated Jesus was a rebel and then fabricated an entirely new set of stories in which Jesus preached peace and was the divine Son of God. They then managed to sell this Jesus, which they made up out of whole cloth, to a population that had witnessed what actually transpired and already had a long oral tradition that fitted precisely with what we find in the New Testament. Aslan offers no explanation of how his supposed original New Testament completely disappeared from the historical record.

To make this thesis work, Aslan has to place the writing of all of the Gospels after the destruction of the Temple in 70 AD in an attempt to wipe out the possibility of the Gospels being eyewitness accounts. Unfortunately for Aslan's argument, plenty of people alive in 70 AD had seen and known Jesus during his lifetime. Moreover, as we have seen, most historians agree that the Gospel of Mark was written prior to 70 AD, possibly as early as the 50s, and was likely taken directly from the Apostle Peter, who was crucified several years before 70 AD. As the similarities between the three synoptic Gospels demonstrate, even the later authors of Matthew and Luke, who tell a story similar to Mark's, clearly did not feel that they were free to change the foundational events of Jesus's life and ministry. This fact alone negates the central core of Aslan's argument, as it does away with his thesis of a concerted effort to remake Jesus's life story after the Great Revolt.

To help prop up his position, Aslan states that Paul extensively reinterpreted the Gospel narratives during his debates with James and some of the other apostles in Jerusalem. But Paul's debates with James, as described in the book of Acts and Paul's letters, centered on food laws, Sabbath observance, and circumcision. They had nothing to do with any disputes about the narrative of Jesus's life, nor did they debate the divinity of Jesus or his message of peace, which neither Paul nor James doubted.

Thus, they argued over how Christians should live, not what they believed.

Aslan also creates a Pauline theological dispute out of his imagination, as there is no record of such a dispute anywhere within the New Testament or any other work. The Paul we see in the New Testament attests to Jesus's teachings and parables, the virgin birth, and Jesus's resurrection. Further, when Paul wrote about theological topics in the mid-50s AD, he explained that he first received this information much earlier. Most scholars have interpreted this much earlier date as being in the mid- to late 30s AD. This is strong evidence that even if, as Aslan falsely contends, the Gospels were all written after 70 AD, there was already a strong oral tradition relating the same stories as the Gospel narratives that began circulating almost immediately after Jesus's death.

Despite finding faults with Aslan's treatment of the New Testament narrative, many critics compliment him on his descriptions of Galilee in Jesus's lifetime. Unfortunately, Aslan presents us with a Galilee that did not exist in Jesus's lifetime. He tells us that a carpenter in Nazareth had little to do to keep him busy and that Jesus "belonged to the lowest class of peasants in first-century Palestine." Nothing in this description is correct. We have already discussed the probability that Joseph should be viewed more as a supervisor of major works—a builder or general contractor—than as a day laborer. But, even if he were only a solitary carpenter or stone mason, he would have rated rather high in the social pecking order of the time by being a skilled artisan. To help build the case that Joseph and his sons toiled in poverty, Aslan places Sepphoris, the city where Joseph and Jesus most likely plied their trade, "a day's walk" from Nazareth. One can actually walk the distance in under an hour. In Aslan's telling, Jesus and his disciples wear linen clothing, as they could not afford wool. He is seemingly unaware that only the relatively rich wore linen in the ancient world. By such sleights of hand, Aslan creates the fable of a poor, revolutionary peasant.

By making Jesus a poor peasant, Aslan perpetuates another commonly held myth: that Galilee was filled with illiterate peasants, of whom Jesus was one. Until recently, the widespread assumption was that literacy rates in first-century Galilee hovered around 3 percent and that a mere carpenter from a small town was unlikely to have received anything more than a rudimentary education.* More generous scholars will sometimes allow that Jesus may have been able to write his name and possibly handle the elementary reading required to run a small woodworking business, but that was the maximum extent of his learning.

But there is much evidence that Jesus was a literate and learned man. As we have done throughout this book, we will first examine what the eyewitness testimony in the Gospels tells us, as only an inept historian discards the testimony of those closest to the story in favor of a narrative made of whole cloth. In the Gospels, we find three direct examples of Jesus being able to read, write, and debate at a level far beyond his supposed educational attainment. We will take each in turn, starting with John:

> The teachers of the law and the Pharisees brought in a woman caught in adultery. They made her stand before the group and said to Jesus, "Teacher, this woman was caught in the act of adultery. In the Law Moses commanded us to stone such women. Now what do you say?" They were using this question as a trap, in order to have a basis for accusing him.
>
> **But Jesus bent down and started to write on the ground with his finger.** When they kept on questioning him, he straightened up and said to them, "Let any one of you who is without sin be the first to throw a stone at her." **Again he stooped down and wrote on the ground.**†

This passage is a clear testimony that Jesus could and did write. Unfortunately, John does not tell us what Jesus was writing, making it possible for many scholars to dismiss this passage as proof of Jesus's literacy by claiming he was only drawing lines on the ground. This is another example of scholars discarding the clear evidence before them in favor of

---

* For what I believe is the best short discussion on this topic, see John P. Meier, *A Marginal Jew: Rethinking the Historical Jesus* (Doubleday, 1991), pp. 253–315. For a more complete analysis, see Catherine Hezser, *Jewish Literacy in Roman Palestine* (Mohr Siebeck, 2001).
† John 8:2–8. [emphasis added]

making up an imaginary event that supports their preconceived notions. If we had a similar narrative telling us that any other person who looms large in the historical record had stooped to write on the ground, historians would have produced multitudes of essays and books guessing about what was written. But, as we are dealing with Jesus, historians feel free to claim that he was not writing anything.

They get another try in a passage from Luke, where we get evidence that Jesus was literate, which is harder to dismiss:

He went to Nazareth, where he had been brought up, and on the Sabbath day he went into the synagogue, as was his custom. **He stood up to read, and the scroll of the prophet Isaiah was handed to him. Unrolling it, he found the place where it is written:**

> *"The Spirit of the Lord is on me,*
> *because he has anointed me*
> *to proclaim good news to the poor.*
> *He has sent me to proclaim freedom for the prisoners*
> *and recovery of sight for the blind,*
> *to set the oppressed free, to proclaim the year of the Lord's favor."*

Then he rolled up the scroll, gave it back to the attendant and sat down.*

To reject this clear statement of Jesus's literacy, scholars have resorted to claiming it is just an imaginative reworking of an event found in Mark, where the people of Nazareth take offense at Jesus's teaching.† There is, however, no evidentiary reason to believe this is the case. But even if we assume that Luke's passage is a retelling of the same event detailed by Mark, it does not discount Jesus's literacy. Instead, Luke's passage would now give us two versions of the same event, written from different sources, thereby strengthening the case for Jesus's literacy, as the Nazarenes in

---

* Luke 4:16–20. [emphasis added]
† Mark 6:1–6.

Mark were astounded by Jesus's "wisdom," which is another way of saying his knowledge.

The last passage attesting to Jesus's having a high level of reading ability also comes from John. In this passage, Jesus is at the Temple Mount
preaching in front of many of the most learned scholars in Judea, where
he clearly impressed the crowd:

> The Jews there were amazed and asked, "How did this man get
> such learning without having been taught?"*

These learned Jews were not amazed that Jesus was able to read or
that he was an educated man. Instead, they are astonished at the scope
and depth of his arguments and his knowledge of the scriptures without
having had any formal training at the feet of a learned rabbi. But as this
passage does not explicitly address Jesus's ability to read, it also has been
too easily dismissed as evidence that Jesus is literate.

Summing up, the New Testament provides at least three direct passages demonstrating Jesus's literacy and high educational accomplish-
ment. Still, Aslan and others reject them all on spurious grounds. This is
in keeping with their belief that only a minute fraction of Jews could
read. But is this true? Historians have long accepted that literacy was
limited to society's rich elites, but recent research has overturned this
conviction. In researching my previous book on the Roman Empire, I was
struck by the high literacy rates of the Roman army and its supporting
contractors, as demonstrated through the Vindolanda tablets, which are
still being unearthed at semi-regular intervals at Hadrian's Wall in Great
Britain. Interestingly, one of the best-known documents is an invitation
to a birthday party, written in the first century by Claudia Severa to the
wife of Vindolanda's commander. This note not only confirms a high
literacy rate in the military, overturning almost all prior scholarship on
this topic, but also establishes that there were far more educated women
in the first century than anyone ever thought.

Other recent research proves that literacy rates in the ancient world

* John 7:15.

were also far higher than historians hitherto credited. One research team, employing an algorithmic approach to some new finds in a Judean fort from the period of the First Temple (circa 600 BC), stated in their initial report that, of the sixteen inscriptions discovered so far, there were a minimum of six different authors. As they concluded:

> The results indicate that in this remote fort, literacy had spread throughout the military hierarchy, down to the quartermaster and probably even below that rank. This implies that an educational infrastructure that could support the composition of literary texts in Judah already existed before the destruction of the first Temple. A similar level of literacy in this area is attested again only 400 years later, *ca.* 200 BCE.*

The study stated that during the period of the First Temple, writing was found everywhere, "from the upper echelons of the Judahite army, down to the level of vice-quartermaster of some remote, isolated fort." Keeping in mind that Jews throughout the region placed a high premium on their children learning scripture taught in synagogues throughout Judea and Galilee, is it likely that the Jews had regressed over the intervening years? One of the crucial findings of this study was that it found high literacy rates across all social classes. As professional ancient armies rarely, if ever, recruited from the best elements of a society, one must ask how likely it would have been for common soldiers to have literacy rates higher than that of skilled artisans and their male children.

A later update of this study discovered there were likely a dozen different writers of eighteen newly discovered texts. When one considers the garrison's small size, we get estimated literacy rates for the remainder of Israel over 50 percent. The authors of the study concluded that: "Someone had to teach them how to read and write, so we must assume the existence of an appropriate educational system in Judah at the end of the

---

* Shira Faigenbaum-Golovin et al., "Algorithmic Handwriting Analysis of Judah's Military Correspondence Sheds Light on Composition of Military Texts," *The Proceedings of the National Academy of Sciences*, Vol. 113, no. 17 (April 11, 2016), pp. 4664–4669. https://doi.org/10.1073/pnas.1522200113.

First Temple period."* That this tradition of teaching and literacy continued through the first century is attested to by many other archaeological discoveries, leading John P. Meier to conclude, "[P]lainly there were special factors in Jewish life that fostered a respect for and a pursuit of literacy, and archaeology provides at least some relics of this pursuit."† Given the weight of evidence, it is long past time to put to rest the myth that Jesus was an illiterate peasant.

Aslan also holds an anachronistic view of the Galilean economy and people's living standards, in which everyone except a few urban elites are poor peasants who are barely surviving. In the next chapter, I address the growing body of work showing that Galilee and its inhabitants were far richer than historians formerly recognized. But, for now, let us content ourselves with the richness clearly visible at the time, as witnessed by Josephus:

[Galilee's] soil is universally rich and fruitful, and full of the plantations of trees of all sorts, insomuch that it invites the most slothful to take pains in its cultivation, by its fruitfulness; accordingly, it is all cultivated by its inhabitants, and no part of it lies idle. Moreover, the cities lie here very thick, and the very many villages there are here are everywhere so full of people, by the richness of their soil, that the very least of them contain above fifteen thousand inhabitants.‡

Those Greco-Roman authors who discuss Galilee—Diodorus, Pliny, Strabo, Tacitus—all commend the richness and productivity of the land.

In summary, Aslan spends considerable time constructing a Jesus who is poor, uneducated, and living in a poverty-stricken world bereft of opportunity. Thus, he created a resentful Jesus who would have been aching

---

* Provided by American Friends of Tel Aviv University, "Study Confirms Widespread Literacy in Biblical-period Kingdom of Judah," Sciencedaily.com. https://www.science daily.com/releases/2020/09/200910110828.htm.
† John P. Meier, *A Marginal Jew: Rethinking the Historical Jesus* (Doubleday, 1991).
‡ Josephus, *The Jewish War*, 3.3.2. Cities averaging over fifteen thousand seems high, but if one counts the surrounding countryside, which any city would have considered part of its domain, the number is not unreasonable.

to overthrow the Roman order in Judea and possibly beyond. Aslan's Jesus never existed.

The real Jesus was literate, relatively comfortable in financial terms, and living in a prosperous corner of the Roman Empire, which, by all indications, was getting more successful. This Jesus was unlikely to have wanted to destroy the Roman political order.

Aslan also conflates two revolts into a single event to build his case that revolutionaries overran Galilee during Jesus's lifetime. Aslan tells us, without any evidence, that after Herod's death, the peasants and day laborers working in Jerusalem were expelled from Jerusalem, creating a hotbed of revolutionary activity. There is no evidence for this invented expulsion in any extant ancient source. What took place was that, after a series of disturbances during Passover celebrations, the authorities ordered all those who were visiting Jerusalem to partake in the religious festival to return to their homes, which they did without causing any further trouble. This is a far cry from the authorities throwing out long-term residents who found themselves without work after Herod's death.

Still, as we have seen, there was a revolt in Galilee, centered on Sepphoris, immediately after Herod's death, but this had nothing to do with Rome and a lot more to do with a Galilean attempt to overthrow the Herodian dynasty and to limit the political power of the Temple. Aslan, however, does not discuss this revolt and, instead, examines a revolt by Judas the Galilean, which took place a decade later—a time difference lost in Aslan's account. This later revolt got underway as the Romans began implementing a new taxation system in Palestine. As we saw in the events in Germany in 9 AD, when Rome lost three legions, implementing a new tax was always a dangerous political time for the Empire, and Judas's revolt must be seen in this light. As Josephus tells us, Judas claimed that Roman "taxation was no better than an introduction to slavery: and exhorted the nation to assert their liberty."* But Judas was not part of any political movement, as one did not yet exist. Nor was he the founder of

---

* Josephus, *Jewish Antiquities*, 18.1.1.

such a movement, as he was soon captured and executed. But Josephus does credit him as the "author" of the Zealot movement.* In this case, Josephus tells us that he inspired a movement that sprang up after his death, as is demonstrated by his two sons being involved in a revolt in the late 40s AD, for which they were executed. Every revolution needs its martyrs, and the Jews would not be the last revolutionaries to reach back in time and fasten an executed and long-dead rebel to a new cause.

Undoubtedly, there was a revolutionary element in many areas of Palestine. In fact, when the Romans refer to bandits, they often mean persons revolting against the established order, such as Barabbas. However, it is also very possible that groups of thieves took on the cloak of rebels to appear more respectable in society's eyes. Also, it is noteworthy that Josephus tells us that the city of Sepphoris and its surrounding region, which included Nazareth, was strongly pro-Roman during the period before and during the Great Revolt. Sepphoris even minted coins during the revolt, calling itself the "city of peace." Having already experienced Rome's wrath in 4 BC, when the Roman general Varus left the city a smoldering ruin, the local inhabitants were in no hurry to endure a repeat performance. Josephus also relates how he and his Jewish forces attempted to take the city but were repelled.† This defeat of the rebels by the people of Sepphoris, no doubt assisted by the towns surrounding the city, is as clear a statement as any that whatever revolutionary undercurrents may have existed in Galilee in the early first century, they made little impact on the area where Jesus was raised. Of course, this does not mean that Jesus could not have been exposed and converted to revolutionary thoughts as an adult and before he began his years of preaching. Still, Aslan's case for claiming that this is what happened to Jesus is thin gruel.

To create a Zealot Jesus, Aslan repeats the mistakes of the Jesus Seminar by picking and choosing only those slight segments of the New Testament that buttress his case. He, thus, declares the bulk of the Gospels, where Jesus is anything but a violent revolutionary, as made-up ad-

---

* Josephus, *Jewish Antiquities*, 18.1.6.
† Josephus, *The Jewish War*, 3.4.1–2.

ditions to the original text. In contrast, anything that can be twisted to support his outlook is declared a reliable truth.

According to Aslan, Jesus never said, "My kingdom is not of this world," as that would show that Jesus was not interested in changing the current order.* Nor, according to Aslan, did he say, "Do not resist the one who is evil" or "Put back your sword . . . For all who take up the sword will die by the sword."† But Aslan has no trouble accepting that Jesus said, "Do not think that I have come to bring peace to the earth. I have not come to bring peace but a sword." In Aslan's telling, this quote is proof of Jesus's violent revolutionary intentions. But as the rest of the verse clarifies, that was not what Jesus was saying. In the earliest Greek versions of the New Testament, the word used is *machaira*, which is not a sword. Instead, it is a large knife used to separate different cuts of meat. The term is also used this way in the book of Hebrews to discuss how scripture can be employed to discern good from evil.‡ Jesus is actually saying that those who follow his teachings will be cut off and separated from those who reject his teachings. His followers would undoubtedly have interpreted Jesus's words as a call to piety, not war.

Aslan set out to place Jesus within the "social, religious, and political context of the era in which he lived" to uncover a Jesus that modern Christians would not recognize.§ Unfortunately, that goal could only be attained by wrongly interpreting almost everything about the social, religious, and political context of the early first century. Aslan, outside of his own unsupported insights, provides no basis for any of his decisions regarding what passages of the New Testament are to be believed and which are to be ignored. Historical research does not work that way. If one wants to discount huge sections of any ancient document, there is a requirement to produce at least some evidential support for one's case other than "My theory does not work otherwise."

* John 18:36.
† Matthew 5:39 and 26:51–52.
‡ Hebrews 4:12: "For the word of God is living and active, sharper than any two-edged sword, piercing to the division of soul and of spirit, of joints and of marrow, and discerning the thoughts and intentions of the heart."
§ Aslan, *Zealot*, xxxi.

EIGHTEEN

Israel: Herod's Death and Jesus as a Child

I n the immediate aftermath of Herod's death, his three remaining sons set off for Rome to either contest the will or, in Archelaus's case, to have it confirmed. With them was a delegation of Jewish leaders who wanted to depose the entire Herodian dynasty and have the kingdom incorporated as a Roman province. While they were in Rome, the Herodian Kingdom, suddenly free of the hated Herod, began slipping into anarchy. Augustus sent a procurator, Sabinus, to take charge of the kingdom until he decided on Herod's will. Unfortunately, Sabinus failed his emperor, as he could not get ahead of a series of revolts erupting at various points within the kingdom. In Peraea, a man known as Simon, at one time one of Herod's slaves, raised the banner of revolt. While in Judea, a local shepherd and his brothers declared themselves as Jewish royalty and rebelled. More troubling was an uprising in Idumea, led by a group of veteran Herodian soldiers, which exposed the weakness of Archelaus's support in his dynastic homeland. The most dangerous revolt, however, erupted in Galilee, where a certain Judas led an assault on the Sepphoris fortress and seized the stockpile of weapons within its armory. Judas was the son of Hezekiah, a senior officer in the wrecked Hasmonean army and a well-known bandit (rebel) who had challenged Herod several decades earlier and was beheaded for his troubles.*

When word reached Syria that Sabinus and a Roman legion entrusted to him were besieged by armed mobs in Jerusalem, the Syrian governor, Publius Quinctilius Varus, acted in the manner expected of any Roman governor facing a revolt: He rapidly gathered his available troops and marched to the scene of trouble. With two of Syria's three remaining legions and a host of auxiliary forces, Varus marched into Israel. A portion of his troops crushed the revolt at Sepphoris, destroying much of the city and enslaving the population. Josephus does not tell us what happened to this revolt's leader, Judas, and a strong case can be made for him escaping and then returning in 6 AD to lead a second revolt.† In the meantime, Varus continued his march on Jerusalem, allowing his soldiers to devastate the countryside and also a few major towns as he marched. Roman armies fought better when they were allowed to enrich themselves through looting while on the march, with a significant portion of the proceeds going to Varus and his officers.

The besieged legion was soon relieved, and order was restored. Varus spent the next couple of weeks searching out the ringleaders of the various revolts, crucifying some two thousand of them, and sending a few of the most influential persons to Rome for judgment. After demonstrating the relentless ruthlessness expected of a Roman official in the face of threats to the Empire, Varus took the bulk of his army back to Syria. He had performed well enough to be entrusted by Augustus with integrating Germany, west of the Elbe, into the Empire. We have already reviewed his abject failure on this assignment when his legions were exterminated at Teutoburg Wald, so we will not linger on that story here. By the time

---

* Hezekiah, a soldier in King Aristobulus's army, took to the hills with the remnant of the Hasmonean army after Pompey had shattered it. In the Galilean hills, Hezekiah, in 47 BC, tried to spark a revolt against Roman rule, but even in this early period of Roman domination, he found little support in the region. When Herod moved against his forces, they were wiped out and Hezekiah was captured and executed.

† J. Spencer Kennard, Jr., "Judas of Galilee and His Clan," *The Jewish Quarterly Review*, New Series, Vol. 36, no. 3 (January 1946), pp. 281–286. This second revolt was caused by the Census of Quirinius, which was a prelude to increased Roman control and taxation.

Varus had finished crushing the Jewish revolts, Jesus was approximately two years old and likely living in Egypt, according to the New Testament. The New Testament also tells us that Joseph returned the family to Nazareth soon after the revolts ended. Therefore, Jesus may have watched the victorious Roman army on the march back to Syria. He surely spent his early years surrounded by the devastation a Roman army left in its wake, which certainly would have left an impression upon him.

These uprisings, against Herodian power and seeking freedom from Rome, were poorly organized and were never a serious threat to the Empire's stability or Rome's domination of Israel. Each of the various rebel leaders had thought himself a king, which would have placed them at each other's throats if Rome had not intervened. Most crucially, none of them appear to have come close to igniting a war of national liberation, such as the Maccabees did a century and a half before. Also missing from any remaining literary tradition are any traces of Jewish messianism in any of these revolts. They were primarily revolts against the Herodians, and only Rome's heavy-handed response turned them anti-Roman. There was no sign of any messianic-inspired zealots in any of these nationalistic movements, which we expect, as their advent remained more than a generation away.*

It is worthwhile taking a short detour to examine how Aslan's book *Zealot* presents these same events:

> Jesus of Nazareth was likely born the same year that Judas the Galilean—Judas, the failed messiah, son of Hezekiah, the failed messiah—rampaged through the countryside, burning with zeal. He would have been about ten years old when the Romans captured Judas, crucified his followers, and destroyed Sepphoris. When Antipas began to rebuild Sepphoris in earnest, Jesus was a young man ready to work in his father's trade.†

---

* For an excellent account and analysis of these revolts, see Eliezer Paltiel, "War in Judaea—After Herod's Death," *Revue belge de Philologie et d'Histoire*, Vol. 59, no. 1 (1981), pp. 107–136. See https://www.persee.fr/doc/rbph_0035-0818_1981_num_59_1_3318.
† Aslan, *Zealot*, pp. 43–44.

First, Jesus was born at least two years before Herod died, and Judas began his revolt. He was not ten years old when the Romans destroyed Sepphoris and possibly executed Judas; he was barely past his second birthday. Destroying Judas and his small band of rebels was a minor event as the legions immediately marched on to relieve their trapped comrades in Jerusalem. It was in Jerusalem and its surrounding Judean hinterlands that Varus captured and crucified two thousand rebels. These executed rebels were not part of Judas's followers in Galilee; they were conducting their own independent revolt. Moreover, Judas the Galilean did not declare himself the messiah; he declared himself king. Nor did his father, Hezekiah, declare himself a messiah. Rather, he was an officer in the Hasmonean army, intent on reestablishing the monarchy, with no intention of making himself the messiah. Josephus, our only source, does not tell us what Judas did after seizing Sepphoris and its fortress, but his most likely action was to try to defend it against the approaching Roman army. Such a defense explains why the Romans thought it necessary to destroy the city. What Judas did not do was pillage and burn the local area. After all, he saw himself as the people's liberator and counted on them for food and other support. It is beyond the pale to believe he deliberately acted to alienate the people he was intent on saving. Finally, when Antipas began rebuilding Sepphoris, Jesus was still a toddler and probably a decade away from being able to work alongside Joseph. Other than these listed errors, Aslan's version is correct in every particular.

As the last of the revolts were crushed, Augustus upheld Herod's final will. Archelaus was confirmed as ruler in Judea, but he was denied the title of king and declared an ethnarch instead. Augustus also removed the cities of Gaza, Gadara, and Hippos from his control. Antipas was given Galilee, and Philip received the wilder northern regions, mostly east of Galilee. Antipas and Philip were made tetrarchs, a title a bit lower than ethnarch, but were given political independence from their brother's rule. Josephus is mostly silent about Archelaus's rule, so we know very little about his short reign. He obviously started in an unenviable position as the son of a hated ruler, now leading a people that Roman arms had only recently violently suppressed. He apparently worsened a bad situation, and by 6 AD, Rome had had enough. Augustus had him deposed and sent off to a leisurely retirement in Vienne, Gaul. Judea was made a province under the direct rule of Rome. Jesus, by this time, was about to enter his teen years.

Archelaus's dismissal did not impact his brothers, who continued to rule in the regions Augustus assigned them. Philip's reign was one of moderation, and he stayed in power until his natural death in 33 AD, the same year as Jesus's crucifixion. Antipas, however, was more audacious, spending lavishly to build a new Galilee and often flouting Jewish law when it pleased him. For instance, he ordered his new capital, Tiberias, named after the Roman emperor, to be built on a graveyard, making the entire city, according to Jewish law, ritually unclean. When most Jews refused to live there, and some even refrained from entering the city, Antipas filled it with Gentiles, and during his reign, the city became the most Hellenistic in Galilee.

Antipas's most serious transgression of Jewish law was setting aside his wife, Phasaelis, in favor of Herodias, previously the wife of his older brother, whom she divorced while the couple lived in Rome. This is the marriage that John the Baptist vehemently condemned in the New Testament, which eventually led to his death. As Phasaelis, the wife Antipas set aside, was the daughter of King Aretas IV of Nabataea, this divorce led to a war between Galilee and Nabataea. Nabataea won some major early victories, but the war ended when Tiberius censured both kings and it became known that the Syrian legions were beginning to stir. Neither Antipas nor Aretas would survive a peace made and enforced by the legions, so they wisely set aside their quarrel. When Herodias pushed her husband above his station and made him demand the title of king in 39 AD, Gaius (Caligula) removed him from office and banished him to Lugdunum (modern Lyon), in Gaul, thus finally ending Galilean independence, such as it was.

The new governor of Syria, Publius Sulpicius Quirinius, immediately ordered a census—this is a second census and not the one mentioned in Luke's birth narrative, also ordered by Quirinius. This census added its citizens to its tax rolls, which sparked a revolt led by a man Josephus calls

Judas of Galilee, possibly the same man who seized Sepphoris in 4 BC. This revolt was quickly put down, and although Josephus does not tell us Judas's fate, he is referenced in Luke's book of Acts: "After him Judas the Galilean rose up at the time of the census and got people to follow him; he also perished, and all who followed him were scattered."[*]

Arguably, Rome, at least until Diocletian's reforms toward the end of the third century, remained a city-state controlling a vast empire. It never truly made the civic reforms necessary to manage and control the Empire its legions had won for it. Hence, the number of persons Rome possessed of sufficient stature and wealth who were also suitably trained to run a province was always small. A province such as Judea would be run by a prefect supported by a small staff, mostly just a few scribes and messengers. The prefect may also have brought a few friends or clients to offer advice and relieve him of some mundane duties. Thus, a governor was forced to focus on just a few crucial Roman concerns, such as the administration of justice, maintaining internal stability, and collecting the taxes due to Rome. Everything else was left to the locals whenever possible.

When one considers Rome's rule of its provinces, it is easy to imagine Roman legionnaires lurking around every corner. This is far from the case, as most of Rome's armies were concentrated, as we have discussed, along the frontiers or, like those in Syria, in large military bases. Thus, the core of the Empire was almost devoid of Roman troops. In fact, during this period, Rome did not maintain a single legion permanently in Judea or Galilee. This is why a prefect of equestrian rank, such as Pontius Pilate, and not a senator, governed Judea. The province was so minor in Rome's military calculations that it was considered beneath the dignity of anyone in the senatorial class. As a result, an equestrian governor would have to rely on auxiliary troops usually recruited from within his governing province. This, however, was not possible in Judea, as the emperor had exempted Jews from Roman military service. Luckily, Roman pre-

* Acts 5:37.

fects in Judea were able to absorb Herod's standing forces and turn them into Roman auxiliaries.

Some of these forces were stationed in the old Maccabean and Herodian forces scattered throughout Judea, although most were stationed in Jerusalem and around the coastal city of Caesarea. As we have seen, on those occasions when auxiliary troops could not maintain order, the Syrian legions were only a short march away. Interestingly, there may not have been a legate in Syria during much of Pilate's time as governor of Judea. This situation would have allowed Pilate a lot of freedom to behave as he wished, as there was no Syrian legate for the people to complain to about his conduct. This being the case, any Jewish complaint about Pilate's behavior or actions had to go directly to the emperor. But this meant such complaints were first seen by Tiberius's gatekeeper and Pilate's patron and protector, Sejanus, who despised the Jews.

A Roman prefect was also responsible for maintaining law and order through a province's judicial system. However, no Roman prefect in Judea had the time or staff to oversee all judicial proceedings. Thus, in most cases, prefects were happy to leave breaches of local laws and customs, both civil and religious, to local courts.

We have previously discussed how Rome collected taxes through a system of tax farmers. What made Judea and Galilee different from many other provinces was the requirement to collect three separate taxes: those due to Rome, those due the Herodian administration, and those that were part of the Temple tithe. Even after Rome took over Judea, there was still a requirement for local taxes to administer the province, as taxes due to Rome went to Rome. Although evidence is lacking, the Temple seemed to have a great deal of trouble collecting its tithes in Galilee after Antipas took over the government.[*]

Galileans may have been lax in their monetary payments to the Temple, but it remained the center of the Jewish faith. According to Jewish law, all males were required to "appear before the Lord your God" during three festivals during the year, and they were explicitly enjoined not to

---

[*] Richard A. Horsley, *Galilee: History, Politics, People* (Trinity Press International, 1995), pp. 140–144.

come empty-handed.* While it may have been easy for Jewish men living in Jerusalem to appear in the Temple three times a year, doing so would have been much more difficult for those living more than a few days' travel from the city. Moreover, if every Jew in the Empire and beyond came to Jerusalem three times a year, that's well over a million visitors traveling simultaneously. Such an influx is so ridiculously beyond the capacity of the period's infrastructure to support as to be unworthy of any consideration. What is much more likely was that travel to Jerusalem was a once-in-a-lifetime quest for most Jews residing outside of Israel. For those within Israel's traditional borders, one can assume that some local leaders regularly made the trip as representatives of the whole. Still, this means that during these three festival periods, tens of thousands of pilgrims were clogging the roads at any one time. It is quite possible that Jerusalem's population more than quadrupled for weeks at a time. It is noteworthy that Joseph, according to the New Testament, made this trip at least annually with Mary and their family, indicating a level of wealth and community stature beyond what is commonly assumed.† Josephus does mention that when the Roman army was advancing on Jerusalem in 66 AD, the legionaries were surprised to find that some towns were empty, as everyone had gone to Jerusalem for the festival. It is, however, a safe assumption that with a rapacious Roman army destroying everything in its path, the walls of Jerusalem had an extra appeal that festival season.

* Deuteronomy 16:16.
† Luke 2:41.

NINETEEN

Economic Growth and Galilee

A t first, much of the Empire's sweeping economic tide had little impact on Galilee, as Herod neglected the province. During the Hasmonean period, when Herod was only the tetrarch of Galilee, he had to fight a number of difficult battles before the Galileans recognized his authority. According to Josephus, Herod was so incensed by the Galileans' attitude toward him that throughout his long reign, he refused to build any significant project within the region, which is borne out in the archaeological record to date.* Even in the regional capital, Sepphoris, no Herodian-period building has yet been found.† This, of course, explains why it was necessary for Joseph to establish his construction business in Judea, where Herod was undertaking massive and expensive building projects.

This does not mean the local farmers missed out entirely on the first

---

* The bulk of the Jewish population in Galilee appears to have been settlers from Judea who were given land and other subsidies by the Hasmoneans. Hence, the Galileans, being strong supporters of the Hasmonean dynasty, which Herod overthrew, never warmed to their new ruler.

† Mordechai Aviam, "People, Land, Economy, and Belief in First-Century Galilee and Its Origins: A Comprehensive Archaeological Synthesis," in David A. Fiensy and Ralph K. Hawkins (eds.), *The Galilean Economy in the Time of Jesus* (Society of Biblical Literature, 2013).

decades of the Empire's prosperity. They all still profited handsomely from the great peace that descended on every province of the Empire. If it was ever true that Galilee was a land of poor peasants just barely scraping by at a subsistence level, which is doubtful, it absolutely was not true in the years of Jesus's youth. Josephus mentions 204 Galilean towns and cities in his books, and at least seven of them were fortified. As a general rule, no town or city fortifies itself unless surplus labor and capital are abundant within the region. This point is particularly true in the era of the *Pax Romana*, when many fortifications throughout the Empire fell into decay, including those surrounding Rome. That local populations could afford fortifications is proof in and of itself that Galileans were living above subsistence levels.

Richard Horsley gives us what, until recently, historians believed was the impact of Herod's taxation and spending in Palestine:

> The general effect of Herod's rule on all subject peoples was extreme economic burden and hardship . . . The Roman imposition of Herod as a client-king added yet a third level of taxation, for the Temple and the priests did not suddenly forgo their revenues. Herod's taxes must have been unusually heavy in order to support his . . . extensive and lavish court that utilized several palatial fortresses, his vast program of cultural building and military fortresses, and the centerpieces of his building projects, the temples Caesar and he rebuilt in Jerusalem. The effect on the peasantry in Galilee, as elsewhere, was increasing indebtedness and even alienation of their ancestral lands, as they were unable to support themselves after rendering up percentages of their crops to tribute for Rome, tithes, offerings to priests and Temple, and taxes to Herod.[*]

All of this might have been the case if these groups hoarded their revenues, as was done before the Empire imposed peace within its frontiers. But it is certainly not what one would expect if the money was

[*] Richard Horsley, *Galilee: History, Politics, People* (Trinity Press International, 1995), p. 60.

being spent as fast as it came in, which is what was happening. And, in fact, the archaeological record does not show any indications that this old paradigm is correct. Rather, it offers just the opposite, such as substantial evidence, in the form of numerous large and expensively constructed homes filled with luxury items, that there was a new large class of wealthy urbanites. These urbanites would have been able to pay handsomely for the local farmers' produce, upon whom their survival depended. Moreover, the discovery of numerous olive presses, clothing manufacturing centers, and industrial pottery and flour-producing sites dating from the Herodian era clearly demonstrates increasing and widespread prosperity throughout the region. There are also signs of extensive trade between the towns and cities of Galilee and other provinces of the Roman Empire. In the ancient era, and even more than today, trade was always the path to riches.

The archaeological record forces us to dispel the lingering myth of Galilee being filled with poor peasants. As Jesus traveled, he was not moving from one blighted area to the next. Instead, he was moving from one prosperous place to another. This growing wealth and expansion of business opportunities helps explain several items, starting with Jesus's recruitment of his apostles. For it is fairly certain that the apostle Peter was married, and Paul references other apostles as being married.* Suppose Galilee was as poor as it has commonly been portrayed. In that case, Jesus taking away probably the only financial support of at least several families appears cruel. But, if we accept a more prosperous Galilee, then Peter and the other married apostles are better thought of as relatively wealthy fishermen, probably outfitting multiple boats. Thus, he can depart for long periods, knowing that he is leaving a going business concern that can provide for his family while he is away. It is certainly beyond the pale that Jesus or his apostles went about their preaching while leaving their families destitute. One would imagine that his enemies would have made much of this. Also, in a later visit to Peter's house, when Jesus reputedly cured Peter's mother-in-law of a severe illness, no one appeared to be in want or in poverty. The fact that Jesus is even there is a testament to the

---

* Matthew 8:14 and Paul in 1 Corinthians 9:5.

fact that the apostles' families were not forgotten and were being cared for.*

Another interesting point is the cost of Jesus's ministry. This is rarely discussed in the New Testament, except in two instances. John tells us that Judas—an interesting choice—was the group's treasurer and carried the money bag, to which he helped himself when it suited him to do so.† We also know the names of several women who traveled with Jesus— Mary Magdalene, Johanna, and Susanna, who were wealthy enough to help "support them out of their own means."‡ Luke states that many other women traveled with Jesus and presumably also offered funds. Still, supporting such a large group for multiple years was costly. Food and lodging expenses alone would have been ruinous. That is unless we accept that Galilee was much more prosperous than commonly attested, and that Jesus and at least some of his apostles were wealthy or had access to more funds than your typical peasant.

Moreover, Jesus grew up and came of age during Galilee's most prosperous decades, as Herod's death presaged a further economic boom in Galilee. As we have seen, the turmoil immediately after Herod's death led to the Romans destroying the city of Sepphoris and probably a number of other towns that have gone unnamed in the sources.§ But, when Herod Antipas succeeded his father as the Roman-appointed tetrarch of Galilee, he immediately ordered Sepphoris rebuilt as his capital. His desire, as stated at the time, was to turn Sepphoris into both a fortress and the "Ornament of Galilee."‖ Such a boast would be remarkably audacious unless Antipas was sure that Galilee's revenues could fill his treasury. For the first two decades of Antipas's rule, Sepphoris was showered in gold and silver for its reconstruction. Antipas probably continued to fund major projects for the rest of his reign, even when he decided to build a new capital city—Tiberias—on the Sea of Galilee, interestingly very close to where Jesus conducted much of his ministry. Is it too much to

* Matthew 8:14–15. Also, 1 Corinthians 9:5 can be employed to build a case that the wives of the apostles often traveled alongside their husbands during Jesus's preaching.
† John 12:6.
‡ Luke 8:1–3.
§ Josephus, *Antiquities*, 17.10.9.
‖ Josephus, *Antiquities*, 18.27.

speculate that Joseph or some of his sons expanded the family business to Israel's newest major construction project? This could explain how Jesus and his apostles maintained themselves for three years and why he preached for so long in one confined area.

All of this spending by the central authorities would have had what we now call a Keynesian effect, where governments spend large amounts of money to grow economic activity. Such huge spending over a long period would have kept money circulating in abundance throughout the Galilean economy, making work plentiful and keeping wages high. Before the Roman Empire, rulers such as Herod Antipas would have stored vast quantities of the silver they collected in taxes in preparation for the next war—there was always a next war. But Rome had ended that particular worry, and rulers could now spend nearly every coin they collected on grandiose projects. As for the taxes paid to Rome, that was the cost of making sure Rome could maintain the wherewithal to keep the peace. Without a hegemon to maintain order and enforce the law, most of the Empire, including Galilee, would have remained poor. Under the Empire's umbrella, society was vastly enriched.

TWENTY

Jesus's Galilee in 33 AD

The Galilee in which Jesus wandered and preached in 33 AD was remarkably different from the one Herod had entered at the start of his political life. When Herod first entered Galilee, he was resistant to the centralizing policies of the Hasmoneans who ruled them from Jerusalem. Before Herod's arrival, the Hasmoneans had mostly left Galilee to be run by its own local leaders and cultural traditions as they focused on continued expansion. Eventually, the Hasmoneans felt a need to consolidate their authority by employing both military power and large numbers of Pharisees, who would assume some administrative control of local councils and preach a Temple-based Judaism in local synagogues. In this role, the Pharisees were likely both respected as scholars learned in Jewish law and simultaneously despised as representatives of the central state.

During Herod's time, the military resistance to his political rule intensified. Still, it appears that the Galileans accustomed themselves to the dictates of the Temple priests when it came to matters of religion. There was one last spasm of revolt in the wake of Herod's death, which the Romans brutally suppressed. After that, Roman military power was rarely, if ever, seen in Galilee until the Great Revolt of 66 AD, almost two generations after Herod's demise. The centurion at Capernaum and the small force likely with him may have been the only Roman soldiers Jesus ever saw, except on visits to Jerusalem. Even then, it would be rare for him to have seen actual Roman legionnaires, as they were almost all in Syria. He would have rather seen Roman auxiliaries, almost entirely recruited within the region. This did not mean there were no soldiers in Galilee. Herod Antipas, once confirmed in power by Rome, would have been allowed to maintain his own local forces to secure the region as well as his hold on power. These Herodian forces would have consisted mostly of Greek mercenaries, although there were probably several units that were entirely Jewish. Most of these forces would have been scattered along the frontiers or in the several fortresses built by Herod. In his younger years, Jesus would have likely run into such soldiers on a regular basis, as they garrisoned the Sepphoris fortress, which Jesus and his father, Joseph, likely helped rebuild, and which was only a few miles from his home in Nazareth. After Herod Antipas had John the Baptist executed, Jesus would surely have felt himself moved to the top of the list of potential incendiaries. Thus, Jesus would have had every reason to avoid those areas where a fortress and soldiers were commanded by Herod Antipas, who Jesus referred to as that sly fox.*

As for the Galileans of Jesus's time, we have already addressed the flourishing economy of the area under Roman rule. The reality was that Galilee contained some of the most fertile lands in Israel and was well cultivated. As Josephus describes it, Galilee was a paradise on earth:

> Its nature is wonderful as well as its beauty; its soil is so fruitful that all sorts of trees can grow upon it, and the inhabitants accordingly plant all sorts of trees there; for the temper of the air is so well mixed, that it agrees very well with those several sorts, particularly walnuts, which require the coldest air, flourish there in vast plenty; there are palm trees also, which grow best in hot air; fig trees also and olives grow near them, which yet require an air that is more temperate. One may call this place the ambition of nature, where it forces those plants that are naturally enemies to

---

* Luke 13:32.

one another to agree together; it is a happy contention of the seasons, as if every one of them laid claim to this country; for it not only nourishes different sorts of autumnal fruit beyond men's expectation, but preserves them a great while; it supplies men with the principal fruits, with grapes and figs continually, during ten months of the year and the rest of the fruits as they become ripe together through the whole year.[*]

Josephus also gives us a description of the area surrounding Capernaum, where Jesus did most of his teaching.

Skirting the lake of Gennesar [Sea of Galilee], and also bearing that name, lies a region whose natural properties and beauty are very remarkable.

There is not a plant which its fertile soil refuses to produce, and its cultivators in fact grow every species; the air is so well-tempered that it suits the most opposite varieties.

The walnut, a tree which delights in the most wintry climate, here grows luxuriantly, beside palm-trees, which thrive on heat, and figs and olives, which require a milder atmosphere.

. . . For not only has the country this surprising merit of producing such diverse fruits, but it also preserves them: for ten months without intermission it supplies those kings of fruits, the grape and the fig; the rest mature on the trees the whole year round.[†]

We must dispel the idea that Israel in 33 AD looks anything like the barren and arid landscape that we see in many current photos of the region. Everywhere Jesus walked, he would see lush fields and groves. In fact, judging from the New Testament narrative, the most challenging task landowners faced was finding enough workers to help harvest the bounty of crops produced.

---

[*] Josephus, *The Jewish War,* 3.10.8.
[†] Josephus, *The Jewish War,* 3.516–521.

One of the reasons that farmers had trouble finding workers is that an ongoing construction boom was occurring throughout Galilee. This was started by Herod with his fortress building and was continued by his son, Herod Antipas, who, among his many other projects, rebuilt the city of Sepphoris and constructed an entirely new city at Tiberias. All of this would have created an employment boom, which would have kept cash circulating at a rapid pace throughout the economy. Of course, Roman taxes were a cause for grievance, as are all taxes at all times. But this must be weighed against the fact that, as Herod Antipas ruled Galilee separate from Judea, the taxes that Judea and the Temple used to collect were now being kept at home. Couple this with the decades of peace enforced by Rome, and the Galilee of Jesus's time was richer than it ever had been.

But by 33 AD, we likely have a Galilee in transition. It is archaeologically clear that the great building programs are coming to an end. This, as we have seen, was taking place throughout the Roman Empire, as the thrifty Tiberius halted the extravagant spending programs of Augustus. This massive spending, first within the Roman core and then within the provinces, had kept the economy from foundering as the civil wars ended, and with them, wartime spending levels. But, as this postwar spending boom ended, it must have set off a deflationary spiral in many regions across the Empire. A deflationary environment, as must have existed in Israel after 33 AD, would have created thousands of unemployed persons, immediately available as recruits for bands of insurgent-minded bandits. Also, the smaller farmers would have been unable to stay afloat, and it is at this time that we start seeing the creation of large estates, as those who still had money started buying up smaller farms. Many farmers would have been turned into rent-paying tenants on their own lands, while just as many would have been totally disenfranchised and joined the bands in the hills.

Did Jesus see any of this happening? Likely he would have witnessed the very beginning of this process, which would have been much further advanced in Judea. His parables make it plain that he can see the change beginning, and he was certainly taking advantage of the rising discontent to spread his own message. He would have seen even greater dissatisfaction in Judea, where the Roman presence was much more keenly felt, and the receding economic tide would have struck with much greater force than it did in remote Galilee. But in neither location had things progressed to the point where there was a real risk of a popular uprising. That would take another generation of increasingly bad economic prospects to ignite enough unhappiness and opposition to Rome to risk all on one throw of the iron dice of war. Still, anyone looking for why the Zealot movement sprang to life in the generation after Jesus's death needs to look no further than the collapsing regional economy and the widespread disenfranchisement of large segments of the population.

Among the 204 villages Josephus tells us could be found in Galilee at about this time, Nazareth was likely one of the smaller. It was certainly not big enough to attract the attention of Josephus when he wrote his stirring accounts of the period. Being so close to the metropolis of Sepphoris, it likely would have been caught up in the same narrative as that city and did not merit a separate mention. It was not, however, a trivial town, as it was close to Sepphoris and the massive building efforts there, and was probably a construction center, all traces of which would have vanished when the rebuilding of the city finished. Moreover, going east to west, important ancient roads passed along the base of the Galilean hills, very close to where Nazareth was situated and through Sepphoris, only a few miles away. The Great High Road, often traveled by Roman armies on the march through Sepphoris on their way to Jerusalem, passes just a short walk from Nazareth, while another major trading road was just east of Nazareth. Thus, Jesus's hometown sits squarely in the midst of the great trading nexus between Jerusalem and Antioch in Syria. This alone would have made it somewhat of a commercial center, even if it was a minor one. Assuming Nazareth's currently identified mountaintop location was employed mostly for defense and that a large segment of the population lived on the surrounding plain, Nazareth likely partook in the huge agricultural bounty for which the region was famous. For, according to the Talmud, out to a distance of sixteen miles from Sepphoris in every direction was a "land of milk and honey." In other words, Nazareth sat in the middle of one of the most productive areas of Galilee.

It has long been traditional to emphasize the remoteness of Nazareth from the great tides of current events sweeping the regions. The truth, however, is the exact opposite: Nazareth, in 33 AD, sits at or near the crossroads of the region's commerce and political life. Thus, Jesus would have had a much more cosmopolitan and sophisticated outlook than is typically attributed to a man many historians insist on portraying as an illiterate and uncultured peasant. As one historian states: "It [Nazareth] was surrounded on all sides by a busy, worldly life, with alien races, languages and customs. To the south were the Samaritans; Carmel, the whole coast plain, and the mountains to the northwest belonged to the Tyrians, enjoying self-government, while Hermon and much of the land to the east of the lake was pagan, Greek or Roman."* From the hills of Nazareth, Jesus could see all of these alien lands and likely came into almost daily contact with peoples from each as they transited from one urban area to the other.

It was long accepted that Galilee was thoroughly Hellenized. Historians no longer believe this to be the case. At its core, Hellenization was a mostly urban phenomenon and appears not to have made a significant impression on the Jewish hinterlands. Here, the peasants clung to their traditional Jewish beliefs, which were not always in accord with what was being espoused by the Temple priests in Jerusalem. Moreover, after the Hasmoneans conquered Galilee, they undertook a program to expel most Greeks from the region's cities. The one location Hellenization, later translated into Romanization, was likely to have clung to was Sepphoris and its immediate surroundings, which would have included Nazareth. As we have seen, Sepphoris was one of Herod's great fortress cities, and Herod himself was a thoroughly Hellenized ruler. The troops he garrisoned there were, in all probability, Greek mercenaries or drawn from distant Hellenized locations. When the Romans marched through in 4 BC, much of the city was destroyed, and the people enslaved. One can assume that the Romans enslaved the rebellious Jewish population, leaving the loyal Hellenized residents alone. When Herod Antipas, who was

* E.W.G. Masterman, "Galilee in the Time of Christ," *The Biblical World*, Vol. 32, no. 6 (December 1908), pp. 405–416.

raised in Rome, rebuilt this city, he definitely copied the Roman mold in its design and architecture, including building a large Roman-type amphitheater, the extant ruins of which almost certainly date to his reign. Moreover, he repopulated the city with people like himself, both Hellenized and thoroughly Romanized. Not only does this Hellenized-Romanized population explain why Sepphoris and the surrounding countryside stayed loyal to Rome during the Great Revolt of 66 AD, but it also tells something important about Jesus.

Jesus was undoubtedly a practicing Jew. But, having grown up in Nazareth and likely having worked in Sepphoris, he would have been exposed to Hellenizing influences almost daily. In other words, he would have been comfortable in both Jewish and Hellenized settings, and it would have been unusual if he could not speak Greek, even if he may not have been able to read in that language. This would explain how he could converse with Pontius Pilate, who was unlikely to speak Aramaic or Hebrew, but, like every learned Roman, he could converse in Greek. This may also explain why Jesus spent so much time preaching in and around Capernaum. We have already discussed why Jesus encountered a Roman centurion in Capernaum, relating that the town sat along several major trade routes. It was also within the economic sphere of the great trading city of Tyre, one of the most Hellenized cities in the east since it was originally conquered by Alexander the Great three centuries earlier. And finally, it was within walking distance of Antipas's recently constructed capital city of Tiberias, which was also thoroughly Hellenized. So, while most of Galilee would have been overwhelmingly Jewish in culture and tradition, the exceptions were Sepphoris, where Jesus spent all of his years prior to beginning his ministry, and the Capernaum–Tiberias region of northeast Galilee, where Jesus spent much of his ministry. That he would pick this area to preach in probably had much to do with its cultural milieu, as he was accustomed to it from his youth. That Christianity was able to so quickly make the leap from its Jewish roots to the Hellenized Jews and Gentiles of the wider Roman Empire has much to do with the faith having been preached to a similar population from its start.

PART VI

TIBERIUS RULES THE EMPIRE

TWENTY-ONE

Tiberius Versus Germanicus

A t its start, Tiberius's reign was plagued with problems. When word reached the Pannonian legions that Augustus was dead, discipline broke down. The aura of Augustus had kept the increasingly restive legions in check, even as the conditions of their service rapidly deteriorated in the final years of Augustus's reign. But Tiberius's accession provided a window of opportunity for the legions to test their political power. Discontented troublemakers seized upon the legionnaires' justifiable complaints to entice the rest of the soldiery to raise the banner of revolt. These complaints included being forced to serve for far longer than the sixteen years that was the established standard, and that legionnaires received only a fraction of what the Praetorian Guard was paid, although legionnaires were exposed to terrifically more risk.

The revolt was particularly worrying for Tiberius, as rumors were arriving that the mutinous legions had offered to declare Germanicus emperor and march on Rome with him at their head. Germanicus did not accept their proposition, but Tiberius had a reason for concern, as his position was not yet secure, and Germanicus, for inexplicable reasons, was beloved by the Roman mob. He must have been tempted to go north himself, to confront the legions he had often led in battle, but that would place too much of his prestige at immediate risk. Moreover, if the situation deteriorated once he was on the scene, there would be no buffer to insulate Tiberius from blame. His personal *auctoritas* would be questioned and, with it, his right to rule. Besides, in Rome, political discord seethed; this was not the time for the newly installed emperor to absent himself.

It was also clear that the legions were not going to be calmed unless they were visited by a person of significant rank with the power to commit the emperor to whatever was decided. Only two persons fit the bill: Tiberius's own son, Drusus, and his adopted son, Germanicus. Germanicus was already at the scene of the emergency with the Rhine legions. So, Drusus was immediately sent north to manage the crisis among the Danubian legions. With him went two cohorts of Praetorians: the Praetorian cavalry and a portion of the emperor's personal German bodyguard. It was enough to make an impression but not sufficient to scare the legions into further rashness.

Several senior advisers, including Sejanus, were accompanying Drusus; Sejanus had recently been raised to the rank of prefect of the Praetorian Guard alongside his father, Seius Strabo. Clearly, Tiberius had not forgotten the man who had befriended him during his Rhodian exile. Sejanus was now the senior commander of the only military force stationed in Italy, a position that an emperor would award only to a man he already held in utmost trust. Unfortunately, there is no record of how Drusus and Sejanus got along on this trip. But, given their later animosity, the two men must have had some trouble. At the least, Drusus likely resented that Tiberius saddled him with a minder who had little more experience than himself.

Drusus's arrival in the mutinous camp did not get off to a good start. After he read a letter from Tiberius, the soldiers made their demands. Their mood turned ugly when Drusus informed them that he was not empowered to make any concessions without checking with Tiberius. Promising violence if their demands were not met, the legionnaires dispersed to consider their next move. It was now that the fates intervened to save Drusus from embarrassment or much worse. As the mutineers plotted that night, there was a full lunar eclipse, a sure sign to the superstitious legionnaires that the gods were angry with them. Drusus took immediate advantage of his good fortune. If the soldiers would return to good order, he would write a letter to his father asking him to look favorably on the soldiers' demands. While the soldiers awaited Tiberius's reply, Drusus had his Praetorians track down and kill the mutiny's ringleaders. The demoralized legions soon returned to discipline and, once again, under their centurions' command, marched off to their winter camps.

The Danubian legions were back in the Roman fold, but Germanicus did not have the benefit of an eclipse to aid him with the Rhine legions. At some point, the mutineers decided they could gain more if Germanicus was emperor rather than Tiberius, and they offered to march on Rome and install him to power. Germanicus jumped down from the podium, claiming he would rather die than adopt such a dishonorable course. His theatrics did not impress the battle-hardened legionnaires, one of whom called his bluff by offering the heir to the throne his sword to commit suicide with. Germanicus tried to put off the soldiers by showing a forged letter, ostensibly from Tiberius, offering to accede to almost all of their demands. The soldiers were not fooled, and Germanicus was soon forced to pay the soldiers out of his own funds and agree, among other concessions, to immediately discharge the longest-serving veterans.

When the crisis did not abate, Germanicus decided to remove his pregnant wife, Augustus's granddaughter Agrippina, and their young son, Gaius—the future emperor Caligula—from the camp. As the pitiful procession was leaving camp, the soldiers, who often displayed a surprising sentimentality, surrounded her wagon and begged her to stay with them. Within the hour, the legionnaires had returned to their standards and even executed the mutiny's ringleaders to prove their loyalty. Before they could change their minds, Germanicus led them across the Rhine on a short but sharp campaign in Germania.

Tiberius was happy to have the mutinies behind him and also to learn that Germanicus had refused the legionnaires' offer to make him emperor. Still, he was convinced that Germanicus had made many concessions to increase his popularity in Rome and garner the loyalty of the legions to him personally. In his report to the Senate, Tiberius attempted to be evenhanded in praising both Drusus and Germanicus, but he could not disguise the fact that Drusus had ended the Danubian mutiny without offering any concessions. Consequently, the Senate and the Roman mob became convinced that Tiberius bore Germanicus substantial ill will. This belief colored all future relations between Tiberius and his apparent heir and, several years later, his perceived dislike for Germanicus was at the core of Rome's next great political crisis.

Germanicus spent the next three years preparing for and conducting annual campaigns in Germany. During this time, Roman arms met with substantial successes but also endured a number of misfortunes, some bordering on disastrous. But the Senate and people of Rome easily forgave the setbacks. After all, Rome endured many reverses along the road to glory and empire. It was the end that mattered. And from the list of battles won, lands ravaged, and Germanic tribes defeated, it appeared that Germania would soon be added to the list of Roman provinces. But from Tiberius's viewpoint, Germanicus's victories were not accomplishing anything of note. Tiberius had inherited the German wars from Augustus and they were a constant drain on Rome's resources. Earlier victories, on the road to empire, had paid for themselves, first in rich booty and then through a steady stream of taxes imposed upon the conquered provinces. As far as Tiberius was concerned, Germania was all cost and no gain. The annual campaigns were vastly expensive, and the returns were slight. Even if Germany immediately turned itself over to Roman rule, it would be many generations before the province would make a valuable economic contribution to the Empire, and it may never have done so.

All of this could not help but raise Tiberius's suspicions about whether the heir was willing to wait for nature to take its course, or if he was laying the groundwork for a coup. Still, there was no clear evidence that Germanicus was set on the latter course. Thus, Tiberius was forced to acclaim his deeds. In 17 BC, Germanicus was ordered to cease operations and return to Rome. Once there, he was fêted as a conquering hero and awarded the first full triumph in almost fifty years. With Germanicus recalled, the annual Roman assaults on Germania ceased, for if Tiberius

had nominated a new commander to replace Germanicus, the Roman mob would have seen it as equivalent to calling their hero a failure. It was safer for Tiberius to end the campaigns east of the Rhine entirely. Of course, this was an action he had long considered prudent, as he never believed Germania was worth the cost. Rome's northern frontiers rested on the Rhine and Danube for nearly a century until a new emperor, Trajan, gave in to the Roman impulse to conquer and marched the legions into Dacia.

The award of a triumph and a host of other honors could not conceal the fact that Germanicus's campaigns had expended vast amounts of blood and treasure for no tangible gain. For a time, Germanicus's popularity and easy way with the people and the support of influential senators would suffice to hold this unflattering truth at bay. But Germanicus surely realized that the longer he was in Rome, in Tiberius's shadow, the faster his personal *auctoritas* would diminish. It was only a matter of time until familiarization bred contempt, and people began to view him as just another in a long line of powerful politicians vying for ultimate power. Tiberius must have also realized this, and he could just as quickly see its danger. Tiberius could not risk Germanicus becoming a pawn to be employed by various senatorial power factions. For Germanicus was a magnet for those opposed to Tiberius's rule, and the longer he stayed in Rome, the more dangerous he became.

From any vantage point, Tiberius could see that Germanicus would become an increasingly robust alternate center of power within a political system not designed to long tolerate multiple centers of political power. Tiberius had come of age as the series of wars that destroyed the Roman Republic were ending. He had seen firsthand the ruin civil wars wreaked upon individuals and society. Allowing the tinder that could ignite a new round of civil wars to pile up would have been anathema to him. The crucial problem was that the Senate and the people of Rome could clearly see the tension growing among Tiberius, Germanicus, and their rival factions. As these tensions grew, Tiberius's popularity sank, as Germanicus was the clear favorite of the people. Moreover, there was no way to strike at Germanicus, assuming Tiberius even entertained such ideas, that would not bring the fearful Roman mob into the street.

There was, however, a solution. With so much in the West to keep Roman elites anxious, growing problems in the East had been left to simmer. Now, many of these problems were ready to boil over. When Augustus ruled, the answer to the issues in the East was to send a person of undisputed authority to the region, with all of the emperor's powers to settle all major outstanding issues. He had first sent his best general and presumed heir, Agrippa, on such a mission. Later, Augustus sent his next presumed heir, Gaius, east. Everyone in Rome knew that it was past the time for someone with imperial dignity to go east, but Tiberius claimed he was too old, and his son Drusus was still too young—that left only Germanicus. For Tiberius, sending Germanicus as his envoy had many advantages. For one, it separated Germanicus even further from the Rhine legions without any hint that he was treated dishonorably. In fact, the mission was viewed as so vital that it honored Germanicus. Moreover, by allowing a potential rival such an honor, Tiberius increased his own *auctoritas.*

By decree of the Senate, Germanicus was granted imperium powers to all areas east of the Adriatic, making him superior to any Roman governor in the east. But before Germanicus left, Tiberius made a horrific political error. In hopes of having someone in the east who could advise the young Germanicus while also keeping a discrete eye on the young heir, Tiberius appointed Gnaeus Calpurnius Piso as governor of Syria, which, after Egypt, was the most important of Rome's eastern provinces. Piso was famous for his haughty arrogance and independence of mind. He, undoubtedly, was given orders directly from Tiberius, who considered him loyal and trustworthy. The extent of these orders will never be known, but it would have been an enormous oversight on Tiberius's part if they did not include detailed instructions on how to deal with Germanicus. Whatever his orders, Piso clearly saw it as his duty to keep the headstrong Germanicus in check. Piso took his wife, Plancina, with him as she possessed an impressive pedigree and was a close friend of Livia's, so it was assumed Agrippina would not overawe her.

But for Germanicus, Piso's appointment must have irked him. At a minimum, it gave the impression that Tiberius was not confident he could be trusted to complete his various missions successfully. Another consideration, undoubtedly not far from Germanicus's mind, was that Piso was put in place to monitor Germanicus's dealings with the Syrian legions. If he could win them over to the same extent that he had done so with the Rhine legions, he would pose a mortal threat to Tiberius.

Piso's overbearing and imperious manner did not help the situation. Upon his arrival in Syria, Piso reportedly offered large donatives—bribes—to the soldiers and their leaders. It was assumed by everyone that this largesse was approved and probably funded by Tiberius to ensure the legions were indebted to him and could not be easily swayed by Germanicus. Piso went further and significantly lessened the legions' ferocious discipline, allowing soldiers to remain idle in their camps or cause trouble in local towns and cities without punishment.

For the moment, Germanicus ignored Piso's actions, as he had more pressing concerns. By all accounts, Germanicus settled many of the outstanding problems rapidly and efficiently; a new ruler was placed on the throne of Armenia, where he ruled peacefully for a decade and a half; Cappadocia and Commagene were reorganized and the first integrated into the Empire as a province. The latter was eventually made part of Syria, and the list of grievances that the east had petitioned Tiberius with were all settled. It was, by any measure, an impressive performance worthy of a future emperor. But the inevitable could not be postponed forever; the collision with Piso that everyone expected was at hand.

When Germanicus arrived in Syria, matters went from bad to worse. From their first meeting in the camp of *Legio* X, their mutual disdain was apparent to all. Moreover, neither man was willing to make any gesture of appeasement to the other. Instead, Piso began to abstain from court when Germanicus was conducting official judicial duties, a calculated insult that Germanicus bore without comment. In turn, and without consulting Piso, Germanicus used his imperium to order the legions' customary discipline revived and enforced. He also ordered several other measures that impacted how the province was run. This usurpation of his authority clearly angered Piso. He, after all, had been appointed governor by Tiberius, and the Senate had confirmed his position and authority.

The province was his to run, and the legions stationed within it were his to command. For a man as proud as Piso, Germanicus's interference must have been galling.

Germanicus now made a mistake. He moved himself and his entourage to Egypt, whether as a vacation or to continue settling the problems of the Eastern Empire is a matter of dispute. But Piso took advantage of Germanicus's absence to reverse all of his orders, including those returning the legions to their former discipline. It was a needlessly provocative move, as Germanicus was sure to overturn Piso's orders upon his return. Germanicus lost no time in doing just that but went further by ordering Piso out of Syria. Clearly, he was testing his power against Tiberius himself, as it was far from clear that his imperium allowed him to summarily remove a governor appointed by the emperor with the Senate's approval.

But the contest of wills was not forced, as Germanicus fell ill in Antioch and died. On his deathbed, he renounced his friendship with Piso and claimed that Piso and Plancina had poisoned him. He died begging his friends to bring the murderers to justice. Although it is much more likely that Germanicus succumbed to one of the many illnesses that ravaged the world in an age where germs were unknown, Germanicus's many supporters were convinced of Piso's guilt. Moreover, many of them suspected that Piso had been put up to his crime by Tiberius and Livia, an idea that soon infected Rome's body politic. When news of Germanicus's death reached Piso at Cos, he and his wife stupidly offered expensive sacrifices to celebrate their deliverance. When word of Piso's celebrations reached Rome, calls for vengeance reached hysterical levels.

Piso did not make matters better for himself by returning to Syria with a hastily collected and somewhat motley force to reclaim his position as governor. However, Germanicus's friends had already emplaced one of their own in this position, and the legions remained loyal to him. The military contest was soon determined, and Piso's small army was quickly annihilated. Piso was captured during the fighting and sent to Rome with a pass of safe conduct. In Rome, Piso found that Tiberius was greatly angered that his "trusted friend" had risked igniting a civil war to reclaim his position. If there was ever a time when it was best to lay low and allow the storm to pass, this was that time. But that was not Piso's way.

When Piso arrived in Rome, emotions were still running hot. Not only was the public demanding Piso's punishment, but matters were so out of hand that Tiberius was willing to offer Piso as a scapegoat for the mob to feast upon. Tiberius was only too well aware that any display of support for Piso would be all the proof the mob, and likely the Senate, required to confirm he had ordered Germanicus's murder. Therefore, throughout the trial, Tiberius remained aloof from the proceedings, further fueling suspicions that the malevolent hand of Tiberius was behind the supposed murder. Only the passions of a mob can explain this, as there was nothing Tiberius could gain from Germanicus's death. If Germanicus had lived, Tiberius could easily have kept Germanicus busy and happy while he waited his turn. More important, he could have used Germanicus to manage the ambitious and forceful Agrippina. But with Germanicus dead, Agrippina was sure to become a focal point of discontent as she maneuvered to ensure that her sons became emperors. If she could not become empress through her marriage to Germanicus, she would work tirelessly to guarantee she was the mother of emperors, a position Livia had used to wield great influence while Augustus ruled.

Despite flimsy evidence of his guilt, there was never any doubt about the outcome of Piso's trial. To forgo such an outcome and to protect his property from confiscation by the state, Piso committed suicide before the trial was decided. The fallout from this entire event, leading to the implacable animosity of Agrippina and her supporters, explains Tiberius's retreat into isolation in his later years and his increasing dependence on Sejanus. It is noteworthy that it was during these years of Tiberius's isolation that Jesus undertook his public ministry.

Tiberius's son, Drusus, now moved into the role of heir apparent. In 22 AD, Drusus was duly awarded tribunician powers, an honor Tiberius had denied to Germanicus. He was also given guardianship over two of Germanicus's sons. But, in only a year, whatever plans Tiberius had for his son dissolved as Drusus died. Although the reason for his death was a mystery at the time, Sejanus's estranged wife, Apicata, later wrote a suicide note accusing Livilla (Drusus's wife and Germanicus's sister) and Sejanus of murdering him. As we will see, there is every reason to believe her accusation.

Hoping to return some level of political stability to a chaotic situation, Tiberius entrusted the Senate with the care of Germanicus's sons. Tiberius was clearly trying to demonstrate his concern not only for the proper upbringing of Germanicus's sons but also that they were being educated to one day become emperors. This may have been enough for anyone else, but Tiberius failed to comprehend Agrippina's need for retribution. Instead, their mutual animosity fed years of insults and political infighting, which the clever Sejanus employed for his advancement and quest for power.

TWENTY-TWO

The Rise of Sejanus

We first met Sejanus when he was part of the entourage that accompanied Gaius Caesar to the East. He stood out because he was among the few ranking Romans traveling with Gaius who treated Tiberius respectfully. Tiberius, now emperor of Rome, had not forgotten Sejanus's kindness toward him. In 14 AD, Lucius Aelius Sejanus was made the joint commander of the Praetorian Guard, alongside his father, Seius Strabo. When, the following year, Strabo was made prefect of Egypt, Sejanus assumed sole command of the Guard. At the time, the Guard consisted of nine cohorts of a thousand men each, billeted throughout Rome and in the surrounding towns. This disbursement was ordered by Augustus to keep their profile within Rome low and to make it difficult to rally the entire guard at one time in support of a coup. For the latter reason, Augustus also ordered that the Praetorians must always be commanded by someone of equestrian rank, making it impossible for a dangerous senatorial rival to control Italy's only organized military force. Although Sejanus was of equestrian rank, he was related on his mother's and father's sides to families of senators who had achieved consular status. Moreover, his adoption by Quintus Aelius Tubero gave him more relatives with senatorial rank, including adopted brothers who had been consuls.

Tiberius's faith in him grew when he was the first to bring the emperor's attention to the dangerous influence Agrippina could exercise over the Rhine legions. Later in his reign, Tiberius made it clear to all where Sejanus stood in the hierarchy of the emperor's court when he called Sejanus the "partner of his toils" and allowed statues of him to be erected in the forum, theaters, and legionary bases.* With Tiberius's permission, it could not have been done otherwise; Sejanus concentrated the scattered Praetorian cohorts into one camp so that they could receive all orders as a single body. Tacitus relates: "That the sight of their numbers and strength might give confidence to themselves, while it would strike terror into the citizens."† Sejanus spent considerable time in the new camp, creeping into their affections and personally selecting their centurions and tribunes. At the same time, he worked hard to ingratiate himself with the senators, employing the trust that Tiberius had in him to ensure the appointment of his favorites to important and lucrative offices in Rome and the provinces. By 30 AD, it seems clear that Sejanus held it within his sway to appoint every governor and prefect within the Empire. Thus, there is little doubt that Pontius Pilate was a creature of Sejanus, totally beholden to him for his position in Judea and whatever other ambitions he had once he returned to Rome.

How did Sejanus attain such power? There was only one way to power in Imperial Rome: through the emperor. One must gain the emperor's trust and then slowly collect power, always in the emperor's name. But who did Tiberius trust? Who could he trust? Surely he had friends from his youth and from his time with the armies. Tiberius did, in fact, place many of these men in positions of power as soon as he returned from his self-imposed exile in Rhodes. But, for his time, Tiberius was already an old man when he assumed the throne, and by 33 AD he was over seventy years old. Many, probably most, of his allies from his generation were already retired from public life or dead. The next generation had almost entirely

* Tacitus, *The Annals*, 4.2.
† Ibid.

cast its lot with the rising stars of their generation, particularly Germanicus and Gaius. Unfortunately for Tiberius, that loyalty had not been transferred to himself after their deaths. Instead, most of it went to Agrippina and her sons, as Tiberius was considered a spent force just waiting to die from old age. One wonders if the rising generation would have made the same choices if they had known he would still be in power a decade hence. Only Sejanus of that younger generation, at great political risk to himself, had befriended Tiberius when he was out of power. That single act had bought Sejanus considerable goodwill.

Sejanus cemented that goodwill by being a tireless and efficient administrator, and, thereby, relieving Tiberius of much tedious work. But if the relationship required more cement, fate provided it. While enjoying dinner in a natural cavern near Naples, a sudden fall of rocks buried many of those present, including Tiberius. When soldiers eventually dug their way through to the emperor, they found him lying on the ground, quite alive. Over him, on all fours, was Sejanus, who, rather than run as many did, had stayed with the aged emperor and used his own body to shield Tiberius from falling debris. When a man saves your life at tremendous risk to himself, one naturally trusts that man. From that moment on, Tiberius's faith in the loyalty of Sejanus was boundless.

In the meantime, Sejanus had done much to secure his position in the firmament surrounding the emperor. As these actions are revealed, one must remember that Sejanus's goal was to isolate the emperor until he was totally dependent upon himself. In many ways, the solitary Tiberius, who was increasingly put off by the never-ending demands placed upon him, made it easy for him. Did Sejanus want to be emperor? The jury is out and must remain out, as the parts of Tacitus's history for a crucial period (30–31 AD) no longer exist. It is known that he coveted an opportunity to marry into the emperor's family. He could have used such a marriage as a springboard to ultimate power after Tiberius's death. At the least, it could have propelled a future son to the throne. After years of diligent cultivation and intimidation of those holding senatorial rank, there certainly would have been many influential senators willing to support such a marriage. He also had the concentrated force of the Praetorians to back up any move with military power. Still, he was not of the senatorial class, and there would be loud opposition to an equestrian elevating himself above his station. There was also a genuine chance that the Roman mob might rebel at the idea.

But when all was said and done, it was the legions that mattered. And the legions still had an almost inexplicable reverence for the Julio-Claudian bloodline. Sejanus's rise to the throne would necessarily mean that Agrippina's sons, who had a direct bloodline to the revered Augustus, would be pushed aside. The legions would surely have been displeased to see Germanicus's sons deprived of their rightful inheritance. If they marched, then Sejanus was doomed, as the Praetorian Guard, used to living a life of considerable ease in Rome, was no match for the legions of the frontiers. The most likely answer then is that Sejanus wanted to exercise ultimate power while Tiberius lived by keeping the emperor isolated and dependent on him, and he hoped to do the same after Tiberius's death in his role as kingmaker. He likely understood that it was impossible for him to be emperor, but with careful political maneuvering and wise marriages, he could make his son or grandson emperor. Many have taken greater risks to achieve much less.

We have already seen the first major step Sejanus undertook to secure his power in Rome: the concentration of the Praetorians in one camp, an act that would have dire consequences for centuries, as the Praetorians set themselves up as kingmakers, subject only to the will of the legions. As commander of Rome's only military force within two hundred miles, Sejanus could physically threaten and intimidate any potential rival.

His next step was fraught with peril. Sejanus made ultimately successful advances to Drusus's wife, Livilla, and then drew her into a plot to murder Drusus, Tiberius's son, and heir. Drusus was a clear obstacle to all of Sejanus's ambitions, for he was younger than Sejanus and had sons of his own who would look to succeed him. If Drusus was alive to succeed Tiberius, Sejanus's role as kingmaker would go up in smoke. Moreover, the two men despised each other. Drusus complained often and bitterly about how close Sejanus was to Tiberius and of the power invested in the favorite when the emperor's son was available for duty. In one earlier incident, Drusus had raised a threatening hand to Sejanus. When Sejanus moved to defend himself, Drusus punched him in the

face. Sejanus wisely desisted from any further violence, but it was a humiliation a man of Sejanus's temperament was never going to let pass.
When Drusus was vested with tribunician powers while Tiberius was
clearly edging toward retirement, Sejanus knew his window to dispose of
a hated rival was closing.

As Tacitus tells it, Livilla, who had been a plain child, had become an
unsurpassed beauty in middle age and was an easy target for someone of
Sejanus's guile. Tacitus minces no words when presenting his thoughts on
the affair:

> When the first infamy had been achieved . . . he moved her to
> dream of marriage, a partnership in the empire, and the murder of
> her husband. And she, the grand-niece of Augustus, the daughter-
> in-law of Tiberius, the mother of Drusus' children, defiled herself,
> her ancestry, and her posterity, with a market-town adulterer, in
> order to change an honored estate in the present for the expecta-
> tion of a criminal and doubtful future.*

To convince Livilla that his marriage proposal was serious, Sejanus
divorced Apicata, the mother of his three children. Livilla's doctor, Eudemus, and a slave, the eunuch Lygdus, were then enlisted in the plot. Soon
after that, Drusus was poisoned with a substance known to mimic the
progress of a natural ailment. It would be nearly eight years before Tiberius learned from a letter sent by Apicata and confirmed in detail by
Eudemus and Lygdus, after they were tortured, that his son had been
murdered.

There remains a good deal of speculation as to the veracity of Apicata's letter, given that she wrote it immediately after her own children
had been executed. She had every reason to cause Tiberius as much pain
as possible while also having the satisfaction of destroying Livilla—the
woman who stole her husband. On the other hand, Sejanus hated Drusus
and needed him out of the way much sooner than Sejanus initially anticipated. Thus, from Sejanus's perspective, the timing of Drusus's death

* Tacitus, *The Annals*, 4.3.

could not have been better. If Sejanus did not have a hand in Drusus's death, then the fates were indeed showing him a benevolence they rarely bestowed on other humans.

Sejanus's next target was Agrippina, who could be counted on to move aggressively to secure the position of her and Germanicus's sons, Nero and Drusus. Clearly, Sejanus could not poison three enemies, all in the same household. Moreover, Agrippina, renowned for her virtue in widowhood, was impossible to seduce. But with Drusus disposed of, there was no need to hurry. If Agrippina could not be attacked directly, indirectly would do. Thus, Sejanus launched a series of judicial attacks on her supporters and close associates. Remarkably, by making it appear to Agrippina that Tiberius was orchestrating these judicial assaults, Sejanus positioned himself as a trusted confidant of Agrippina without losing the confidence of Tiberius.

There is no need to detail the many prosecutions that Sejanus engineered during these years. It is enough to say that his attacks were successful in removing many of Agrippina's most powerful supporters from the political chessboard, as a result of execution, suicide, or exile. Sejanus was so overwhelmed by his success that he made a rare political mistake: In a letter, he asked Tiberius for the hand of his mistress, Livilla. If he was successful, Sejanus would have placed himself squarely in the middle of Tiberius's reduced family, gained some control over Tiberius's only grandson, Tiberius Gemellus, and further isolated Agrippina. Tiberius did not forbid the marriage but clearly demonstrated his displeasure at the suggestion. In a letter of his own, Tiberius reminded Sejanus that he had many enemies and that it was only Tiberius's continued friendship that kept him from danger. Thoroughly alarmed, Sejanus put aside his ideas for marriage and returned to his patient removal of his enemies and further isolation of Tiberius.

He was successful on both fronts, as Tiberius found Rome and its environs increasingly wearisome. In 26 AD, the emperor, in the twelfth year of his reign, departed Rome for Capri. He never returned to the Eternal City. For the next eleven years, Tiberius ruled from afar, and until his downfall, the emperor ruled mostly through Sejanus, who now controlled access to Capri. Before he departed, Tiberius had one final run-in with Agrippina, which proved disastrous to her future, as it turned Tiberius decisively against her. Sejanus's spies in Agrippina's household had convinced her that Tiberius was looking for opportunities to poison her. So, the next time she was invited to court for dinner, she made a show of refusing to eat. Tiberius took note and personally offered her some apples from a nearby basket. More suspicious than ever, Agrippina refused the offer. Disgusted, Tiberius turned away, commenting that people should not be surprised that he was ill-disposed to someone who openly accused him of such villainy.

With Tiberius in a self-imposed exile to Capri, Agrippina was exposed. Sejanus immediately pounced, accusing Nero, Agrippina's oldest son and the closest to succession, of a litany of crimes, even employing his brother, Drusus, to inform on Nero's most indiscreet comments. These comments and many others fed to Sejanus by his numerous spies were enhanced and then forwarded to Tiberius in Capri. Of course, since Sejanus controlled all information leaving Rome for Tiberius, the emperor never heard Agrippina's side of the story. Tiberius seemed all too willing to have his suspicions of Agrippina, her family, and her supporters confirmed, all the more so if the reports came from Sejanus, the "partner in his toils."

However, Augustus's widow (and Tiberius's mother), Livia, had remained in Rome, and only she could keep Sejanus's ambitions in check. Despite her detestation of Agrippina, she would not countenance a direct attack on the family of Germanicus. As she was impossible to sway or intimidate, Sejanus bided his time. When she died in 29 AD, Agrippina lost whatever protection Livia afforded her.

With Agrippina and Nero busily defending themselves from direct accusations, their remaining supporters became easy targets, allowing Sejanus to use the courts to rapidly remove them from the playing field. Finally, in late 29 BC, he judged the time right for a direct assault on the family of Germanicus. During the trial of one of the last remaining supporters, Titus Sabinus, charges were made that implicated Agrippina and her sons in treacherous plans to overthrow Tiberius. Orders soon came from Capri that eventually led to the arrest of Agrippina, Nero, Drusus, and their few remaining supporters.

How all of this was resolved is now lost to history. Tacitus's chapter dealing with this crucial year no longer exists; Dio's account is only available in small fragments, leaving only a brief report from Suetonius to finish this horrid tale. Agrippina was exiled to Pandateria, where she continued to reproach Tiberius until a centurion beat her so severely that she lost an eye. After this, she attempted to starve herself to death, but, according to Suetonius: "her mouth was pried open, and food crammed into it."* She eventually died of starvation in 33 AD. Her son Nero was accused of shameful sexual activities, declared a public enemy, and was taken in chains to the island of Pontia, where he either was killed or committed suicide. Drusus was imprisoned on the Palatine and reportedly died of starvation after being reduced to eating the straw in his bedding. Only two male members of the Julio-Claudian line were still alive: Germanicus's surviving son Gaius (Caligula) was now eighteen, but not considered, as of yet, a serious political player, and Drusus's son, Tiberius Gemellus, was only ten years old.

As the year 31 AD began, all treated Sejanus as the first man in Rome. He was at the height of his power and had only to wait for the aged Tiberius to die to start placing his own offspring in the line of succession. His opportunities for doing so had hugely enlarged, as Tiberius had finally allowed his betrothal to Livilla. As a final mark of his success, word came from Capri that Sejanus would be one of the two consuls for the year 31 AD, joined by Tiberius. Only twice before had Tiberius joined another consul—in 18 AD with Germanicus and 21 AD with his son Drusus—both, at the time, widely recognized heirs to the throne. Just possibly, Sejanus must have thought, it was possible to make himself an emperor.

---

* Suetonius, *The Twelve Caesars*, 53.

The Fall of Sejanus

We know nothing about the exact circumstances that turned Tiberius against his most trusted subordinate, leaving one historian to ask: "Why did Tiberius destroy the man he had raised above all others, the one man he had trusted in his loneliness and fear?"* Reportedly, Tiberius wrote in his autobiography that he turned on Sejanus when he discovered his role in the punishments accorded Agrippina and her family. But, as Agrippina, Nero, and Drusus were all still alive when Sejanus was executed and were not released from captivity afterward, it is difficult to credit Tiberius's veracity. There is fragmentary evidence indicating Sejanus was planning a coup, but this is hard to believe, as Sejanus's power still rested on Tiberius's active support. Even in 30 AD, with his power at its pinnacle, neither the Roman mob nor the legions were inclined to accept him as emperor. Moreover, the speed with which the Praetorian Guard later deserted him—after Sejanus spent over a decade cultivating their support—indicates that they always viewed his command over them as derived from the emperor.

But what is possible, even probable, is that Sejanus saw that his future was tied to achieving the guardianship of Tiberius Gemellus. But in that

---

* Robin Seager, *Tiberius*, 2nd ed. (Blackwell Publishing, 2005), p. 180.

case, the next in line of Germanicus and Agrippina's sons, Gaius (Caligula), who was now reaching adulthood, had to be disposed of, probably in much the same way Sejanus had destroyed the rest of the family. A letter from Antonia, Gaius's grandmother and Tiberius's sister-in-law, warning Tiberius that Sejanus was planning to move against Gaius and that the youth needed protection, forced the emperor to shake off his sloth. Tiberius immediately sent for Gaius to be brought to Capri, where he was secure from any attack Sejanus had planned.

Antonia's letter also sparked Tiberius to further action. For over a decade and a half, Tiberius had trusted Sejanus above all else, but for the first time, he realized he had been duped. He now comprehended that he had not been the guiding force of the partnership, allowing Sejanus to do his bidding. Instead, Sejanus had led him about by the nose with a single-minded determination to increase his *auctoritas* and power. Once the suspicion that Sejanus had outsmarted him was planted in Tiberius's mind, Sejanus's days were numbered.* Assuming Antonia's warning was the driving force behind Tiberius's destruction of his previous favorite makes sense, at least as an ex post facto justification. Tiberius clearly saw himself as protecting Agrippina's children by taking in Gaius. Moreover, he could claim that his continued persecution of Germanicus's son Drusus, who died in 33 AD, was a consequence of Drusus allying with Sejanus to help bring down his brother, Nero.

Tiberius's long brooding silences could easily be interpreted as his being slow-witted, likely making it easy for Sejanus to forget that Tiberius was far more intelligent and cunning than his slow and often plodding manner let on. Only a few Greek philosophers Tiberius always kept in his court were ever treated to the full range of his gifted intellect. For many, though, his constant huddles with learned Greeks seemed un-Roman, even unmanly. But, at his core, Tiberius was always a man of action. One is left to wonder how those around him allowed themselves to forget that Tiberius spent over two decades of his life fighting on Rome's many battlefields. He was, after Agrippa, Augustus's finest military commander. Once he had decided upon action, Tiberius planned

---

* Seager, *Tiberius*, p. 182.

meticulously, prepared for every eventuality, and then struck with such ruthless efficiency that his enemies were often defeated before they fully comprehended their peril. Sejanus was about to be treated to a display of the Tiberius that had commanded the Rhine frontier against Rome's most vicious and brutal enemies.

Plan, prepare, act; it was a mantra Tiberius had followed his entire life. In taking down Sejanus, the first two items of this mantra were crucial, for Sejanus was now the power in Rome. As Dio relates:

> Sejanus was growing greater and more formidable all the time, so that the senators and the rest looked up to him as if he were actually emperor and held Tiberius in slight esteem . . . Sejanus had completely won over the entire Praetorian guard and had gained the favor of the senators, partly by the benefits he conferred, partly by the hopes he inspired, and partly by intimidation . . . [Senators] sacrificed to the images of Sejanus as they did to those of Tiberius.[*]

First, Sejanus was lulled into a new sense of security. So, besides announcing that Tiberius had deigned to share the consulship with Sejanus in the next year, rumors were also allowed to circulate that Sejanus would be given tribunician powers, always before reserved to those destined to rule the Empire. Once bestowed upon him, Sejanus would have virtually the same legal powers as Tiberius. Therefore, Sejanus must have felt pretty good about his prospects in the days and hours before Tiberius struck.

Events now happened very quickly. During the night of October 17, 31 AD, Naevius Sutorius Macro arrived from Capri. He carried a letter from Tiberius removing Sejanus as Praetorian prefect and naming Macro as his replacement. He entered the city before dawn and went directly to the most loyal of the current consuls, Memmius Regulus. Regulus also commanded the night guard, which acted as a police force and was armed. It could not stand against the Praetorians but could make its presence

* Dio, *The Roman History*, 58.4.

felt, particularly if the Roman mob rallied to Tiberius's support. As dawn approached on October 18, Macro made his way to the Palatine, where the Senate met at the Temple of Apollo. At the temple's entrance, he ran into Sejanus, who had not yet entered the building. In a private discussion, Sejanus expressed his disquiet about not having heard anything official from Tiberius about granting tribunician powers. To put Sejanus at ease, Macro confided that he carried with him Tiberius's instructions to the Senate to bestow that singular honor upon him.

An ebullient Sejanus then strode confidently into the temple, taking his accustomed place of honor among the senators. Macro then showed the Praetorians guarding the Senate, and those personally guarding Sejanus, Tiberius's orders placing him in command of the guard, and ordered them to return to camp. He also informed them that the same letter from Tiberius bestowed a large donative that would be distributed to the guard soon. Tiberius fully comprehended that if the Praetorians' loyalty were torn, financial gains would sway them in his favor. As his compatriot Graecinius Laco, commander of Rome's night watch (the *vgilum*), placed his forces on guard in place of the departing Praetorians, Macro entered the Senate and handed Tiberius's letter to the other consul to be read aloud to the Senate. Before a word was read, however, he rushed to the Praetorian camp to ensure they had gotten word of Tiberius's generous donative and stave off any revolt in favor of Sejanus.

While Macro rushed to appease the Praetorians, Tiberius's letter was read. It was a long read that took time to reach its main points. First, it addressed other matters, and then there was a slight censure of Sejanus, followed by another switch in topics, and then another rebuke of the favorite. As the letter progressed, it became increasingly clear that Sejanus was being condemned, so much so that the sycophants surrounding Sejanus moved to the far corners of the room. At the letter's conclusion, Tiberius ordered the punishment of two senators who were Sejanus's closest associates and that Sejanus be kept under guard.

The assembled senators were shocked. Just moments before, they had surrounded Sejanus, cheering and congratulating him on the expected bestowment of tribunician powers. They all vied for his acknowledgment, telling him they fully concurred with Tiberius's decision to award him this new honor. But Tiberius's final instruction to hold Sejanus under guard was all that was needed for the senators to understand what was expected of them. As soon as the letter was read, praetors and tribunes surrounded Sejanus, preventing him from causing a disturbance or rushing out of the building. They need not have worried, as Sejanus was frozen in place as he tried to process his sudden fall from grace.

Eventually, Regulus summoned him to go forward. Sejanus, in shock, remained seated. According to Dio: "[Regulus] called the second and third time, 'Sejanus, come here.' He merely asked him, 'Me? you are calling me?'" Sejanus slowly rose, allowing Laco to move behind him, intending to lead him away. But the assembled senators, determined to demonstrate their loyalty to Tiberius, started shouting denouncements. With the help of the night watch, Laco eventually led the condemned man to prison.

It was a remarkable reversal of fortune. As dawn broke, Sejanus had been the man of the hour, surrounded by fawning sycophants and supplicants. But by afternoon, he was being dragged off to prison while the mob assailed him with insults and rotten food. Sejanus could see his statues being pulled down and his portraits being dragged through the mud as he walked. This was but a foretaste of what lay ahead for him. The Senate, recovering from the morning's shock, reconvened at the Temple of Concord, not far from the prison where Sejanus awaited his fate. Although Tiberius had not stated what to do with Sejanus after he was arrested, the senators were very well aware that this was Tiberius's way. Virtually all of Tiberius's instructions were opaque, as he expected his subordinates to divine his intent from whatever information he deigned to give them. Few doubted what was expected now, but they hesitated, waiting to see which way the mob was tilting and how the Praetorians would react to Sejanus's arrest. But the mob quickly revealed its mind, as the streets were soon occupied with tens of thousands screaming for Sejanus's death. More crucially, as the hours passed and the Praetorians remained in their camp, the senators increasingly discovered some small reservoirs of courage. It helped that most realized that after the course of events had played out, their own safety might depend on how quickly they changed sides and how vocal they were in Sejanus's condemnation.

The order for Sejanus's immediate execution was given, as well as instructions for the body to be thrown down the stairs of *Scalae Gemoniae*. This last order was meant as a message to Tiberius, as only the most heinous criminals were thrown down the stairs and their bodies left exposed to the abuse of the mob, before being torn apart by the dogs that prowled Rome during the night. What little remained of Sejanus was thrown into the river three days after he was executed. Not sure they had done enough to appease Tiberius, the senators also condemned Sejanus's children to death.

His son, Captio Aelianus, was old enough to understand what was happening and stoically awaited his fate. Sejanus's daughter, Junilla, was too young to grasp what was going on. Tacitus says, "[She was] so innocent that she kept asking what she had done wrong and where they were taking her, that she would not do it again and surely could be punished with a trivial beating."* Because it was against Roman law to execute a virgin, a rope was tied around Junilla's neck before she was raped and then strangled. The bodies of both children were thrown down the *Scalae Gemoniae*.

Sejanus's former wife, Apicata, was not condemned, but when she learned of her children's executions, she immediately went to view the bodies lying at the bottom of the stairway. Unable to remove or protect the broken bodies, the distraught mother withdrew to compose a letter to Tiberius. In it, she revealed that Sejanus had conspired with Livilla to murder Drusus, Tiberius's son. She then committed suicide. Upon reading the letter and verifying it through the tortures of other persons implicated in the plot, Tiberius's wrath was fearsome. Livilla and everyone mentioned in Apicata's letter were immediately put to death. Then, Tiberius struck out at Sejanus's supporters. Sejanus's death was followed by a wide-sweeping purge of anyone deemed a Sejanus partisan. The mob lynched some in the days following Sejanus's fall, and many others were

---

* Tacitus, *The Annales*, 5.9 (fragment).

killed during a long series of trials and executions that lasted well into 32 AD, and possibly far into the next year.

This last point is crucial to our understanding of Jesus's crucifixion. As we shall see, Jesus was likely crucified early in April of 33 AD, about eighteen months after Sejanus's execution in mid-October of 31 AD. At the time, it took an average of about three months for news to reach Judea from Rome, although important news could be carried somewhat faster. As winter was approaching, when almost all sea travel ended, it is fair to say that Pontius Pilate in distant Judea may not have heard about Sejanus's fall until the late spring of 32 AD, or later. Keeping in mind that many of Sejanus's supporters and acolytes were spread throughout the provinces and had to be recalled for trial and probable execution, the post-Sejanus purges could not possibly have ended until late in 32 AD at the earliest, and they likely continued beyond that date. But, if we assume an early end to the purges, in November or December of 32, then it was quite probable that when Jesus went on trial, Pilate believed the purges were continuing. And even if he knew they had ended, he would still have been looking over his shoulder, as any disturbance in Judea would attract Tiberius's watchful eye. As a friend and appointee of Sejanus, Pilate could not afford for anyone, particularly Tiberius, to harbor any doubt that he could control the always troublesome Jews. Pilate was only too aware that it would take very little for Tiberius to order him home for a fast trial and a slow execution.

TWENTY-FOUR

33 AD's Other Great Catastrophe

Economic crises, such as the ones the world has become accustomed to since the near-total collapse of the global financial system in 2008, are nothing new to history, and the ancient world was not immune from such crises. In 33 AD, one of the few financial crises that made it into the ancient historical record began in Rome and possibly spread across the Empire. Unfortunately, only a few specifics of this event are known to historians. Still, this lack of information has not stopped pundits from elaborating at great length about the crisis's course and its impacts across the Empire's breadth. Anyone undertaking some basic research comparing economic crises across the ages would soon come across this story of what took place in 33 AD, which has been widely reprinted across the internet, even by many reputable persons and journals:

> Tiberius also saw the contagion spreading from the Senate's corruption that crippled the banking system. The firm Seuthes and Sons, of Alexandria, was a firm facing difficulties because of the loss of three richly laden ships in a Red Sea storm, followed by a fall in the value of ostrich feathers and ivory. Nearly at the same time, there was the house of Malchus and Co. of Tyre with branches at Antioch and Ephesus. They suddenly became bank-

rupt as a result of a strike among their Phoenician workmen and the embezzlement of a freedman manager. These two failures also affected the Roman banking house Quintus Maximus and Lucious Vibo operating in the Roman forum.

These events set in motion bank runs, which then impacted another major Roman banking house of the Brothers Pittius. The Wall Street of the day in the Forum was the Via Sacra, which erupted in panic as merchants were now impacted by the collapse in banking and money supply. There was then also a rebellion among the people of northern Gaul, so now the emerging markets went into crisis as well. Money was contracting as nobody would lend and hoarding soared.

When Publius Spencer, a wealthy nobleman, requested 30 million sesterces from his banker Balbus Ollius, the firm was unable to fulfill his request and closed its doors. Over the next few days, prominent banks in Corinth, Carthage, Lyons, and Byzantium announced they had to *"rearrange their accounts,"* i.e., they had failed. This led to a banking panic and the closure of several banks along the Via Sacra in Rome.

This is both a magnificent and harrowing story of financial contagion running out of control. But not a word of it is proven true. The source can be traced to two economic historians, William Stearns Davis and Otto C. Lightner, one building upon the other at the start of the twentieth century.* As Davis admitted in his work, he was presenting what he found in Tacitus's and Suetonius's work "a little expanded." By "a little expanded," Davis told an entirely new story. This is what is known from Tacitus, Suetonius, and Dio:

Hence followed a scarcity of money, a great shock being given to all credit, the current coin too, in consequence of the conviction of so many persons and the sale of their property, being locked up

* See William Stearns Davis, *The Influence of Wealth in Imperial Rome* (Macmillan, 1910), and Otto C. Lightner, *The History of Business Depressions* (Northeastern Press, 1922).

in the imperial treasury or the public exchequer. To meet this, the
Senate had directed that every creditor should have two-thirds of
his capital secured on estates in Italy. Creditors however were
suing for payment in full, and it was not respectable for persons
when sued to break faith. So, at first, there were clamorous meetings and importunate treaties; then noisy applications to the prae-
tor's court. And the very device intended as a remedy, the sale and
purchase of estates, proved the contrary, as the usurers had hoarded
up all their money for buying land. The facilities for selling were
followed by a fall of prices, and the deeper a man was in debt, the
more reluctantly did he part with his property, and many were utterly ruined.*

Suetonius and Dio agree with Tacitus without adding any new crucial
information. Suetonius states: "He [Tiberius] had ratified a decree of the
senate obliging all money-lenders to advance two-thirds of their capital
on land, and the debtors to pay off at once the same proportion of their
debts, and it was found insufficient to remedy the grievance.† According
to Dio, one senator poisoned himself, while another, Nerva, "who could
no longer endure the emperor's society, starved himself to death, chiefly
because Tiberius had reaffirmed the laws on contracts enacted by Caesar,
which were sure to result in great loss of confidence and financial
confusion."‡

It is necessary to closely examine what little Tacitus has left for us to
understand what was happening. First, the underlying law that Tiberius
set out to enforce was passed nearly fifty years before. It ordered that
two-thirds of any wealthy person's capital must be invested in land and
forbade anyone to hold more than sixty thousand sesterces in ready cash.
This was clearly a wartime measure meant to stop the wealthy from
hoarding cash and to prevent a precipitate collapse in land values. Why
Tiberius sought to start enforcing a fifty-year-old law that no one had
paid attention to for over five decades is a mystery, only explainable by

* Tacitus, *The Annals*, 6.17.
† Suetonius, *Tiberius*, 48.
‡ Dio, *The Roman History*, 58.21.

two factors: first, that he had no conception of the economic impact of such a move, and second, Tiberius's well-known reverence for all laws.

The first thing to consider in such a situation is the state of Roman finances at the time and what had changed. Here we must remember the financial impact of the Roman civil wars, which forced both sides to coin huge amounts of ready cash and to spend liberally. In doing so, they flooded the economy with cash, lowering interest rates and artificially raising the price of real estate. One might have expected this excess spending to end when the civil wars ended, but Augustus was a liberal spender. He had taken the Egyptian treasuries of Cleopatra, and according to his personal testament of his life, the *Res Gestae*, he spent six hundred million sesterces—double the cost for funding Rome's entire military for a year at the start of the first century—purchasing plots of land for tens of thousands of discharged veterans, sending real estate values soaring. By his own testimony, he also lavished huge sums on the people of Rome, rebuilt all of the roads in Italy, restored eighty-two major temples, and built many new ones. Moreover, he provided for the building of aqueducts, public baths, and temples in many of Italy's cities. Such extravagant spending, likely more than twice Rome's previous non-wartime spending levels, was paid for first by what was taken from the east, second by the opening of new mines and mints in Spain, and finally by increasing the tribute required from the provinces, particularly Gaul.

By the end of his reign, Augustus was slowing his spending, but the amount of coin in circulation continued to expand. All of this came to an abrupt halt during Tiberius's reign. Tiberius was notorious for his miserly attitude toward the public purse. While Augustus had left him with an almost bare treasury, Tiberius left nearly three billion sesterces for his successor.* This large contraction of government spending would have made itself felt under any circumstances. It was worsened by the fact that huge sums required to pay the legions were now being spent far from Italy, along the Roman frontiers. Moreover, there is evidence that large sums of capital were leaving Italy and being invested in the now peaceful and stable provinces, where returns were better. Tenney Frank blames

* Suetonius, *Gaius*, 37.3.

Rome's love of eastern luxuries for creating a trade imbalance with India, continually draining gold and silver from the Empire.* Frank probably overstates this case, but it was perhaps a minor contributing factor to a general decrease in coin within the Empire, particularly in Italy.

The currency contraction, when added to a government-induced slowing of the economy, was almost certainly causing increasing economic pain throughout the second half of Tiberius's reign. The crises began when Tiberius tried to command a lowering of interest rates, which always rose when there was a large and sustained currency contraction. When the Senate decreed that the old laws dealing with land investments would be enforced, it added fuel to the fire.

Land prices had been falling for decades, likely in a direct ratio to the dwindling currency in the economy. Tiberius likely thought enforcing Julius Caesar's defunct law would prop up prices by forcing large investments into real estate. Unfortunately, it had the exact opposite effect. Most of Rome's rich, particularly the senatorial class, disdained industry and avoided buying land for many years, which they viewed as a constantly depreciating asset. Many of them turned to lending money to others to make a profit. Often, they were so desperate to lend out their accumulated cash that they would force borrowers to take their funds, which was relatively easy to do in the provinces, where local elites were constantly on the lookout for ways to curry favor with influential Romans. Thus, when the order came to invest their fortunes in land, the rich were forced to call in almost all of their loans to raise the money for land investments. Many borrowers could not meet the sudden payment demands and were immediately bankrupted. Others began selling off their lands to raise cash to pay back their loans, creating a glutted real estate market and a price collapse. Even those who had cash now held off on buying land as they waited for rampant deflationary pressure to do its job and further lower prices.

It was the perfect financial storm, and Tiberius acted with dispatch. Channeling his inner Keynes, nearly two thousand years before the econ-

---

* Tenney Frank, "The Financial Crisis of 33 AD," *The American Journal of Philology*, Vol. 56, no. 4 (1935), pp. 336–341.

omist John Maynard Keynes explained his ideas for fixing the Great Depression, Tiberius broke open his piggybank. According to Tacitus, once again supported by the testimony of Dio and Suetonius:

> The destruction of private wealth precipitated the fall of rank and reputation, till at last the emperor interposed his aid by distributing throughout the banks a hundred million sesterces, and allowing freedom to borrow without interest for three years, provided the borrower gave security to the State in land to double the amount. Credit was thus restored, and gradually private lenders were found. The purchase too of estates was not carried out according to the letter of the Senate's decree, rigor at the outset, as usual with such matters, becoming negligence in the end.[*]

In other words, Tiberius used government funds to bail out the rich to forestall a further economic collapse. Does this sound familiar?

It is difficult to determine the long-term impact of the crisis as we have no information on its aftermath. We can assume that Tiberius's massive addition of liquidity to the system worked, as we would expect our ancient commentators to have given us more information if it had failed. We can, however, make several assumptions based on what we now know about economic theory, and couple that knowledge with what we know about later events. First, Tiberius's cash infusion would have been about the same as half the cost of Rome's entire military establishment for about a year. So, it was by no means insignificant. Still, it represented less than a twentieth of the funds he had accumulated in the treasury, meaning he had tremendous financial ammunition to spare, and he never considered the crisis so bad that it was necessary to deploy any of his remaining cash hoard. That tells us that the crisis was sharp but of short duration. From this, we can probably say that the crisis was also likely limited to Italy, although one wonders if distant governors, such as Pontius Pilate, who had left the bulk of the wealth in Italy, were seriously impacted.

---

[*] Tacitus, *The Annals*, 6.17.

Tiberius's actions, however, did nothing to address the underlying cause of the crisis. Moreover, he risked reigniting the crisis by demanding that the hundred million sesterces he loaned out be repaid in three years. Consider what is going on in the global economy today, when after over a decade of easy money—quantitative easing—the world's central banks have several times tried to remove excess cash from the system to hold inflation in check. In doing so, they are knowingly risking collapsing global markets and pushing the world into a painful recession. The same is true of Tiberius's time. As that cash was removed, and with no indication that he would increase spending, the Roman economy was courting a prolonged recession and possibly a destabilizing depression. This never occurred, as Tiberius died before the debt was called, and his successors opened up the spending spigots. In fact, Tiberius's colossal accumulation of financial reserves was spent in a historical twinkling. Clearly, his immediate successors did not consider their hold on power as secure as Tiberius thought his. They certainly were not secure enough in their positions to willingly risk another financial crisis.

PART VII

PASSION WEEK

TWENTY-FIVE

Reconstructing Jesus's Last Week

The events of the first three days of Jesus's last week are easily summarized. Six days before Passover, he arrived in Bethany, a two-mile walk from Jerusalem's walls, where he visited with close friends: Mary and Martha, and their brother, Lazarus. He quickly went to Jerusalem, where he was greeted as a conquering hero. Then that same night he was back in Bethany. He left early the following day for Jerusalem, where he created a disturbance at the Temple, before again returning to Bethany. Once again, he made his way back into Jerusalem the next day, where he escaped an ambush set by the Sanhedrin. That's the gist of it, but what happens when historians unpack these isolated events within the context of Jesus's time?

SUNDAY

As Jesus approached Jerusalem from the east, through nearby Jericho, crowds gathered around him. As he approached the city gates, thousands of Passover pilgrims, already within the city's environs, rushed to greet him. There was a reported miracle worker from the House of David, referring to himself as the Messiah while hinting at being a king and promising a new kingdom free from Roman rule, making his way toward Israel's capital city, escorted by a core of loyal supporters, some of whom were armed. Taking all of these items together creates quite a calling card. If Jesus aimed to attract Rome's attention, he was making an excellent start.

At least a few times along the route, Jesus stopped to address the crowds. During these talks, often delivered in parables, Jesus never gave his followers any reason to doubt their hopes and preconceptions that he was a man of the sword. For instance, he ended his Parable of the Ten Servants (Parable of the Minas) by saying: "But as for my enemies, those who had not wanted me to be king over them, bring them here, and slay them in front of me." Many explanations have been presented over the centuries for this comment, but we should interpret it within the context of Judea in 33 AD. His audience would clearly have heard a call to arms from someone they sincerely believed was their savior.*

At some point, a couple of his apostles had procured a donkey and a colt for Jesus to ride into Jerusalem. Interestingly, Jesus could tell the apostles he sent to retrieve the animals exactly where they would be found. If we remove divine knowledge from the process, as we should, then clearly, Jesus had coordinated earlier with someone within the city to have the animals ready. The choice of a donkey rather than a horse is another thing that has sparked centuries of debate, leading to a shaky scholarly consensus that riding a donkey was a sign of peaceful intent. Why such an act would be perceived as peaceful is never adequately explained. We should probably take Matthew at his word when he tells us it was meant to fulfill a prophecy made by the prophet Zechariah, one that every Jew would have known: "Rejoice greatly, Daughter Zion [Israel]. Look your king comes to you, righteous and victorious, lowly riding on a donkey."† For a Jew watching this event, the fulfillment of the prophecy meant that a king that would lead them against Rome had arrived. They believed this because, besides the lines from Zechariah, quoted by Matthew, they also knew the rest of the prophecy. For Zecha-

---

* Many scholars believe the Parable of the Minas refers to Herod's son Archelaus's trip to Rome to get the emperor's approval for him to rule Judea in the wake of his father's death. Even if Jesus was anchoring this parable in a story that his listeners would have known, I believe the message they would have taken from it remains the same.
† Matthew 21:1–5.

riah had told them their king would rule to the ends of the earth and make the sons of Zion "like a warrior's sword."*

Jesus may very well have been talking about the Kingdom of Heaven or a distant judgment day, but that is not what a Jew, under Roman rule, would have heard. Instead, they were hearing a rallying cry to war. For, Zechariah continues: "Then the Lord will appear over them; his arrow will flash like lightning. The Sovereign Lord will sound the trumpet; he will march in the storms of the south . . . They will destroy and overcome with slingstones . . . The Lord their God will save his people on that day.†

Peaceful prophets are rarely allotted triumphal entries on the scale Jesus received. As the gospel traditions tell us, thousands of people lined the road's sides, throwing their cloaks and palm leaves on the ground before Jesus's advance. Christianity has reinterpreted palm leaves as a symbol of peace, but no one in the ancient world would have thought that. The Jews who greeted Jesus threw their cloaks before him—a symbol of submission to a king. They also threw palm leaves, which throughout the ancient Mediterranean symbolized glory and victory. For instance, in ancient Greece and Rome the gods of victory, Nike and Victoria, are almost always pictured carrying palm leaves as a symbol of victory in sport and war.

As Jesus rode the donkey down into the Kidron Valley, he followed the same route that King David's son Solomon had traveled centuries before when he arrived on his father's mule to be proclaimed king. Zadok the priest and Nathan the prophet anointed Solomon and the assembled people shouted, "Long live King Solomon!"‡ As Solomon rode into Jerusalem the people were playing flutes, rejoicing, and shouting "so that the earth shook at their noise." Now, in 33 AD Jesus was riding across this same valley and on up into the city of Jerusalem—atop the clothing, the palm fronds, and the leafy branches, and surrounded by the people's loud welcome. Those who knew the history of the Davidic dynasty, as most Jews did, would have understood Jesus was arriving as a king.

Supposedly, as he got close to the city, Jesus wept and predicted a

---

* Zechariah 9:10–13.
† Zechariah 9:14–16.
‡ 1 Kings 1:32–40.

harsh future for Jerusalem: "For the days will come upon you that your enemies will throw a palisade up against you, and encircle you, and press in on you from every side . . . you and your children within you, and there will not be left within you a stone upon a stone . . ."* Many biblical scholars claim that Jesus was predicting the destruction of the city and the Temple that took place during the Great Revolt that began in 66 AD, thirty-three years after Jesus's death. But why would Jesus make a statement that none of his followers could possibly have understood as a prediction for an event a generation hence? Such an interpretation had no relevance for the thousands listening to him.† On the other hand, it makes more sense within the context of the time, particularly if he was talking or warning his followers of the consequences they would suffer if they revolted against Rome. Remember that Jesus had grown up near Sepphoris, which was destroyed by Rome the last time the Jews had revolted. The destruction was so complete that those who returned to the rebuilt city, previously a hotbed of insurrection, refused to join the Great Revolt of 66 AD. Even if a contemporary Jewish revolt in 33 AD could easily have seized Jerusalem, Jesus was not under any illusion as to the results of the Roman counter-attack. When the legions arrived from Syria, which they were sure to do, it would have meant the end of Jerusalem. In any event, as Jesus's followers could not possibly have comprehended that he was talking about an incident still a generation hence, what they heard was a call to war and a warning that it was going to be a hard and destructive struggle.

According to Matthew, Jesus's arrival in Jerusalem threw the city into an uproar. At some point, a group of Pharisees, scared that the growing disturbances would force a Roman reaction, begged Jesus to rebuke his followers and get them under control. Jesus's answer was simple: "I tell you, if these [his followers] go silent, the stones will cry out."‡ Again, religious scholars have tied themselves in knots trying to explain Jesus's

---

* Luke 19:43–44.
† We have already discussed the fact that the Gospels were most likely written before the destruction of the Temple. Thus, this is not a concoction of later authors who may have been traumatized by the destruction of Jerusalem by the Romans.
‡ Luke 19:40.

meaning. The current consensus is that Jesus's words mean that the truth will always win out, even if human voices are silenced. There is, however, a simpler answer, and it is probably the one the Pharisees believed Jesus intended to convey. Keep in mind the passage from Zechariah above: The enemies of the king will be "destroyed and overcome by slingstones." Everyone who heard Jesus speak that day would have understood Jesus's reference to the "stones crying out" as a direct threat, for an easy interpretation within the context of the moment is: If you Pharisees try to stop what is going on, stones will fly. This is the same as if, in our own time, someone says, "If you stop the people from demonstrating, then the guns will speak."

Still, Jesus did not tarry for long in Jerusalem. He got as far as the Temple, but as evening approached, he and his apostles turned back toward Bethany. His trip that day was obviously planned; if it was not, how did he know where to send his apostles to pick up a waiting donkey and its colt? But then why did he not leave at an earlier hour that morning, allowing him time to accomplish more than just a walk to the Temple and then a walk back to Mary's and Martha's farm? Given what occurred at the Temple the next day, is it unreasonable to conclude that he had come to Jerusalem to conduct a final coordination meeting for the main event?

MONDAY

The next morning, Jesus set out again for Jerusalem, only stopping once to deliver another parable and to curse a fig tree. According to all four canonical Gospel accounts, upon arriving at the Temple, Jesus drove out all those selling and buying in the Temple courts, starting with an assault on the money changers' tables. John adds that Jesus employed a whip to drive the money changers out of the Temple.* All of the gospel writers also agree that this act triggered the arrest, trial, and execution of Jesus.

Why?

---

* John 2:15–16. Some historians believe that John was recounting a separate incident at the Temple, when Jesus was just starting his public ministry. If this is true, one wonders why he did not suffer severe consequences at that time, when he could have been taken and executed before he became famous.

For one, the Temple was not only a center of both religious activity and commerce. During Passover, thousands of sacrificial animals were purchased within or near the Temple courts. Several hundred thousand pilgrims entered the city every Passover, many of them from distant lands, carrying money from their homeland with varying levels of silver purity. Specialist money traders would take these funds and, for a small commission, give their bearer Jewish or Tyrian coins, which, as they had no representations of persons or animals on them, were considered religiously clean.* Every Jew was also required to donate a half shekel to the Temple each year, and these pilgrims would also need money changers to handle such transactions. Where you have people and massive amounts of currency in one place, you will also have many other forms of commerce being simultaneously conducted. Passover was the one time each year when merchants and traders from throughout Palestine and the wider Roman world would all be in one place to settle accounts, make and take orders, and obtain financing for future endeavors.

What Jesus overturned was not a few table-holding coins. He had attacked the entire region's commercial center at what many merchants considered the most crucial time of the year. Thus, for the Jewish leadership and, more crucially, the Romans, this attack on the Temple appeared like someone trying to drive a stake through the heart of commerce. And anything that reduced commerce, by definition, reduced the taxes Rome could collect. Again, if Jesus was hoping to attract Rome's interest, he was doing brilliantly. Fewer things were more likely to attract Rome's negative attention than someone cutting into the tax base.

No single man, even if supported by a dozen apostles, could possibly accomplish what the Gospels claim took place. First, the Temple complex was gigantic, and the courts where the money changers and other men of commerce conducted business could have covered more than thirty acres. One can also assume that men carrying as much ready cash as the money changers would necessarily have also hired their own personal security. In addition to this personal security, the Temple had its

---

* Coins minted in Tyre were renowned in the first century for their purity of silver content, with little or no debasement. These are the coins that Judas was probably bribed with.

own guards. No one is sure about the size of this guard, but as it would have to secure a large area and manage hundreds of thousands of pilgrims, it must have numbered in the high hundreds. There was still more for Jesus to worry about. The Antonia Fortress stood right beside the Temple, housing, on a permanent basis, at least a full cohort of Roman auxiliary troops. Most of this cohort was probably on duty in and around the Temple throughout Passover. From the Roman perspective, Pilate was on hand to keep an eye on things as Passover was the most likely time for a revolt to start. It is nearly inconceivable that he arrived without at least two cohorts of infantry and an *ala* of cavalry that were customarily stationed in Caesarea.* In all, there may have been as many as two thousand Roman soldiers in or near the Temple during Passover. This does not account for the Jewish Temple guard and the strong possibility that the four legions in nearby Syria may have sent a cohort or more to keep an eye on the Jews during the most turbulent time of the year. We should remember what happened when Herod was near death: A mob attacked the Temple at night to remove a golden eagle. Forty of them were easily captured and later burned alive. That mob was routed by a security force that would have been a small fraction of what was immediately available during Passover.

Given the security forces in and around the Temple, some historians have claimed that Jesus's cleansing of the Temple is pure fiction. But to believe that means we would have to say that all four canonical gospel writers got it wrong, an improbable circumstance. A much more likely scenario was that Jesus's trip to Jerusalem the day before was employed in coordinating this exact action.

Jesus would have required thousands of supporters to have any chance of clearing the Temple courts. We can assume from his welcome the day before that those needed thousands were standing ready to support him. He merely needed to give the word. As in the wake of the Temple cleans-

---

* For an interesting analysis of the size and composition of Roman forces in Judea, see Michael P. Speidel, "The Roman Army in Judaea Under the Procurators: The Italian and Augustan Cohort in the Acts of the Apostles," *Ancient Society*, Vol. 13/14 (1982/1983), pp. 233–240; and Christopher B. Zeichman, "Military Forces in Judaea 6–130 CE: The *status quaestionis* and Relevance for New Testament Studies," *Currents in Biblical Research*, Vol. 17, no. 1 (October 10, 2018). https://doi.org/10.1177.1476993X18791425.

ing, Jesus stayed to preach; he would have required those same thousands of persons to protect him from immediate arrest. Luke attests to the fact that the Jewish leaders wanted him arrested or dead: ". . . he was teaching daily in the temple. And the chief priests and the Torah scholars, along with the leaders of the people, were trying to kill him. Yet they were not finding any way they could do it, because the entire crowd was hanging on him, listening to him."*

These events tell us several things. First, organized and trained military forces, like those that the Jewish leadership and the Romans possessed, rarely feared mobs. Thus, those around Jesus must have been well-organized, numerous, and likely armed. If they had not been numerous and armed, the Temple guards would have moved to arrest Jesus. Moreover, if the Roman cohorts in the Antonia Fortress were immediately available, they would have waded in. Finally, no matter how numerous or well armed Jesus's supporters were, the Romans would have taken the fight to them. Doing so was rule one in the Roman playbook when facing an insurrection. There was something or someone holding the Roman troops back.

So, if we believe that Jesus was not a revolutionary in the sense that he was trying to overthrow Roman rule, how do we square this belief with the above narrative? There are only two ways. The first and simplest is to affirm that he was a revolutionary of the classic mold. But this goes against everything we know about Jesus before he arrived in Jerusalem. Moreover, Jesus's behavior after his assault on the Temple is the opposite of what one would expect of a revolutionary, as he once again transitions to a man of peace.

His actions were those of a man shouting "Take notice of me," but once he had gotten the desired attention, there was no reason to do anything further. This leads us to the second option: Jesus was a man set upon a particular mission. Whether God truly ordained his mission or he is only a man who believes that he is on a divine mission does not truly matter. The only way to see his mission through was to martyr himself. There were many ways to accomplish this, but the surest of them was to

---

* Luke 19:47–48.

anger Rome. The fact that the Roman authorities had not acted so far only shows that Pilate was willing to wait and see if the Jewish leadership could handle the situation without the messiness of Roman involvement. It in no way demonstrated that Rome was not interested. As we shall see, they most surely were.

TWENTY-SIX

Jesus's Trial

TUESDAY

After cleansing the Temple, Jesus once again spent the night in Bethany, only to return to the Temple the next day. We hear nothing about any triumphant arrival this time, likely because the mob expected more from him after he had run off the money changers and was now disappointed that nothing much had come of it. Instead of summoning the mob to complete the day before's work by marching on the Praetorium—the palace where Pilate was residing—or leading attacks against the Jewish elites who were cooperating with the Romans, or even assaulting the gates of the Antonia Fortress, Jesus appears to have entered the city, toured the Temple grounds, and almost immediately returned to Bethany for a good night's sleep.

Mobs are very fickle and emotional. They are easily carried to the heights of exultation, as they were when they were convinced that Jesus was the Messiah come to throw off the Roman yoke. But, instead of the attack on the Temple heralding a revolution, they were handed what amounted to a temper tantrum. Throughout history, mobs have raised leaders to lofty pinnacles, only to cast them down at the first disappointment of their hopes. For anyone looking for an explanation as to why the mob rapturously greeted Jesus in one moment, only to violently turn against him soon after his arrest and trial, look no further. When Jesus allowed himself to be taken meekly into custody, the passion of his emotionally crushed believers switched to a new course. They turned on the leader who had failed them.

But on that Tuesday of Holy Week, Jesus still had enough core supporters, and the memory of what happened the day before remained strong enough to cause the authorities to move carefully. At first, Jerusalem's religious elites limited themselves to questioning Jesus about his authority to act as he was. Then, instead of giving them an answer, Jesus told them that tax collectors and prostitutes would go ahead of them into the Kingdom of God. But just in case that did not sufficiently raise their ire, Jesus also told them that God's kingdom would be taken from them and given to the people, as anyone who opposed the rejected stone (a metaphor for Jesus) would be broken and crushed. According to Matthew, the religious leaders rekindled their efforts to arrest him after hearing these insults, but they were too "afraid of the crowds" to make an overt move.*

Jesus eventually left Jerusalem but stopped on the Mount of Olives, about halfway to Bethany, to teach and entertain a few more questions while also avoiding a series of verbal traps offered by spies placed by the Jewish leadership among his followers. These traps included the famous question about whether it was permissible for Jews to pay a tribute tax to Caesar. After asking them whose picture and inscription was on a Roman coin—a *denarius*—and hearing them reply "Caesar's," Jesus instructed them to return to Caesar things that belong to Caesar and give to God what is God's. The reply must have frustrated those trying to trap Jesus, but for us, his words are the foundation for the Western concept of a separate church and state. Finally, Jesus ended his workday with what is now called the Mount of Olives Prophecy, where he predicted his imminent death and eventual glorious return.

---

* Matthew 21:45 and Luke 20:18–19.

WEDNESDAY

By nightfall, Jesus was back in Bethany. He apparently stayed in the town all the next day, although little is known about what Jesus did this day. One can assume he needed a day of rest after an eventful seventy-two hours, as he readied himself for the ordeal ahead. If Jesus was resting, Jerusalem's religious leaders certainly were not. They spent the day concocting plans for capturing Jesus and putting him on trial. But all of these plans foundered upon the same problem: They needed to anticipate where Jesus would be at a time when he also separated from the bulk of his followers. But, without a spy within Jesus's core circle of followers, there was no way to know Jesus's schedule ahead of time.

Enter Judas Iscariot, one of the core twelve apostles, who was ready to make a deal to betray Jesus in return for thirty pieces of silver. For those who have wondered how much Judas was enriched by his betrayal, thirty pieces of silver approximated six weeks of salary for a single Roman legionnaire. It was also about how much it would cost to feed a family of four for about same time period. As Judas was also the treasurer for Jesus and his apostles, one can assume he further compensated himself by making off with the group's savings. One may wonder if his true reason for betraying his friends was to ensure that there was no pursuit once they realized he had made off with all their money. Scholars have long debated Judas's motive for his treachery. One scholar claims that Judas was disenchanted by Jesus's refusal to assume "the role of a political-military messiah," or that he was trying to force Jesus to call for an immediate uprising to avoid arrest.* Others claim that Judas was captured during Jesus's assault on the Temple and threatened with death if he did not betray Jesus.† This hypothesis cannot, however, explain why Judas still betrayed Jesus after he was free of the Temple authorities, or why his captors thought they needed to add thirty pieces of silver to their threats to kill him. Still, this is all mere speculation with no basis in the histori-

---

* Bart D. Ehrman, *Jesus, Apocalyptic Prophet of the New Millennium* (Oxford University Press, 1999), p. 219.
† John Dominic Crossan, *Who Killed Jesus?: Exposing the Roots of Anti-Semitism in the Gospel Story of the Death of Jesus* (HarperSanFrancisco, 1995), p. 81.

cal record. Whatever Judas's ultimate motivation for betrayal, it is lost to history. No matter his motive, Judas had set the stage for Jesus's arrest.

THURSDAY

On Thursday morning, Jesus told the apostles Peter and John to go and prepare the Passover meal. When they asked him where he wanted to eat this meal, Jesus gave them detailed instructions for going to Jerusalem, including whom to meet once there, and informed them that they would be directed to a large room, already set up and furnished to receive them for the meal. Jesus had clearly done a good deal of pre-coordination. Interestingly, he managed to arrange for a large room at a time when space in Jerusalem was at an absolute premium, and apparently did so without involving any of his most trusted apostles.

It is worth noting that there is a person mentioned in the Gospel narratives who was particularly well placed to assist Jesus in his ultimate designs: Joseph of Arimathea. We know very little about this man, but from what can be pieced together from the canonical Gospels, we can deduce several crucial points.* For one, we know that he was a man of substantial wealth and influence, possessing enough of each to become a member of the Sanhedrin, which governed Judea under Pilate's rules and was responsible for condemning Jesus. We also know that he voted against condemnation at Jesus's trial.† And finally, we know that he had enough influence to get an immediate audience with Pontius Pilate, which he used to ask Pilate for Jesus's body after the crucifixion. Crucially, according to John, he was a "secret" disciple of Jesus.‡ Therefore, his support for Jesus was unknown to his fellow Sanhedrin members, meaning he was particularly well placed to keep Jesus informed of what the Jewish leaders were planning. One of the few Pharisees in the Sanhedrin, Nicodemus, was also known to have assisted Joseph in preparing Jesus's body for burial and taking Jesus's side during his trial. Nicodemus was also a man of some wealth and influence, but as a known supporter

---

* I do not place any faith in the stories told in the Gospel of Nicodemus, nor do I give credence to myths that arose during the Middle Ages.
† Luke 23:50–56. Mark 15:43 tells us that he was a "respected" member of the council.
‡ John 19:38.

of Jesus, he was unlikely to be privy to the Sanhedrin leadership's plotting. Nicodemus is only mentioned in the Gospel of John, so he is not as
well attested as Joseph. In any case, the members of the Sanhedrin were
clearly not unanimous in their desire to arrest and prosecute Jesus, which
may have been another reason that they moved slowly and carefully.

If we accept that Joseph was keeping Jesus informed, many mysteries
become explicable without resorting to divine knowledge. It explains
how Jesus escaped the multiple traps set by Jewish authorities, who were
continuously looking for ways and opportunities to arrest him. Having
an inside informer also explains how on the Mount of Olives he could
predict his own death and how he knew that one of his apostles planned
to betray him to the Jewish authorities. Finally, Jesus would have needed
someone with Joseph's influence and wealth to secure a large enough
room in Jerusalem to accommodate his entourage and pay for the food.
Joseph of Arimathea fits the bill nicely.

That evening, Jesus sat down with his apostles for Passover dinner.*
During the dinner, Jesus told his core followers that this would be his last
Passover meal with them. He then offered them bread and wine, telling
them that this was his body and blood, which was being offered up for
them. They were instructed to perform this ceremony on a regular basis
to remember and commemorate his memory and sacrifice. Finally, Jesus
must have left his apostles dumbfounded when he informed them that
his expected death was occurring as planned, while also cursing the apostle who was about to betray him.

What we know from all four Gospels is that Jesus knows he will soon
be arrested, tried, and executed. In any event, Jesus has an early enough
warning to escape Jerusalem easily. But he does nothing to avoid his fate,
which leads to a single conclusion: His arrest and eventual martyrdom all
happen as part of a design, then known only to him.

---

* The timing of this dinner, as well as much of what is now called Holy Week, has been
a matter of debate by historians and biblical scholars for centuries. I am presenting what
I believe is the most accurate reconstruction, based on the source material available to
us. For a thorough examination of the debate from one of the greatest scholars of ancient Rome, see Fergus Millar's "Reflections on the Trials of Jesus," in Fergus Millar,
Rome, the Greek World, and the East, Vol. 3, *The Greek World, the Jews, and the East,* Hannah M.
Cotton and Guy M. Rogers (eds.) (University of North Carolina Press, 2006), pp. 139–163.

Jesus also told his apostles that one of them was a traitor, which caused no small amount of consternation at the table. Each began protesting his innocence and asking Jesus if he knew who the traitor was. Jesus's reply, according to Matthew: "The one who has dipped his hand into the bowl with me will betray me."* This was not enough information to figure it out, as it was common to dip pieces of bread into a bowl filled with various mixtures of herbs and nuts, or to dip the bread in the wine to cut its bitter taste. Doing so together was an act of friendship, and every apostle had likely done so with Jesus during the dinner.

As the answer was unsatisfactory, at the urging of John, Peter asked the direct question: "Lord, who is it."† Jesus told Peter that "it is the one I give a piece of bread dipped in wine." Jesus then dipped the bread and handed it to Judas, who immediately protested his innocence. Jesus cursed him and ordered him to depart from their company immediately. After Judas departed, Jesus turned to the other apostles and said: "It would have been better for that one not to have been born." Unless we again credit divine knowledge, someone is clearly keeping Jesus well informed. He not only knows who will betray him, but also when and where he will be betrayed. More crucially, Jesus clearly could have thwarted this plot to arrest him, as he had done all the other times throughout the week. He had the manpower—eleven other apostles—to detain Judas for as long as was required to get safely away. That he did not is further historical evidence that his arrest, trial, and execution are part of a larger design of Jesus's making.

As the dinner concluded, Jesus demonstrated a keen insight into human frailty when he told his apostles that they would all desert him. When Peter objected and said, "Even though all become deserters, I will not," Jesus rebuked him, saying he would deny their association three times before dawn.‡ The others joined Peter, claiming they would all die for Jesus rather than deny him. Given who he was talking to and how long they had remained loyal to him, Jesus's accusation is rather remarkable. These apostles were the men who had defended him in the past and

* Matthew 26:22.
† John 13:26.
‡ Mark 28:21.

had led the masses of followers he counted on to keep the Temple guards and Roman auxiliaries from attacking him. There are two things that are going on here. First, there is a big difference in the type of courage it takes to stand and fight when you have a significant numerical advantage over your enemies or when a charismatic leader leads you. But on this night, the apostles, with Judas gone, numbered but eleven, and they were separated from the mob that had supported their triumphal entry, all of whom were celebrating their own Passover meals. These facts were surely known to the Jewish leadership, who could be counted upon to bring an overwhelming force with them. And then, like any group under mortal threat and deprived of a leader willing to fight, they would scatter upon Jesus's arrest. Courage is tough to maintain when hope is lost.

Jesus retreated after dinner to the Garden of Gethsemane, likely at the foot of the Mount of Olives. Depending on what Gospel you credit, he took all of his apostles or just a select few with him. No matter the number, Jesus soon separated himself to pray alone, asking his accompanying disciples to remain awake. Certainly, he was hoping for some warning if Judas arrived with soldiers at his back, hence his anger when he returned and found them sleeping. The apostles were asking his forgiveness when Jesus cut them off, saying the time had come. In the next moment, they were surrounded by soldiers.

According to Luke, those around Jesus asked if they should draw their weapons, indicating that all or most of the party was well armed.* Peter did, in fact, draw his sword and wounded one of the Temple guards before Jesus ordered him to cease fighting and for his other disciples to stand down. In the dark, Judas had to identify Jesus to the soldiers with a kiss. Afterward, Jesus scolded the soldiers for not daring to arrest him during the day when thousands of supporters would have been watching: "As though after a bandit, you have come out with swords and clubs. Every day with me being next to you in the temple you didn't lay your hands on me. But this is the hour for you, and the authority of darkness."† It is left to John to make it clear that Rome was already taking an interest,

* Luke 22:45.
† Luke 22:52.

as Judas arrived with the Temple guards sent by the priests and a detachment of soldiers from the Roman cohort.*

After his arrest, Jesus was brought before the high priest, Caiaphas, at
his home, probably near Mount Zion in the western portion of the city,
not far from where Pilate was residing.† Caiaphas and his father-in-law
before him, Annas, had been the Jewish high priests for most of the prior
two decades, ever since Rome had taken over appointing persons to fill
that position. As such, both men had a long experience of working with
the Roman governmental apparatus and were supremely sensitive to
Roman concerns. They were particularly concerned about Rome's reaction to a revolt that could lead to the near destruction of the Jewish
people, an action Rome had carried out many times in the past and
would do again in Judea in 66–71 AD. When a people rose against Rome,
they were, by definition, placing their future survival at serious risk. Not
for nothing did Tacitus write: "You Romans create a desert and call it
peace." Thus, according to John, Annas advised killing Jesus, as it was
better to kill one man than to see a people destroyed.‡ Such talk betrays
the fact that, at least in the priest's mind, Jesus had sufficient influence to
raise the Jewish people in a major revolt.

Joining Caiaphas were members of the Sanhedrin, best described as
an integrated governing and judicial body. The Sanhedrin was first mentioned by Josephus as having been reconvened by the Romans in 56 BC.§
Every major town or city in Israel had its own Sanhedrin, but the Great
Sanhedrin, consisting of seventy-one of Israel's most learned sages, met
in the Chamber of Hewn Stones, carved into the side of the Temple
Mount in Jerusalem. The entire seventy-one members would typically
meet as a body only for the most important of cases—the overthrow of
a king, or to declare war. Bodies as small as three would hear lesser cases
and twenty-three were considered necessary for a capital offense. The
number was always odd to make sure there were no ties.

* John 18:3.
† The Gospel of John states that he was brought before Caiaphas's father-in-law, Annas,
before being brought to Caiaphas.
‡ John 18:4.
§ Pompey had outlawed the Great Sanhedrin, and it was left to Julius Caesar to allow
its revival.

One of the problems historians have had with the Gospel accounts of Jesus's first interrogation is that there were no supporters of Jesus present to witness the events. Thus, how could the gospel writers have such detailed knowledge of what transpired within Caiaphas's home that night? For many, this has presented a sufficient reason to claim that the gospel stories for at least this part of Jesus's life are fiction. Of course, this problem vanishes once we take account of Joseph of Arimathea as well as Nicodemus being members of the Sanhedrin. That both were present for Jesus's interrogation is a certainty, as the Gospels clearly state that Joseph did not agree with the council's decision, and Nicodemus pleaded with the other council members to listen to Jesus's version of events. Moreover, Joseph and Nicodemus were probably not the only Sanhedrin members who had some sympathy for Jesus. It is feasible, even likely, that Joseph kept the apostles informed of what was happening outside their view. Also, Jesus's trial was the event of the year in Judea. Thus, everyone in Jerusalem would be hanging on every detail and rumor. There would have been no shortage of persons keeping the gospel writers and their informants up to date on the latest information. Finally, this was an official judicial interrogation involving key members of the Sanhedrin. Thus, a record of events was likely to have been kept and was probably still extant, at least until the Temple was destroyed in 70 AD. What would have been truly remarkable is if the apostles did not get a complete description of the events at Caiaphas's that night.

Other historians have claimed that the interrogation broke several trial rules, as laid out in the Mishnah, particularly for a capital offense. Thus, they feel free to discard the entire gospel tradition. But it is crucial to note that the Mishnah is a record of the Jewish oral religious tradition written down for the first time centuries after Jesus's death and just as many centuries after the Romans destroyed all Jewish documents from the period. The Mishnah almost certainly represents the structure and actions of the Sanhedrin after the Temple was destroyed in 70 AD.* But nothing is known for certain about the rules the Sanhedrin followed in

---

* It was a full generation after the Temple was destroyed before the Sanhedrin was reconvened at Yavneh, but even then their procedures were not recorded.

Jesus's time. Moreover, Jewish law made many allowances for periods of crisis. After Jesus's triumphal entry into Jerusalem and his overthrow of Temple commerce, many in the Sanhedrin were certainly convinced that Jesus was pushing Judea toward a crisis with Rome.* Another argument can be made, and it comes from Jewish tradition. Rabbinic Judaism rejects any connection with the trial of Jesus with or without the Sanhedrin. Modern or Rabbinic Judaism, as we noted earlier, claims descent from the Pharisees, a group often at odds with the Sadducees. Many Jews believe it possible that Jesus's trial was before a Sadducean illegal court. If so, an illegal court would certainly not consider itself bound by traditional rules.

Is this possible? Josephus tells us it is. He details the trial and execution of Jesus's brother, James, with details that are very similar to what the Gospels describe for Jesus's trial. In this latter case, James was arrested in 62 AD and tried before a Sanhedrin, consisting entirely of Sadducees, convened by the high priest Ananus. Just as Jesus's was, James's trial was held in the high priest's home, and it was there that James was condemned to death by stoning.†

Finally, we are not even sure that what took place at Caiaphas's home was even a trial. Instead, it may have been an interrogation with a trial to follow. Caiaphas and the Sanhedrin certainly conducted a long-lasting interrogation of Jesus, mostly centered upon whether he had predicted the destruction of the Temple and had also referred to himself as the Christ. It took some time to find witnesses to accuse Jesus of either, but the priests finally asked the question directly once they were found. Jesus refused to deny that he had said everything that he was accused of. Upon hearing this, Caiaphas tore his clothes and exclaimed that no further witnesses were needed.

Much has been made of the notion that the Sanhedrin could not conduct trials during the night. Even if this was true of the pre–70 AD

---

* As an example, Mishnah Sanhedrin 4:1 says it is illegal to have a trial at night. Whether this was true in Jesus's time is unknown. Still, it is easy to see Jesus's time at Caiaphas's home as an interrogation and not a trial. When Pilate told the priests to take Jesus away and try him according to their own laws, he clearly did not think a trial had been conducted already.

† Josephus, *Antiquities*, 20.9.

Sanhedrin, there is no reason to believe that what took place at Caiaphas's home was a trial. By all appearances, it was an interrogation of Jesus and several potential witnesses in preparation for a trial to be held at a later time. Almost certainly, no one attending the interrogations planned to order a public execution based on a secret tribunal consisting of a small cabal of persons, particularly if their vote was not unanimous. When the chief priest consulted with the "elders and scribes, and the whole council" the following day, the topic was almost certainly whether there was sufficient evidence of wrongdoing to proceed to a formal trial.*

FRIDAY

During this meeting, Caiaphas would have gone over what had been said during the interrogation and revealed that Jesus stood condemned by the majority of those present. But there was hesitation when Caiaphas asked the others what was to be done with him. Certainly, most of the Sanhedrin agreed that Jesus should be executed, but they were in no hurry to conduct a formal trial or to order an immediate execution. Instead, the Sanhedrin decided to take him before Pilate and have Rome judge him. If the events of the night before were an actual trial, there would have been no need for a retrial in front of Pilate. As we shall see, given the circumstance, Pilate would have strongly preferred that the Sanhedrin handle the entire affair without Rome's involvement.

The Gospels all state that Pilate was hesitant to condemn Jesus, going so far as to tell the Jewish leaders to take him back and judge him according to their laws. John tells us that the priests told Pilate they could not do so because Roman law forbids local authorities to try someone for a capital offense.† Forget for a moment that Pilate would certainly have known if Rome had any such law—and it did not. In fact, Rome, knowing its representatives were spread thin, encouraged local authorities to handle all such matters on their own. Just as certainly, neither before nor after Jesus's trial had the Sanhedrin ever hesitated to order a judicial execution. So, what is going on here?

* Mark 15:1.
† John 18:31.

Once again, there is an easy answer but one that is all too often overlooked. Just days before, Jesus had entered Jerusalem as a conquering hero. Before forty-eight hours had passed, he had rallied enough persons to his cause to launch an assault on the Temple of sufficient ferocity to give the Temple guards and the Romans in the Antonia Fortress pause. The priests and elders may have wanted Jesus dead, but with the mob's reaction still unknown, they did not want to be held responsible for it. In that regard, the decision to hand Jesus off to Roman justice, which was always severe and prompt, was a no-brainer.

But what of Pilate? As we will see, he never hesitated to use violence to maintain order before Jesus's trial. And three years after Jesus's execution, he was removed from his position due to his overfondness for employing violent measures against the Jews. Refusing to judge and then execute Jesus goes against everything we know about Pilate. But events speak for themselves. Pilate did everything possible to avoid condemning Jesus. In one Gospel account, upon discovering Jesus was from Galilee, he ordered him sent to Antipas, the Roman-appointed tetrarch of Galilee, who was in Jerusalem for Passover. Had Pilate pulled it off, this would have been a neat trick, as he could have had a Jewish ruler settle the matter. But Herod certainly knew all that had transpired that week and was no more willing than Caiaphas and the Sanhedrin to have the mob turn on him. Unwilling to execute him and possibly rile the mob, but just as unwilling to release him and make enemies of the high priests and the Sanhedrin, Antipas did what any good politician would do: He passed the buck. After he and a few members of his court had amused themselves at Jesus's expense, he returned Jesus to Pilate for judgment.

The Roman prefect had one last trick up his sleeve. According to all four Gospel accounts, Pilate offered the crowd a choice between Jesus and another prisoner, Barabbas, one of whom he would release. The Gospels agree that such a release was part of a tradition, although there is no hint about when it would have started. As there is no record of any such tradition in either Jewish or Roman law, many historians have found this story very troubling. Those scholars who have defended the biblical passages relating to the event have tortured the historical record in search of other Greek or Roman examples of prisoner releases, particularly any related to religious festivals. Some have been found, but in each case, the prisoners were only released for the duration of the festival and expected to turn themselves back in afterward. This is not what is happening in this case, as Pilate is offering to release either Jesus or Barabbas free and clear.

To summarize the findings of dozens of scholars, no tradition in the ancient literature supports what Pilate was offering. But there is another major problem particular to the Roman Empire: No Roman governor or prefect had the power to release a condemned prisoner, which would have been even more the case if the prisoner was charged with sedition against Rome, as Barabbas likely was. Only the emperor could pardon a condemned prisoner.

If we use the Gospels as historical works, as we should, it is perilous to disregard a story that appears in all four Gospels, as we then have to admit we know absolutely nothing. We also must never lose track of the fact that the first three synoptic Gospels were circulating when there were still many living witnesses to the recounted events. These witnesses would not have hesitated to call foul at any attempt to insert a fictional tale into the narrative. If we then accept that the Barabbas story is true, how could it have happened? Certainly Pilate was not going to unilaterally usurp the power of Caesar?

But he did not have to.

One of the most important duties a Roman governor or prefect had was to act as the primary judicial officer within a province, and there was no appeal from his judgments short of the emperor. Thus, a governor or prefect would spend considerable time on a circuit around his province hearing cases and dispensing justice. As Pilate had to be in Jerusalem for Passover, it only made sense that he would schedule this trip as part of his regular judicial circuit. Hence, Pilate was available on such short notice to hear Jesus's case because he likely already had his calendar for the day filled with other cases to be heard. Barabbas's case was probably also already on the day's docket; otherwise, it is unlikely that a man as busy and as usually disinterested as Pilate would even be aware of it. And this is the crux of the matter. Barabbas had not yet been found guilty of any crime. He was not a condemned man. As the Gospels make clear, he was in prison awaiting Pilate's justice. This is proven by the fact that he was still alive. Roman justice was always swift. Once a prisoner was condemned, he was immediately taken away for execution, as happened to Jesus once Pilate made his decision. Thus, if the local elites did not strenuously object—threaten to appeal to the emperor—it was easy for Pilate to judge the evidence against either Barabbas or Jesus as insufficient for conviction, and to release either prisoner. This was not only within the power of a governor or prefect but also an expected part of his regular duties.*

But was it customary? Doubtless, in cases where the parties on trial were clearly guilty, there were often persons pleading special circumstances and begging for clemency or mercy. No Roman governor or prefect was immune from such pleading, particularly when it came from the powerful local elites who governed in conjunction with him. Without their cooperation, the proper governing of a province quickly became an insurmountable ordeal. Pilate was no different; he needed at least the tacit cooperation of the Jewish leadership. If that meant indulging their judicial pleading now and again, that was a small price to pay for smooth governing relations.

As Pilate was in Jerusalem every year for Passover, and he almost certainly took the opportunity to conduct his judicial duties, what would it have taken to establish a custom? If he released one prisoner a year at the behest of the Jewish elites, it could have been considered customary in a mere two years. He may even have announced it: "What scoundrel are you begging me to release this time around?" It would take only a small leap in logic to assume that before Jesus's arrival in Jerusalem, some persons were already pleading Barabbas's case to Pilate or his assistants. This explains how Pilate was able to offer a choice of whom to release so quickly, as well as how quickly the crowd made their choice; they clearly knew who Barabbas was and that his case was pending. Many of them probably also knew that the ground had already been prepared for Barabbas's case to be dismissed.

---

* After reading dozens of learned accounts on the topic, I believe this to be the most comprehensive and informative: Richard Wellington Husband, "The Pardoning of the Prisoners by Pilate," *The American Journal of Theology*, Vol. 21, no. 1 (January 1917), pp. 110–116.

This also tells us something about the crowd gathered at Herod's former palace, now Pilate's *Praetorium*. Most crucially, this is not the same mob that greeted Jesus on his triumphal entry into Jerusalem just days before. We must remember the size of the space with which we were dealing. Although the place was built on a grand scale, we are told that the Jewish leaders and whoever else had gathered were limited to the courtyard, as a Jew who wandered too deeply into the palace's environs risked becoming religiously unclean, with no time to purify himself prior to Passover. Although the courtyard was large, its capacity was limited; at most, several hundred people could have crowded into its precincts.*

Moreover, this is still the morning after Jesus was secretly arrested in the middle of the night, while in a secluded garden. The Jewish leadership would have done its best to keep any word of the arrest from spreading, a task made much easier by the majority of Jerusalem's population being focused on Passover preparations. Thus, the Jewish leadership would have had no trouble filling this courtyard with several hundred paid supporters told to yell whatever the priests wanted them to.

As Jesus is transferred from the control of the Jewish elites to be judged by Rome, we must pause the narrative of events to take a deeper look at Rome's representative in Judea: Pontius Pilate, for in Pilate's hand rested the full power of Roman might. Without some comprehension of Pilate, his outlook on the world, and how his mental universe changed after Sejanus's death, it is impossible to make sense of Jesus's trial and eventual crucifixion.

---

* Excavations between the Jaffa Gate and the Zion Gate by Shimon Gibson reveal a wealth of information that might place the home of Caiaphas in that area as well as the Praetorium. For one report of this online, see https://biblearchaeologyreport.com/2022/04/14/behold-the-man-where-did-pilate-sentence-jesus/. Shimon Gibson's report is available at https://www.academia.edu/22894409/The_Trial_of_Jesus_at_the_Jerusalem_Praetorium_New_Archaeological_Evidence. The latter is published as "The Trial of Jesus at the Jerusalem Praetorium: New Archaeological Evidence," in *The World of Jesus and the Early Church: Identity and Interpretation in Early Communities of Faith*, Craig A. Evans (ed.) (Hendrickson Publishers, 2011), pp. 97–118.

TWENTY-SEVEN

Pontius Pilate:
What Do We Know?

Pontius Pilate was the Roman governor of Judea, with the rank of prefect, from approximately 26 to 36 AD. He is, of course, infamous today for presiding over Jesus's trial and execution. But who was he? Although we have more information about Pilate than we do about almost any other Roman governor, the sources remain scant. But we can fill in some gaps with careful inference from what we do know.

No sources tell us anything about his early life, but we can make a few deductions based on his name and achievements. First, the name Pontius tells us that he was from the Pontii family, centered on Samnium in central and southern Italy, although he may have been born elsewhere. The Pontii led the Samnite resistance to Roman expansion in an earlier century. Pilate could even boast of a famous relative, Gaius Pontius, who inflicted upon Rome one of its most humiliating defeats at Caudine Forks in 321 BC. But by the time Pilate was born, Samnium had long ago been conquered and Romanized.

Pilate clearly came from a wealthy family, as no one became a Roman governor without a claim to significant wealth. A governorship could also be very profitable, and more than a few Roman senators and equestrians took advantage of the lucrative opportunities such an appointment presented to rebuild dwindling family fortunes. Pilate was born into the equestrian order, which sat in the middle, between the senatorial class and the poorer plebeians. Still, many equestrians had fortunes as great or greater than any senator, blurring the lines between the two strata. Augustus insisted on keeping the equestrian order as militarized as possible, meaning equestrians made up the bulk of the officers in the Roman army. For Pilate to have become a governor, he almost surely had to have had a military background and distinguished himself in that role. He certainly governed with the harshness of a man with considerable time in the legions.

The one final point, which is crucial to the story of Jesus's crucifixion, is that no one rose to the rank of Roman governor without a great deal of patronage involved. In 26 AD, there was only one source of patronage at this level: Sejanus. Thus, Pilate was almost certainly a client of Sejanus, as was virtually every governor and high Roman official appointed during this period. Moreover, even if he was appointed to the governor's position without Sejanus's approval, he certainly could not have remained in that role, as Sejanus's power over such crucial appointments grew, unless he had Sejanus as a patron.

Once Pilate becomes governor, there is a little more primary evidence to go on besides the gospel texts. Pilate is mentioned by both Philo, a Jewish philosopher living in Alexandria, and the historian and former revolutionary Jewish leader Josephus. The Gospels portray Pilate as a weak, vacillating, and often indecisive governor. But this is at odds with how Philo and Josephus describe him. In both non-Gospel accounts, we see a decisive, tough, and often cruel Roman governor. In this regard, he is much like any Roman governor, but for reasons of his own, Philo depicts him as unusually cruel, even by Roman standards.

According to Josephus, Pilate once used a part of the Temple's sacred treasury—the Corbonas—to construct an aqueduct to supply much-needed water to Jerusalem. There is no indication that he stole the money, meaning the Jewish Temple authorities would have had to agree to its use. If they had done otherwise, Josephus probably would have mentioned the fact that Pilate stole it. According to Jewish law, this money was set aside for social welfare. As the aqueduct would have led to a massive improvement in the lives of many of the city's residents, it is hard to specify what Pilate had done wrong. Possibly, he was only guilty of being a Roman and using Jewish funds. A better approach would have been for Pilate to direct Jewish leaders to use the funds to build an aqueduct instead of seizing the funds and contracting it himself. Rome had long ago learned that it was best to put a local face on every major initiative, but no one seems to have explained that to Pilate, who was learning on the job.

In any event, while he was in Jerusalem, likely for another feast, someone used the confiscation of Temple funds to turn the mob against Pilate. As a result, a threatening mob formed around his tribunal, where Pilate was conducting judicial proceedings. But Pilate had either been forewarned of trouble or he was an exceedingly cautious man. He had placed numerous disguised soldiers throughout the crowd, carrying heavy cudgels under their robes. Josephus tells us it was in the tens of thousands as the crowd formed, and other soldiers in full battle array moved into position around the crowd's edges.

At first, the crowd demanded that he give up on his construction plans and return the funds to the Temple. But it soon began to hurl insults and became dangerous. Josephus picks up the story:

> "When the furor hit a fever pitch, Pilate gave the soldiers a prearranged signal for the soldiers to strike. Many Jews were killed on the spot, as a mob has little chance against trained soldiers. Like any mob that suddenly meets an unexpected check and then a violent reverse, it first staggered and then panicked. Hundreds, possibly thousands more were killed in the crush at the exits.*

In a later occasion, three years after Jesus's crucifixion, Pilate again unleashed his troops against civilians. This time a Samaritan, claiming to be the reincarnated Moses, rallied the mob by announcing he knew where Moses had buried the sacred vessels on Mount Gerizim. For Samaritan Jews, Mount Gerizim was considered the holiest place on earth, and in their tradition, it is where God is supposed to have ordered his temple

---

* Josephus, *Antiquities of the Jews,* 18.60–62; *The Wars of the Jews,* 2.175–177.

built. For hundreds of years, the temple built on Mount Gerizim was in direct competition with that built on Temple Mount in Jerusalem. The Gerizim temple was destroyed in 112–111 BC, on the order of the Hasmonean John Hyrcanus. To this day, the few remaining Samaritans continue to ascend the mount three times a year—Passover, Shavuot, and Sukkot.

Those who believed this new Moses's story armed themselves and gathered at a village named Tirathana, at the foot of the mountain. It appears they camped there for some time, as they welcomed newcomers until they were a vast multitude. Unfortunately, such an armed gathering could never have escaped Roman notice. Before they began their ascent, Pilate blocked them with a detachment of cavalry supported by heavily armed infantry. A pitched battle ensued, which had the predictable out-come of what happens when a mob runs into trained Roman soldiers ready to greet them. The first ranks of the Samaritans were cut to pieces, sending the rest into panicked flight. During their pursuit, the Romans captured many prisoners, and Pilate immediately executed the most influential of them.

Josephus tells us that after the uprising was quelled, some of the surviving Samaritans went before the Syrian governor, Vitellius, to charge Pilate with an illegal and cruel slaughtering. They claimed they were not rebels against the Romans but were refugees trying to escape Pilate's persecution. Vitellius supposedly sent one of his friends to take charge of Judea while ordering Pilate to return to Rome and account for his deeds before Tiberius.[*] This is probably a misunderstanding of what actually happened, as no governor, unless given special powers by the emperor, could relieve another governor of his position. On the other hand, Vitellius had just been a consul of Rome and was trusted by the imperial family, so he probably wielded more power than a typical governor. Besides, he controlled three Roman legions. Still, if we keep in mind that the average Roman governor served fewer than three years and that Pilate had been governor of Judea for over a decade, the much more likely scenario

---

[*] Josephus, *Antiquities of the Jews*, 18.85–89.

was that Pilate was called as part of a regular rotation and allowed to retire to his estates. That he had to report to the emperor was not unique, as returning governors would routinely make a final report to the Roman Senate and the emperor. Besides, it is hard to see what Pilate would have had to account for unless Josephus is not telling the full story. Faced with a formidable mob that had armed itself, Pilate had only done what was expected of any Roman governor. He assembled whatever forces were immediately available and crushed the disturbance. Rome was always ready to forgive a bit of zealousness in the quest to maintain the general order.

But in another, and final, mention of Pilate, Josephus relates an earlier incident when Sejanus was still in power. On this occasion, Pilate, although his first instinct was to employ the state's military force at the first sign of trouble, demonstrated that he could accept a peaceful outcome when he could see a benefit to doing so. Roman governors were certainly harsh masters, but they were not often stupid. In this case, Pilate had ordered several of his troops to leave Caesarea and go into winter quarters in Jerusalem, likely in and about the Antonia Fortress. According to Josephus, Pilate ordered the soldiers to march into the city with busts of the emperor upon their standards, an act that violated Jewish laws forbidding the making of images.

Upon discovering the images, which were likely placed at the gates of the Antonia Fortress, which stood alongside the Temple, the population became irate. According to Josephus, nearly the entire population of Jerusalem marched to Caesarea to beseech Pilate to remove the statues. For six days, their entreaties continued, and one wonders how such a multitude was fed. Either Josephus hugely exaggerated the number of persons who marched from Jerusalem, or Pilate drew out the negotiations, expecting the crowd to start dispersing in search of food and water. Whatever the answer, Pilate refused to budge, and on the sixth day, he acted. The Jews were surrounded by fully armed and armored Roman cohorts, and Pilate threatened to have them hacked to pieces if they did not immediately disperse. But instead of going home, they prostrated themselves on the ground and bared their necks, welcoming the executioner's blade. Finally, after a moment's pause and reflection, Pilate called off the soldiers and ordered the offending images returned to Caesarea.*

Why did Pilate back off? Given all we know about him, such a retreat was not part of Pilate's constitutional makeup. There were likely a few crucial reasons, none of them having to do with Pilate being struck by a moment of softheartedness. First, unlike the Samaritans at Mount Gerizim, none of these persons were armed. Even Pilate, with the full support of a Jew-despising Sejanus, could not expect to survive an inquiry into the deaths of thousands of unarmed citizens.† The emperor and Senate back in Rome would sanction even the harshest measures against armed insurgents; it would not, however, countenance the mass slaughter of unarmed civilians, offering their necks to Roman blades. Few things would inspire an undying Judean rage against Rome more than a merciless slaughter of unarmed innocents protesting against an insult to their religion.

Philo relates a similar instance, this one apparently taking place during Passover the year before Jesus's execution, when all of Herod's remaining sons joined Pilate in Jerusalem. Pilate had decided to place gilded shields honoring Tiberius in Jerusalem. This time, Pilate was careful to avoid placing any images on his tribute to Caesar, putting only his and Tiberius's names upon the shields. Despite Pilate's attempt not to cross any Jewish religious boundaries, the population still rose in protest. This time, the protesters were represented by all of Herod's living sons. This was likely enough to ensure that Pilate could not employ violence, as he knew these sons had been raised in Rome. That means they were likely

---

* Josephus, *Antiquities of the Jews*, 18.55–59; *The Wars of the Jews*, 2.169–177.
† Philo claims that Sejanus was plotting to destroy the entire Jewish nation. See Philo, *In Flaccum*, i, 1; and *Legatio*, 24, 159–161. A number of historians have claimed that Sejanus was not an anti-Semite and did not pursue any anti-Jewish policies, as there is no extant record of him having done so while at the heights of his power after 26 AD. Of course, there has been so much lost to history that such a policy could certainly have existed without leaving any trace for modern historians. Still, the reason he may have not bothered much with Rome's Jewish population is that he was instrumental in having the bulk (possibly all) of the Jews expelled from Rome and four thousand of them being forcibly enrolled into the army in 19 AD (Suetonius, *Tiberius*, 31).

Roman citizens, and citizens abroad always had to be treated with special care by governors. Moreover, they had been raised alongside the children of Roman nobility and still counted many of these persons, including Caligula (the emperor-in-waiting), as their friends. No ancient author tells us what influence Herod's sons had on Pilate, but, at the very least, he would have to tread very carefully around men who personally knew the emperor. Still, Herod was reluctant to retreat. Philo tells us that this was because of Pilate's flawed character. According to Philo, Pilate was a man of "very inflexible disposition, and very merciless as well as very obstinate." Philo also informs us that when the Jews threatened to send an embassy to Rome to plead their case before the emperor, Pilate feared such a mission would reveal his "corruption, and his acts of insolence, and his rapine, and his habit of insulting people, and his cruelty, and his continual murders of people untried and uncondemned, and his never-ending, and gratuitous, and most grievous inhumanity."[*] This is a very interesting assessment of Pilate's character, one that, even if exaggerated, likely presents Pilate as most Jews viewed him. In the end, the Jews settled on sending a letter to Tiberius, and Pilate appears to have given them his permission to forward the letter through the imperial post. An angry Tiberius ordered the shields brought to Caesarea and set up there. Pilate had likely already concluded that this was the best course, but he could not accept the loss of face and prestige if he had done so because of Jewish pressure. It was quite another thing to follow the orders of the emperor. Both sides got what they wanted or needed; the Jews got the shields removed, and Pilate got to accommodate them while appearing not personally to have given in to the protesters' demands.[†]

So, how do we reconcile the indecisive, weak, and merciful Roman governor with the descriptions left to us by the only non-Gospel accounts we have about Pilate? For that answer, we must return to Jesus's ongoing trial.

---

[*] Philo, *Letter to Gaius*, 1.298–308.

[†] The fact that Tiberius supported the Jewish position is strong evidence that Sejanus had already been executed; otherwise, the complaint never would have made its way to Tiberius. The fact that Pilate gave his approval for the letter's dispatch is a strong indication that he was not yet aware that Sejanus was no longer in place to protect him.

Jesus on Trial

No contemporary source, including the Gospel accounts, ever hinted at Pilate being a fool. So, as he looked over the crowd in the Praetorium's courtyard, he knew that he was facing a carefully selected audience. These were not the same people who were part of the Jewish mob that had rapturously greeted Jesus during his triumphal entry into Jerusalem just days before. At any other time, this would hardly have mattered. As we have seen, the Pilate presented in Josephus's and Philo's accounts, and who had over a half-dozen years of experience before Jesus's trial, would not have given a second thought to ordering Jesus's execution. He was also not someone who would decide based on the threats of a small and curated mob. But this time, Pilate hesitated, despite the execution being the expressed desire of the Jewish leadership. Moreover, the harder the Jewish leadership pushed for an immediate crucifixion, the more Pilate resisted:

According to Luke:

"I have found in this man no basis for the charges you are bringing against him. And neither has Herod, for he has sent him back to

us. So you see, nothing being done by him is worthy of death. Therefore, having scourged him, I will release him."*

And

But a third time, he said to them, "Why? What crime has this man committed? Having scourged him therefore, I will release him."†

According to Matthew:

"Why? What wrong has he done?"‡

And

When Pilate saw that he could do nothing, but that instead, a riot was starting, he took some water, washed his hands before the crowd, and said, "I am innocent of this man's blood. You take care of it yourselves!"§

According to Mark:

Pilate asked them, "Why, what evil has he done?"₵

According to John:

"I find no basis for an accusation against him."**

* Luke 23:14.
† Luke 23:22.
‡ Matthew 27:23.
§ Matthew 27:24.
₵ Mark 15:14.
** John 18:38.

And

Again, Pilate went out and said to the Jewish leaders, "Look, I am bringing him out to you, so that you may know that I find no reason for an accusation against him."*

The reason for Pilate's reluctance is easy to determine once the context is established. It is very similar to why the Jewish leaders were determined to make Rome responsible for Jesus's death. The crucial concern for both is that the Jerusalem mob had not weighed in yet. Pilate was certainly aware of how the mob greeted Jesus when he first arrived in Jerusalem only a few days before. He was also well briefed on the events at the Temple two days later, as his soldiers and officers must have watched it all unfold from the walls of the Antonia Fortress. So, Pilate knew several things: The mob supporting Jesus was massive, they were in a riotous mood, and many were armed. Compared to that, the crowd in the Praetorium courtyard was rather pitiful. Still, it was always in Pilate's best interest to appease the Jewish leadership. But appeasement was not worth risking potential riots in Jerusalem, which had a way of rapidly spreading into the hinterlands. Still, Pilate had never before demonstrated a reluctance to bait the mob and then violently crush its first stirrings. What changed? Why was a man as demonstrably ruthless as Pilate suddenly displaying weakness and indecision?

The most probable answer is that the execution of Sejanus in October of the preceding year changed everything. By this time, Pilate was aware of three crucial events. The first was that Tiberius, free of Sejanus's malevolent influence as to how the Jews should be treated, had ordered that all Jews be treated with more leniency and understanding than they had while Sejanus was at the height of his power. This imperial order had gone out to the provinces in the immediate aftermath of Sejanus's execution and, by now, was surely in Pilate's hands. Thus, news of Jews being

---

* John 19:4.

slaughtered in the middle of celebrating their most important holy day was unlikely to be well received in Rome.

Second, Pilate also knew that his patron and protector, Sejanus, had been brutally overthrown in Rome. Without such a patron, Pilate was politically exposed to attack by his enemies, and no Roman of high rank was without enemies. To be so exposed, when also far from Rome and unable to offer a personal defense, could mean financial ruin and often death.

Finally, Pilate knew that the post-Sejanus purges were continuing. The fear that these purges must have engendered in all of Sejanus's supporters should not be minimized. As Tacitus says of the period:

> Executions were now a stimulus to [Tiberius's] fury, and he ordered the death of all who were lying in prison under accusation of complicity with Sejanus. There lay, singly or in heaps, the unnumbered dead, of every age and sex, the illustrious with the obscure. Kinsfolk and friends were not allowed to be near them, to weep over them, or even to gaze on them too long. Spies were set round them, who noted the sorrow of each mourner and followed the rotting corpses, till they were dragged to the Tiber, where, floating or driven on the bank, no one dared to burn or to touch them. The force of terror had utterly extinguished the sense of human fellowship, and, with the growth of cruelty, pity was thrust aside.*

Even if Tacitus, who clearly despised Tiberius, was exaggerating, there is no doubt that the ongoing purges were a constant threat to Pilate's continued well-being. Pilate, therefore, had to tread very lightly. But his immediate path was clear: He had to find a way to get Jesus's case off his docket.

The Jewish leadership must have sensed Pilate's hesitation, for they now unleashed the most potent threat at their disposal: *"If you release this*

---

* Tacitus, *The Annals,* 6.19.

man, you are not Caesar's friend; everyone who makes himself a king sets himself against Caesar." * The gloves were now off, as this was no veiled threat. The Jewish authorities were clearly saying that if you do not do as we wish, we will send a letter or a delegation to Tiberius telling him of your willingness to tolerate an enemy of the emperor and Rome. This would have been a useless threat if Sejanus had still been in power and controlled who had access to Caesar and what correspondence he saw. With Sejanus's backing, Pilate would have inflicted a high price upon the Jewish leadership for such insolence. But without such a protector, a Jewish embassy informing Caesar that one of his governors had stayed the hand of justice against a rabble-rouser declaring himself a king placed Pilate in mortal peril. Pilate had locked his fate too closely to Sejanus. Thus, he could ill afford any hint that he was not wholly loyal to Tiberius. But, before him, and much to his horror, were the Jewish authorities threatening to cut the string holding the Sword of Damocles that had hung over Pilate's head since Sejanus's fall.

Pilate's resistance crumbled. Despite the genuine risk of further uprisings, Pilate handed Jesus to the Jewish authorities for immediate crucifixion. Sejanus's fall had opened a pathway for the Sanhedrin to blackmail Pilate into acquiescing to their demands. Free of such threats, Pilate likely would have continued to ignore the Jewish authorities and released Jesus rather than risk a general rebellion.

That risk had not disappeared, which explains why Pilate handed him back to the Jewish leadership to execute. Pilate still did not want the mob to blame Rome or himself for Jesus's death, although Jesus was led to Golgotha by an entire cohort of Roman soldiers, which was about the size of a force one would need to intimidate any local crowd. Pilate also ordered that a sign be placed upon the crucifix declaring Jesus as the "king of the Jews." The Jewish leaders asked that the sign be replaced by one saying that Jesus "claimed" to be king of the Jews, but Pilate refused the request. It appears to be a small issue and one not worth antagonizing the Jewish authorities about—Pilate still needed them to help him in the peaceful governance of Judea. The only reasonable explanation for his

* John 19:12.

refusal to grant their request is that Pilate was still looking over his shoulder, back at Rome. If the mob did revolt and had to be bloodily suppressed, then it would be crucial for Pilate to portray them as led by a king, admittedly of their own making, whom he was forced to crush. Surely Tiberius would understand that he had no other choice.

TWENTY-NINE

Aftermath

By this point in the book, we can confidently say that Jesus's existence and crucifixion are historical facts. But now we have arrived at a final crucial question: Did Jesus rise from the dead three days after his crucifixion? Let's start with what historical evidence exists in the core of the Gospel stories.

After Jesus was taken down from the cross, Joseph of Arimathea took control of his body and had it buried in a nearby tomb. A heavy rock was rolled in front of the cave, and Roman soldiers were placed at the tomb to guard it. On the following Sunday, several of Jesus's female followers discovered the rock rolled back and the tomb empty. That this is female testimony gives this story a lot of credence. At the time, women were not allowed to serve as witnesses in a Jewish court of law. If this story had been invented decades or centuries after Jesus's death, one or more apostles would have discovered the empty tomb. For the gospel writers, using women's testimony would only be acceptable if they believed their narrative of events was the absolute truth. If they were telling an invented story, the end of every Gospel account of the resurrections would be radically different from what we have.

Historians have disparaged this version of events, because some of the details in the Gospels conflict. But these conflicts, such as how many and which women were with Jesus at the crucifixion, are minor and incidental. They are the kinds of disputes we expect in any historical event with multiple attestations. But the core of the story is found in every Gospel; Jesus died on the cross, was buried, and the tomb was found empty three days later.

So, we have a historical event, but what explains it? The apostles found their explanation in the resurrected Jesus. There have been many attempts to explain away what the apostles unanimously claim to have experienced, and these counter-arguments are discussed in detail below. Historians claim that such an event was impossible, as a divine resurrection cannot be countenanced in any historical work. Still, it is abundantly clear that the apostles believed they had seen and interacted with a resurrected Jesus multiple times over the days and weeks after his execution.

Moreover, these interactions profoundly changed their lives. Remember that until Jesus was led off to Golgotha, the apostles had no clue that the Messiah would be shamefully executed as a common criminal. Moreover, Jewish beliefs about the afterlife centered upon all of the deserving being resurrected at the end of times. There was no allowance in these beliefs for someone defeating death before the world ended. Nevertheless, they all accepted that they had met resurrected Jesus and were willing to give their lives rather than deny their experience. It would take a massive transformative experience to provide the energy and commitment that sent the apostles throughout the Empire, and possibly as far as India, to preach a set of ideas that would have been foreign to almost all who heard them. As the theologian and New Testament scholar N. T. Wright has written: "That is why, as an historian, I cannot explain the rise of early Christianity unless Jesus rose again, leaving an empty tomb behind him."[*]

Now let us examine the three most common reasons presented for disbelieving the resurrection narratives. The first and most easily disposed

---

[*] N. T. Wright, "The New Unimproved Jesus," *Christianity Today* (September 13, 1993), p. 26.

of is that Jesus did not die on the cross. Instead, he had passed out or
fallen into a coma and was thought dead—Heinrich Paulus's "swoon
theory," mentioned earlier in this work. After being removed from the
cross and placed in his tomb, he revived on the third day, escaped from
the tomb, and convinced his many followers that he had risen from the
dead. To accept this explanation, we must also accept that his Roman
executioners did not know their business, which is unlikely. According
to the Gospel of John, the soldiers could see that he was dead, but just
to be sure, one of them thrust a spear into his side, and "immediately
blood and water flowed out."* Is this medically believable? The answer is
yes, as torture and crucifixion could easily create enough cardiac stress for
pericardial effusion (a liquid buildup around the heart that can cause
cardiac arrest) to form. A spear driven into Jesus's side could easily pierce
the cardiac cavity, causing blood and water to flow from the wound. Further, the chances of surviving a spearpoint penetrating the cardiac cavity
are nil.

Jesus, however, had to survive much more than a spear thrust into his
side. He also endured the damage caused by brutal torture, dehydration,
nails driven into his wrists and heels, and three days of exposure in a cold
cave. That is a lot to ask of anyone. Still, let's assume Jesus survived all of
that and somehow found the strength to roll back a heavy stone and
crawl into town. What kind of reception would he have received? Would
a bloodied, close-to-death Jesus, in dire need of a twenty-first-century
trauma center, have convinced his apostles that he was resurrected from
the dead and inspired them to preach a new religion to the world? Any
fair-minded person would have to judge that unlikely. A beaten and
bloodied Jesus may have aroused some sympathy, but he could not inspire a movement.

Others have postulated that the disciples stole Jesus's corpse and then
lied to everyone about seeing a resurrected Jesus. To judge the reasonable-
ness of this explanation, we must first overcome the historical testimony
found in Matthew's Gospel. Members of the Sanhedrin had petitioned
Pilate to place a Roman guard on the tomb, specifically to prevent Jesus's

---

* John 19:34.

disciples from stealing the body and claiming he was still alive.* Roman soldiers were unlikely to desert their post because a few disciples arrived to steal the body. But the Sanhedrin had little to worry about and were surely overestimating the capacity of Jesus's apostles to carry out such a plan. They had deserted him during his arrest and trial, and only Jesus's female followers, possibly joined by the Apostle John, were recorded as nearby during the crucifixion.† His other followers, mostly women, appear to have stood some distance off.‡ But after Jesus died, the apostles retreated to Jerusalem, where they cowered together in a single room. Could this dispirited, fearful group have organized such an operation? Without their charismatic leader, the apostles fell into a depressed lethargy; they had no plan for what to do in the event of their leader's death.

One also has to ask why they would try to perpetuate such a hoax. The apostles did not know they were a global faith's progenitors. Is it reasonable to expect a small group of men to make a plan to steal a body, claim Jesus had been resurrected, and then try to build an Empire-spanning religion on that lie? A lot could go wrong there. One wonders what they would gain from such an endeavor. Preaching what became Christianity did not make any of the apostles rich. Instead, it made them outcasts who were almost all regularly beaten, jailed, and martyred. Would anyone pay such a high price for a cause they knew to be a fraud? For these reasons, I believe the speculation of the apostles building a religion based on grave robbing is untenable.

The final reason for disbelieving the Gospels' resurrection narratives is that the apostles and many others who witnessed a resurrected Jesus hallucinated. As hallucinations don't typically spread from person to person, many have changed this explanation into a claim of some form of mass psychosis or hysteria. Such a claim has the benefit of being unfalsifiable, which does not mean it is correct. Even if it cannot be proven as complete nonsense, the psychosis theory remains highly unlikely. For one, such a psychosis typically strikes people experiencing heightened social excitement. The depressed group of apostles hiding and fearing

---

* Matthew 27:62–66.
† John 19:25.
‡ Luke 23:49 and Matthew 27:55.

retribution by the Sanhedrin were most certainly not experiencing social excitement. Such a euphoria-induced psychosis would be far more likely after they had seen a resurrected Jesus; it is almost impossible as a prelude to it. Moreover, a psychotic experience of this kind varies for each individual. In the Gospel narratives, everyone sees the same thing simultaneously. Moreover, euphoria is passing, making it implausible that such hysteria could have maintained itself for days or weeks. Again, we are presented with an explanation for disbelieving the resurrection stories in the Gospels that fails to hold up when scrutinized.[*]

Demonstrating the weakness of the arguments most commonly put forward by those skeptical of the Gospels' resurrection narrative does not prove that the resurrection took place. It does, however, mean that the skeptics must do a better job of providing practical reasons for doubt. Without such new reasons, which have not been forthcoming, the questions as to whether Jesus was resurrected after death remains a matter of faith. But from a historical point of view, it is a faith supported by an amazing amount of eyewitness testimony. According to Paul, Jesus was "seen by Cephas, then by the twelve. After that, he was seen by over five hundred brethren at once, of whom the greater part remain to the present, but some have fallen asleep [died]. After that, he was seen by James, then by all the apostles. Then last of all, he was seen by me also, as by one born out of due time."[†]

Paul wrote this letter in about 55 AD, just twenty-two years after Jesus's death. He does not ask any of his readers to take his word for it about the resurrection. Instead, he invites them to seek out those who witnessed a resurrected Jesus and were still alive. Hence, we have a testimony of the resurrection, supported by over five hundred witnesses, that was written during the lifetime of almost all of those who personally

---

[*] For a much more detailed analysis of the science behind this line of argument, see Joseph W. Bergeron and Gary R. Habermas, "The Resurrection of Jesus: A Clinical Review of Psychiatric Hypotheses for the Biblical Story of Easter," *Irish Theological Quarterly*, Vol. 80, no. 2 (2015), pp. 157–72, and Joseph W. Bergeron, *The Crucifixion of Jesus: A Medical Doctor Examines the Death and Resurrection of Christ* (CrossLink Publishing, 2019).
[†] Paul, 1 Corinthians 15:5–8.

knew Jesus. In fact, Paul claims that he was the last person whom the risen Jesus appeared to after his death. When he brought that story to the new leaders of the fledging Christian Church, none of them doubted his experience, for they shared it. In short, when Paul was teaching about the resurrection, many persons close to Jesus when he was alive could have called foul. That they did not demonstrates that many witnesses to Jesus's life and death sincerely believed they had experienced a risen Christ. The apostles believed so fervently that they almost all died gruesome deaths as martyrs rather than deny what they had witnessed. Only the Apostle John died a natural death, but according to the early Church father Tertullian, he survived being boiled in oil.* The resurrection may not have taken place, but historians have to then deal with the fact that we have more contemporary evidence that it did happen than for almost anything else we know about the ancient world. Only the fact that it is medically impossible to rise from the dead keeps historians from entering Jesus's resurrection into the history books. Hence, Christians profess the resurrection as a matter of faith.

---

* Tertullian, *The Prescriptions Against Heretics* (*De Praescriptionibus adversus Haereticos*).

Acknowledgments

First and foremost, I want to thank my wife, Sharon, who provided all the emotional (I can get needy when writing) and logistical support (especially feeding me) required to complete this book!

I also want to thank Uri Kaufman, author of *American Intifada* and *Eighteen Days in October*, for many valuable suggestions and for being particularly helpful on the topic of ancient Jewish history. I also want to thank Dr. William Barrick, who made a number of important suggestions that hugely improved this work. Of course, if any errors remain, I am entirely responsible.

I want to give a short shout-out to Kip Braily, the draft's first reader. His encouragement meant more than he knows.

No book gets published without massive support from the publisher. My first thank-you goes to Emily Hartley, who acquired this book for Ballantine—thanks for your belief in its commercial success.

I also want to thank my current editor, Anusha Khan, who took over this book when Emily departed. She has done a magnificent job shepherding the book through the often-trying production process. She made it all easy for me if not so much for herself.

Of course, this book would not have gone forward without the approval of Editor-in-Chief Jennifer Hershey, Kim Hovey (deputy publisher), and Kara Welsh (Ballantine President). As this book entered production, the design work was done by Jo Anne Metsch and the cover by Carlos Beltran.

Finally, although I have not met the marketing manager for this book as of this writing, I hope that by the time the book reaches bookshelves, Emma Thomasch and I will be best of friends!

ABOUT THE AUTHOR

Dr. James Lacey is the professor of strategy at the Marine Corps War College. He also holds the Horner Chair of War Studies at Marine Corps University. Prior to taking this position, he was a widely published senior analyst at the Institute for Defense Analyses in Washington, D.C. His previous works include *Rome: A Strategy for Empire*, *Moment of Battle*, *The First Clash*, *Great Strategic Rivalries*, *Gods of War*, and *The Washington War*.

ABOUT THE TYPE

This book was set in Centaur, a typeface designed by the American typographer Bruce Rogers in 1929. Rogers adapted Centaur from a fifteenth-century type of Nicholas Jenson (c. 1420–80) and modified it in 1948 for a cutting by the Monotype Corporation.